Date Due

A PECULIAR KIND OF POLITICS

DESMOND MORTON

1726385711

A Peculiar Kind of Politics: Canada's Overseas Ministry in the First World War

UNIVERSITY OF TORONTO PRESS
Toronto Buffalo London

© University of Toronto Press 1982
Toronto Buffalo London
Printed in Canada

ISBN 0-8020-5586-9

To Barbara Wilson

the source of as much of this book as the author

Canadian Cataloguing in Publication Data

Morton, Desmond, 1937-
A peculiar kind of politics

Includes index.
ISBN 0-8020-5586-9

1. Canada. Ministry of Overseas Military Forces.
2. Canada – Politics and government – 1911-1921.*
3. World War, 1914-1918 – Canada. I. Title.

FC557.M67   971.061'2   C82-094346-0
F1034.M672

Contents

Preface

In the years before 1914 Canadians appeared to have two options in their future relations with the world. They could continue the role that, for many of them, seemed inevitable: Canada would remain the senior white dominion in the greatest empire the world had ever seen. Canadians would remain safe behind the power of the Royal Navy and aid, with increasingly self-confident voices, in the management of the empire's affairs. Alternatively (though outside French Canada the option commanded a much quieter following) Canada could seek her own independent sovereignty, perhaps within the British family, perhaps outside it, but in all its external policies autonomous.

In the years after 4 August 1914 that choice was made. The Canada that went into war as a proudly loyal colony of a world-wide empire emerged less than five years later with its future direction clearly delineated. Canada would be autonomous.

That decision was the result of many dramatic changes, not least in the mind of her wartime prime minister, Sir Robert Borden. It was also the result of internal political crises, notably the bitter dispute over conscription, which transformed the balance of forces in Canadian domestic politics. However, the most significant transformation occurred in the minds of the men who represented Canada's most tangible contribution to the idea of empire. The soldiers of the Canadian Expeditionary Force went to England in October 1914 as an integral part of the British army; they returned half a decade later as soldiers of a junior but essentially sovereign ally. In their eyes, if not in the more refined perceptions of constitutional lawyers, Canada now managed her own affairs.

Put to the test, Canadians were unwilling to surrender control over their own war effort. They had, in a gesture almost unnoticed at the time, promised to meet the financial as well as the human burden of their contribution. The result, inexorably, was involvement in administrative decisions and, eventually, control over all but the tactical deployment of their forces in the theatre of war.

For such responsibilities, Canada had neither experience nor machinery and the process of developing them was notably retarded by the extraordinary figure who managed Canada's war effort during its formative stages. If it is true that Sir Sam Hughes's nationalism contributed to the assertion of Canadian military autonomy, it is even more true that his personality made the process more costly and humiliating than the most supercilious Englishman could have wished. A political problem was resolved by political means, however, and in their very different ways both Sir George Perley and Sir Edward Kemp developed the institutions which, belatedly, gave Canadians increasingly effective control over their own overseas forces.

In the initial excitement of August 1914, most Canadians saw no alternative to a unified imperial war effort. In time, as historians like R.A. Preston and C.P. Stacey have demonstrated, the Borden government insisted upon and achieved some share in imperial policy making. However, historical change is rarely achieved by mutation; most often it occurs through complex, connected episodes, some of them with unexpected outcomes. It is the result, to paraphrase the late Donald Creighton, of the interplay of many characters and innumerable circumstances.

That is the real significance of the creation and work of the Ministry of Overseas Military Forces of Canada. It was by solving the problem of Canadian military administration in England and of Canadian authority over the CEF in France that the symbolic victories of autonomy were made possible. Behind the achievements of the Canadian Corps at Vimy Ridge or Amiens was a complex network of human and institutional problems to be solved. Wars involve more than fighting; history is about more than great moments.

Those principles were consciously held by most of the members of the small, congenial group I joined in Ottawa in September 1963 as the newest member of the Army Historical Section. It was in a stuffy little office, sandwiched between Frank McGuire and the late John Swettenham, that I was set to my apprentice task of reading and revising Captain L.R. Cameron's study of Canadian command and administration in the First World War. My neighbours in that informal graduate school taught me most that I ever learned about the practical approach to historical research. The late J. Mackay Hitsman was a more theoretical mentor, but that single year with the Historical Section was enough to convince me that historical scholarship was as fascinating and congenial an undertaking as could be imagined.

In the past nineteen years, through a procession of academic and political distractions, the issue of Canadian autonomy in the First World War, opened during those first weeks in Ottawa, has continued to fascinate me. Continuing my research in Ottawa and London provided a welcome distraction from more immediate projects. It was also a logical completion of other work on political-military relations in Canada in the post-Confederation period.

One good reason for my fidelity to the project has been the friendship and encouragement of other members of Canada's community of military historians. The atmosphere in the Army Historical Section was only a sample of a climate of mutual support which may explain the strength of military history within the broader domain of Canadian studies. Under Alec Douglas, the Directorate of History at National Defence Headquarters continues to serve as a focus for innovative scholarship and research for all in the field. At the Public Archives of Canada, Barbara Wilson, with her encyclopedic knowledge of our military records, has probably helped to inspire more innovative research in the field of military history than any Canadian except Charles Stacey. Both of them have provided me with advice, encouragement, and much practical help in this lengthy labour. So have many individual colleagues, notably Jack Hyatt of the University of Western Ontario and Craig Brown of the University of Toronto. Both possess a rare familiarity with Canada's military and political experience during the First World War.

All books are collaborative enterprises. This one, stretched over so many years, has involved more people than most. My wife, Janet, has suffered my absences and, even more, my presence during the throes of literary frustration. Clara Stewart typed the manuscript and the revisions and the revisions of the revisions, adding her own welcome improvements. My colleagues at Erindale College, in particular, Paul Fox, have provided the stimulation and friendship implied in the highest sense of the concept of collegiality.

Research for this book was supported in 1976 by the Canada Council. Its publication has been assisted by a grant from the Social Science Federation of Canada, using funds provided by the Social Sciences and Humanities Research Council of Canada, and by a grant from the Publications Fund of University of Toronto Press.

Mississauga, 13 June 1981

A Note on Military Terms and Values

Like the civilians who joined the Canadian Expeditionary Force, even some of those invested with colonelcies and commissions, readers of this book may be bewildered by a host of unfamiliar terms and concepts. It was as hard for a newly enlisted private to realize that he could no longer call by his first name a boyhood chum who happened to be a lieutenant as it was to learn to roll puttees up his calf. It was just as hard for an aggrieved new lieutenant to realize that he should no longer appeal to his MP or his influential father to redress some military grievance.

What made the army even stranger for Canadians in 1914 than for their descendants three generations later was that for many it was the first experience of a structured, regulated bureaucracy. What Max Weber had defined in the Prussian civil service was, after all, more principle than practice in Canadian public administration. The militia, with its aura of amateurism and its close association with political patronage, only pretended in 1914 to be rational as well as bureaucratic. The war, as the ensuing pages will argue, set a hot pace for change.

Readers who may share the bewilderment of the CEF recruits may be willing to submit themselves to a short and wholly theoretical course of basic training. The basic fighting unit of the CEF was the infantry battalion, approximately a thousand strong and commanded by a lieutenant-colonel. Cavalry and mounted rifle regiments were much smaller but, with their horses and expensive saddlery, still ranked as a lieutenant-colonel's command. Four infantry battalions formed a brigade, under a brigadier-general. Three brigades, accompanied by artillery batteries, engineers, pioneers, machine gun companies, and a contingent of army service corps and medical corps units, made up an infantry division, commanded by a major-general. The Canadian Corps would eventually have four such divisions. A corps was commanded by a lieutenant-general. Throughout the war, organizations changed steadily as generals experimented and as new weapons, like trench mortars, poison gas, and tanks, became available. A division might muster anywhere between eighteen and twenty-five thousand soldiers. Heavy artillery, intended mainly to attack the enemy's guns and rear areas, was commanded directly by the corps headquarters.

The main role of the Canadian military organization in England was to channel a steady flow of trained reinforcements to the divisions fighting in France. The British peacetime organization, based on regiments which recruited their men from specific districts of the British Isles, proved to be remarkably adaptable to the huge wartime expansion. Canada had no such system and its peacetime militia regiments were deliberately ignored in the 1914 mobilization. Not until 1917, on the eve of the conscription crisis, was a serious effort made to reorganize the CEF reinforcement system in Canada and England so that a recruit from, say, New Brunswick, would eventually find his way to a New Brunswick battalion in the Canadian Corps. Instead, for two critical years, hundreds of CEF battalions were organized in Canada, sent overseas, and dispersed.

For the individuals involved, that could be a painful experience. A soldier's wartime home and almost his family was his battalion, his company, and especially his platoon, the little body of twenty to forty men in which an individual could be more than a statistic or a body. Discipline, morale, and fighting efficiency, as the British army had long since discovered, depended on the bonding of small military units. Sam Hughes's recruiting system was not only a confidence trick, betraying promises made to prospective colonels and their men, but also it threatened the efficiency and morale of the CEF, particularly in England, where the painful break-ups occurred.

Those affected by the experience, like young Captain Leslie Frost, were less likely to blame a distant minister of militia than the officers of the hated staff, with their pretentious manner and their distinguishing red cap bands and collar tabs. As Shakespeare noted in *Henry IV*, soldiers have always regarded staff officers with contempt, but the static warfare of 1914-18, with its dramatic contrast between the death and squalor of the trenches and the tranquil safety only a couple of miles to the rear, made staff officers even more detested than usual. When the men were safely in England, their mood translated easily into insensate fury. Resentment was not alleviated when inexperienced staff officers covered their uncertainty with brusque officiousness.

Canadian soldiers, as virtually every account from the ranks makes clear, rarely liked any of their officers although most managed to secure a tolerant acceptance and a few even won grudging admiration. One problem was that officers automatically enjoyed privileges – higher pay, a soldier servant, a lighter load on the march – which nothing in their training or in Canadian social attitudes could justify. Another problem was that the more senior officers, particularly generals, were almost compelled to remain remote from their men by the rigidity of telephone communications. Senior commanders, like Major-General M.S. Mercer at Mont Sorrel in 1916, who joined their men in the front line and shared their suffering lost control of their commands. In a later war, wireless would allow commanders to move forward; in 1914-18 it was still too primitive, heavy, and unreliable to free commanders from their tangle of telephone lines. The result was that generals were known only as remote, unappealing figures, visible mainly at formal inspections and suspected (falsely as A.M.J. Hyatt has demonstrated) of living in safety and dying in bed.

Ordinary soldiers had, of course, good reason to suspect generals and staff officers. By the standard of earlier wars, and particularly in the British army, detailed staff work reached a level of perfection. Never before had soldiers in action suffered so little from disease or so rarely from hunger. Despite the inevitable confusion and miscalculations of war, staff officers perfected techniques for hurtling unprecedented numbers of men and munitions at the enemy. Never before had the products of technological ingenuity been so quickly adapted to the problems of the trench warfare stalemate. The problem was not that staff officers were, on the whole, bunglers but that they were appallingly efficient because at the end of their minute calculations and detailed orders lay the unbridgeable abyss of no man's land with its guardian machine guns, barbed wire, gas, and artillery barrages.

That barrier was proof against all the ingenuity generals, staff officers, and scientists could bring to bear. It could only partially be bridged by the tracked but mechanically defective monsters called tanks. In March 1918, German storm troopers showed that infiltration could succeed when massed assaults had failed, but their valour could not overcome physical exhaustion and defence in depth. In the end, as the Polish banker, Ivan Bloch, had predicted, victory was the product of exhaustion, not of tactical brilliance. On both sides, millions paid the price of so dreary and ugly a solution.

Out of that war came a lesson which even the most civilian of nations has never quite forgotten: never again, even among Canadians, would war ever be portrayed as a bright summer adventure. In the end, that was a far more important lesson than the correct way to fit Webb equipment or the proper style for a military memorandum.

Never happier than with 'his boys,' Sir Sam Hughes finds a congenial group at the
Canadian Cavalry Brigade. From left to right, Hughes with Brigadier-General
J.E.B. Seely, Lord Rothermere, a British press baron, an unidentified staff officer
and a demure-looking Lieutenant-Colonel Max Aitken. (PAC PA 608)

Ever watchful of 'your good self,' Major-General John Wallace Carson helps a visiting Sir Sam Hughes into a staff car outside his headquarters in the Hotel Cecil. (PA 4776)

Trouser cuffs rolled up for the mud, a helmeted George Perley inspects a dugout near recently captured Vimy Ridge. Perley's willingness to delegate responsibility to competent Canadian officers won their loyalty. (PA 1770)

Sir Edward Kemp presides over a meeting of the Militia Council. Major-General Sir Willoughby Gwatkin turns the same quizzical eye to the camera that he did to most of his colleagues, including the octagenarian Major-General D.A. Macdonald on the far left. (PA 42826)

'Inclined to suffer from a swollen head' was the resentful judgment of Sir Douglas Haig on his plump Canadian subordinate, but he also backed Sir Arthur Currie's promotion in 1917 and the refusal to reorganize the Canadian Corps in 1918. As for Currie, he had better relations with Haig than with some of his Canadian superiors in London. (PA 2497)

Sir George and Lady Perley chat with Lieutenant-General Sir Richard Turner at an investiture for colonial soldiers in London. Both of the Perleys were suspected by Hughes of subordinating Canadian interests to the dictates of London society. The charge lacked nothing but evidence. (Ont Arch Acc 11595 Alb 3, p. 42)

Major-General Sidney Mewburn, Sir Robert Borden, and Sir Edward Kemp during the 1918 visit to London. Though Kemp developed some trust in his successor as Minister of Militia, he could never forget that Mewburn's friends were Grits. (PA 5725)

Sir Edward Kemp and a crippled Brigadier-General A.H. Macdonnell review troops at the Canadian Training School in Shoreham, Kent. Kemp found wartime England a trial. Even the wealthy, he discovered, could not necessarily get enough to eat. (PA 5158)

A PECULIAR KIND OF POLITICS

1

The Contingent

The fourteenth of October dawned as a clear, crisp autumn morning for the people of Plymouth. More than the weather tugged people from their beds, however. The rumours were true. The old Devon port where Sir Francis Drake had waited for the Spanish Armada would again be part of history. From beyond the Atlantic, the young men of Britain's largest colony were coming to lay down their lives for the mother country. The threat of German submarines had diverted their huge convoy to the security of the West Country naval port.

As a light mist lifted from the Hamoaze, cadets at the Royal Naval College dressed ship and mustered on the green lawn to cheer the arrivals. At the town hall, officials fretted that Mayor Baker was out of town for Plymouth's grand occasion. By 7 AM the first dark shapes emerged from the mist on Plymouth Sound. Led by the light cruiser *Diana*, the big grey-painted Atlantic passenger ships edged cautiously upstream. From vantage points in the old town, women in smocks and girls in pinafores fluttered handkerchiefs. On command, the cadets of the naval college raised caps and cheers. The sound rose, high-pitched and faint across the water to be answered by the khaki-clad men who crowded the ships' railings. Some in the crowd began singing 'Tipperary,' already the theme-song of the British at war. More joined but the men on the ship did not respond. 'Tipperary' had yet to reach Canada.

Instead, the Canadian Expeditionary Force had come to England.[1]

The leader writer of *The Times* responded, like most of Britain, to the imperial symbolism of the occasion. The Canadian contingent was only part of the response of the self-governing colonies: 'The coming of the Colonial troops is the proof that the people of this Empire understand each other better than all the spies and investigators which Germany has sent out to study them.[2]

The confident pronouncement of *The Times* was predictable but premature. In the headlong, instinctive rush to send volunteers to the great European conflict, Canadians had not paused to ask whether their force would be Canadian or British. Was Canada involved in the war because she was a colony of a great empire or did her commitment rest on her own will?

Even raising such questions in August or September of 1914 might have provoked indignation in much of English-speaking Canada. In 1885, Sir John A. Macdonald had met an Anglo-Egyptian crisis in the Sudan with a blunt refusal to help 'Gladstone & Co.' out of a mess of their own making.[3] In 1899, dispatch of an official Canadian contingent to the South African War had provoked deep differences in Canada – by no means exclusively in Quebec. In 1914, objections were instantly stifled. Returning to Ottawa on 4 August, Sir Wilfrid Laurier promised his full support for the war and called for a political truce with Sir Robert Borden's Conservative government: 'I have often declared that if the Mother Country were ever in danger, or if danger ever threatened, Canada would render assistance to the fullest extent of her powers.'[4]

Laurier's comments, like his cry of 'Ready, aye, ready,' on 19 August came not from a veteran prime minister but from an aged opposition leader, determined to save his Liberal party from cries of disloyalty on what might well be the eve of a general election.[5] The 1911 general election had given power to a Conservative party determined, for the most part, to strengthen the bonds of empire. Its leader, Robert Laird Borden, was a cautious, uncharismatic Nova Scotian who harboured few romantic ideals. Among the few was a faith in the British Empire. After his unexpected feat in uniting French and English-Canadian nationalists for his 1911 victory, Borden proceeded to sacrifice his party's Quebec wing in an unavailing drive to tax Canadians to reinforce Britain's fleet of dreadnoughts.[6]

For Borden and his colleagues, the events of August 1914 posed no questions about Canada's role. When the British ultimatum to Berlin expired, Canada found herself at war as fully as Great Britain herself or her smallest dependency. However, being at war did not necessarily compel Canada to fight. Thanks to the work of a pre-war committee, a 'War Book' dictated a long series of precautions, from the guarding of canals and railway bridges to the creation of an examination service for Halifax harbour.[7] However, no one interfered with any German or Austrian reservists sufficiently patriotic to slip discreetly into a neutral United States. Commerce raiders like the *Karlsrühe* or the *Dresden* might have sunk Canadian ships. German or Irish filibusters might launch trifling raids across the American frontier. Otherwise, there was no way for the Kaiser to extend the war to Canada.[8]

For most Canadians in 1914, commitment to the war seemed inevitable: even in French Canada early dissent was muted. The national response arose from widespread illusions about war among people too young to remember the American Civil War or the Franco-Prussian War. The frantic haste in mobilizing a Canadian contingent was spurred less by anxiety for Britain's desperately overstrained little army than from anxiety that the war would be over by Christmas.

In the circumstances, the status of the soldiers of Canada's First Contingent seemed wholly appropriate. The troops might have been enlisted under the Militia Act. Section 69 did make it lawful for militiamen to serve in the defence of Canada beyond its borders.[9] No such nationalistic quibble was even considered. The Canadians were attested as 'Imperials' – soldiers of the British army recruited from the empire.[10] If there was any doubt about the integration of the Canadians in Britain's army, it was laid to rest by the minister of militia, Colonel Sam Hughes: 'We have nothing whatever to say as to the destination of the troops once they cross the water,' Hughes informed the Canadian House of Commons on 21 August 1914, 'nor have we been informed as to what their destination may be.'[11] In London, Canada's acting high commissioner, the Hon George Perley, stated: 'that as soon as the Canadian troops arrive here they will be entirely under the authority of the War Office and become part of the Imperial army in every sense of the word.'[12] In 1914, no one presumed otherwise.

The war did not, of course, end at Christmas. It continued for more than four terrible years, time enough for the ambiguities and differences in the Canadian response to the war to be wrenched into the open and to shape a very different Canadian consciousness. The silent, sullen acquiescence of French Canada in the wartime commitments of English-speaking neighbours grew slowly into the collective resistance of the conscription crisis of 1917. However, it is no longer adequate to portray that conflict as a struggle of French-Canadian nationalism against a dying Canadian imperialism.[13]

Reality was more complex. The First World War had a heavy impact on Canada. It accelerated changes in the country's industrial capacity, her transportation system, and her agricultural industry. The war changed the legal status of women, the role of the labour movement, and the structure and responsibilities of government. It left no significant social institution, from the churches to the taverns, untouched.[14] Among the most significant developments of four crucial years was the emergence of English-Canadian nationalism from an intellectual chrysalis into an unarticulated major premise for most Canadians. In 1914, Laurier's cry of 'Ready, aye ready' in response to Britain's crisis had echoed the feelings of most Canadians (and robbed the Conservatives of their case for an early election). Only eight years later, when Arthur Meighen, as Conservative leader, offered the same slogan in his response to the Chanak crisis, the cheers were limited to his audience of Toronto Tory businessmen. The phrase haunted and embarrassed him across the country.[15] Most Canadians had stopped responding instinctively to appeals for British patriotism.

English-Canadian nationalism was not, of course, born during the war years. It had existed in the speeches of Thomas D'Arcy McGee and Edward Blake, in the writings of John Skirving Ewart, and in the naïve, sometimes perverse doctrines of Canada First and its heirs. Yet, as French-Canadians like Henri Bourassa would forever complain, its exponents never really did put Canada first. Carl Berger, in *The Sense of Power*, has recorded the intermingling of nationalism and imperialism among many of the exponents of a Canadian identity. To those, like Ewart, who offered a future as an independent 'Kingdom of Canada,' the 'imperial-nationalists' held out an infinitely grander vision of Canada sharing and perhaps even coming to dominate a worldwide empire upon which the sun never set.[16]

Such dreams undoubtedly influenced the government of Sir Robert Borden in 1914. Later, drafting his manifesto for the 1917 election, the prime minister would claim that Canada had gone to war on the decision of Parliament, admittedly without dissent. Borden was re-writing history.[17] On 1 August, even before the issue of peace or war was finally settled, Borden and his ministers had guaranteed Canada's loyal support. The Duke of Connaught, Canada's governor general, assured the colonial secretary in London that his government would offer every assistance: 'They are confident that a considerable force would be available for service abroad.'[18]

However, even in 1914, there were some Canadians who interpreted Canada's involvement in much the same spirit that would strike Sir Robert Borden as appropriate for the very different Canada of 1917. John Wesley Dafoe, editor of the Manitoba *Free Press*, proclaimed to his readers that Canada had entered the war not as a colonial dependency but as an ally. 'All the world knows,' Dafoe insisted, 'that Canada, like the other self-governing Dominions, has gone into this war with the determination to fight shoulder to shoulder with Great Britain to the finish, under no compulsion save that of conscience and duty and devotion to the ideals of civilization of which the British flag is the symbol.'[19] For Dafoe and those who shared his thoughts, there might be limits to what might be demanded of a colony; there could be no compromise for a Canadian nation pitted against Kaiserism and Prussian militarism.

In his own visceral and explosive fashion, Colonel Sam Hughes was the archetype of the 'imperial-nationalist.' His response to the August crisis reflected some of the contradictions of his faith. A quick reading of the Ottawa morning newspapers on Monday, 3 August, convinced Hughes, in his own words, that Britain's Liberal government was going to 'skunk it.' The French would be abandoned. Colonel Winters, Hughes's military secretary, was commanded to haul down the Union Jack that fluttered over Militia Headquarters. The horrified staff officer reluctantly obeyed orders. 'Oh!' moaned Hughes, 'what a shameful state of things. By God, I don't want to be a Britisher under such conditions.' Cooler heads prevailed. The venerable quartermaster-general, Major-General D.A. Macdonald, a special favourite of Hughes, persuaded the minister to wait for the afternoon papers. The flag was restored. The news improved. The empire would go to war and Canada could go along.[20]

Hughes's manic wilfulness would embarrass many more Canadians than his immediate staff officers. His determination to impose his will on every conceivable aspect of Canada's war effort would result in costly and humiliating errors. At the same time, it undermined his own claim that the Canadian Expeditionary Force had passed into British control. Almost from the outset, Hughes's insistence on personal control established a pattern which later and abler successors could use to transform the CEF from a British to a Canadian organization.

By 1918, with little formal or negotiated change of legal status, Canadian troops in France and England had become members of the militia serving abroad. The battle-hardened Canadian Corps remained under the operational control of the British General Headquarters but the Canadians had their own commanders, their own organization, and their own tactical doctrines. They were now part of a Canadian, not an imperial, army, with a chain of authority which stretched from the Corps through a Canadian section at General Headquarters and a Canadian cabinet minister in London to a prime minister who insisted on a voice in the higher strategy of the war. The British commander-in-chief, Field-Marshal Sir Douglas Haig, grumbled that the Canadians had come to see themselves as junior but sovereign allies. His political superior, the Earl of Derby, could only counsel resignation to altered circumstances: 'we must look upon them in the light in which they wish to be looked upon rather than the light in which we would wish to do so.'[21]

The transformation of the Canadian Corps and of the Canadian overseas military administration from a colonial to a highly autonomous status marked a crucial practical development in the growth of genuine Canadian sovereignty. Canada's military contribution to the Allied war effort, including the trauma of the conscription dispute and the sacrifice of more than sixty thousand young lives, was the foundation for subsequent marks of international status, from the placing of signatures on the Covenant of the League of Nations to the famous Halibut Treaty of 1923. In this case, symbolism was built on hard reality. In the practical test of wartime co-operation, the faith of many leading Canadians in some form of imperial federation was tested and demolished. The overseas experience of close to half a million Canadians drove home a common sense of nationality and a painful awareness of how little sentiment most of them still shared with a former mother country.

Since 1914 Canadians have often been reminded that their country was almost wholly unprepared for war. The claim adds glory to the achievements of soldiers who, within months, would match their valour against that of the finest German regulars. It encourages a fond Canadian notion that pre-war military preparations are largely superfluous. In fact, Canada's expeditionary force had precedents and could have been based on a detailed mobilization plan. If both were overlooked, it was because the minister of militia insisted on exercising enormous and illegitimate authority and neither his cabinet colleagues nor the country possessed the knowledge or the will to stop him.[22]

The world, as Hughes boasted in his valedictory to the CEF on 3 October, might regard it as a marvel that thirty-three thousand men had been assembled and dispatched within six weeks.[23] In October 1899 it had taken two weeks to recruit, organize, equip, and embark a regiment of one thousand Canadians destined for the South African War. Moreover, that feat had been accomplished amidst unprecedented political divisions. 'Never since 1899,' according to Charles Stacey, 'has the outbreak of a war found the national government so deeply and gravely divided.'[24] Although the Canadian House of Commons had offered unanimous support for the British policy in South Africa, a British invitation to offer an official contingent split Sir Wilfrid Laurier's cabinet. French-Canadian ministers, prodded by an articulate young backbencher, Henri Bourassa, opposed an official contribution to a conflict which neither affected Canada nor threatened Britain. English-speaking ministers, led by Ontario's William Mulock, demanded official action. Major English-language newspapers in Montreal and Toronto echoed and amplified the demand.[25]

The intense controversy shaped the resulting Canadian contingent. The British promise to meet the full costs of the force once it reached South Africa robbed Laurier of his best argument to English-speaking ministers – the burden of military expenditure. An initial plan for a small mixed force of cavalry, infantry, and artillery was altered to a single battalion of infantry commanded by a veteran Canadian-born professional soldier, Lieutenant-Colonel William Otter. Laurier might well have preferred the original British request for little units of 125 men, commanded by junior officers, easily integrated into British regiments. That might have made it easier to persuade French-Canadian critics that the government had done no more than acquiesce in British recruiting in Canada. It was the governor general, Lord Minto, who insisted that anything less than an official force would be unworthy of Canada's dignity.[26]

Britain's initial desire for a colonial contingent had nothing to do with military necessity. Experience with a small Australian contingent at Suakin in 1885 had suggested to the War Office that raw colonial volunteers needed several months of training before they were fit for active service. What Joseph Chamberlain, the imperial-minded colonial secretary, badly wanted was a symbolic gesture to show that the empire could respond as a unit to military crisis. Sam Hughes, then a turbulent Conservative backbencher, had responded to the South African crisis by proclaiming to Chamberlain, Laurier, and Militia Headquarters that he could recruit and lead ten thousand Canadians to Britain's aid. For Laurier, the Hughes offer answered his political problems and might well have furnished a precedent for all subsequent Canadian overseas contingents. For Chamberlain and his associates in Canada, Lord Minto and Major-General E.T.H. Hutton, commanding the Canadian militia, the Hughes offer might be well intentioned but it was a dangerous threat to an imperial purpose.[27]

Frustrating the Hughes scheme provided a discordant counterpoint to the struggle for an official Canadian contingent. When Hutton threatened heavy-handed military sanctions against Hughes as a militia colonel, the irrepressible Sam responded with a defence of his rights as an MP and a citizen of the empire. Hutton reacted with personal fury at Hughes's insubordination; Hughes replied with claims that Hutton had sneered at Canadian military prowess. Hughes, a former teacher, athlete, and railway promoter, a newspaper editor of unbridled vituperative power, a leading Orangeman and a highly independent Tory, became a key figure in the debate over Canada's South African contingent. General Hutton, who might well have driven his outspoken adversary from the militia, was eventually compelled by Minto and the government to allow Hughes to travel unofficially with the Canadian contingent.[28]

When the *Sardinian* berthed at Cape Town on 4 December 1899, disembarking the Second (Special Service) Battalion of the Royal Canadian Regiment, assorted chaplains, nurses, newspaper correspondents, and a still-fuming Lieutenant-Colonel Sam Hughes, Ottawa had discharged its full responsibilities. Otter and his men found themselves part of the British army, subject to its discipline and to its frugal scales of rations, pay, and pension. Otter was content with the arrangement. An austere disciplinarian, he shared the common view that a British line regiment was a worthy military model. To the dismay of his politically-appointed officers and his raw, self-confident soldiers, Otter set out to drill the Canadian contingent into a reasonable facsimile. Otter's responsibility was heavy: he must bring his regiment home with its military honour intact. His means was to be uncompromising discipline.[29]

Back in Canada, early British defeats persuaded Laurier's government to offer a second official contingent. A number of military disasters in early December persuaded Whitehall to accept the offer. Two battalions of mounted infantry and three batteries of field artillery left Canada in January 1900, having survived the rigours of recruiting and organizing during a Canadian winter. As a final official contribution to a suddenly overstrained Britain, Canada recruited a third battalion of the Royal Canadian Regiment to replace the regular infantry in the Halifax fortress.[30]

Almost from the outset Ottawa had discovered that it was politically troublesome to lose contact with its contingents overseas. Relatives of Canadian soldiers in South Africa pestered the Militia Department and then turned to members of parliament for up-to-date news of their next-of-kin. When Otter's battalion set off under Lord Roberts for the long march to Pretoria, Canadians demanded instant reports of casualties. Official reports, travelling through leisurely British channels to the War Office in London, were no substitute. As a patriotic gesture, Hugh Graham of the jingoistic Montreal *Star* had promised life insurance coverage for every man of the contingent. When the Canadians suffered heavy losses at Paardeberg, the insurance company demanded better proof of death than a mere British casualty list. In Ottawa, an indignant MP demanded that Parliament give the minister of militia the power to get information to bereaved families without delay.[31]

In South Africa, Colonel Otter was in a poor position to help. To the British, he was simply another regimental commander. His base at Cape Town consisted of a few officers sent south to recuperate from ill health. While some extra officers had accompanied the contingent, most of them found staff positions. Only Colonel Hughes, denied employment by a private letter from Hutton to the British base commander, fretted in idleness. Once on the march, Otter had to travel light. Huddled under a wagon, sometimes soaked by driving rain, armed only with the stub of a pencil, the sixty-year-old veteran had reason to grumble at his burden of correspondence. 'No one has any idea of the troubles I have in serving two masters, the Imperial people and our own,' Otter complained to his wife, 'I would not undertake such a thing again for a great deal more than I shall ever get out of it.'[32] His only support in dealing with the flow of dispatches, telegrams, and letters was a quartermaster-sergeant. Penuriousness, ingrained by years of peacetime service, undoubtedly added to Otter's problems. After Paardeberg, Otter sent his report of the battle to Kimberley with eleven pounds to cover the telegraph charges. Military authorities treated the dispatch as a civilian message. By the time the censors had done their work, the money was insufficient to pay for both censorship and transmission. Otter's message, desperately awaited in Canada, languished until a passing Canadian chaplain was invited to find the extra cash.[33]

Belatedly, Otter and other contingent commanders were firmly instructed by Ottawa on the reports and information they must submit. Colonel George Sterling Ryerson of the Canadian Red Cross and Dr William Barry of the YMCA provided comforts and services for the Canadians. The Laurier government overcame its aversion to military expenditure sufficiently to make up the difference between Canadian and British pay and pension scales. When the contingents returned to Canada, their Canadian-made uniforms and equipment were evaluated and, in some cases, found wanting. Canvas uniforms, water bottles, greatcoats, blankets, and the specially-designed Oliver equipment had failed the test of active service but little was done to replace or improve them.[34]

Answering critics like Bourassa, Laurier had assured Parliament that the cabinet decision of 14 October 1899 did not constitute a precedent. In fact, as Bourassa appreciated, it was to prove the most important precedent in modern Canadian military history. It determined the response Canada would adopt in two world wars and in the Korean conflict. It added a new and far more realistic function for which Canadian military forces could prepare. Until 1899, the Canadian militia existed for two essential roles: war with the United States or aid to the civil power. The former was increasingly unlikely and even more certainly bound to be unsuccessful as American military power grew. The latter role was uninspiring and, in the long run, utterly repugnant. The prospect that future British wars would involve Canadian expeditionary forces offered realism and a sense of purpose for militia training. The military enthusiasts who carried the burden of such a voluntary organization could now dream of fulfilling their warlike ambition.[35]

In the wake of the South African War, Canada's militia underwent a drastic overhaul and modernization. Old values and attitudes could not easily be abandoned. Political influence, quarrelsome rivalries, and much of the social ritual of militia summer camps survived reforming efforts. South African experience gave some of the participants – and many more who never went – an inflated sense of Canadian military competence. The Boer farmers, as Sam Hughes had warned, gloriously vindicated amateurism over military professionalism. However, in the post-1900 period, Canadians could have both. Between 1897 and 1913, Canadian defence spending rose from $1.8 million to $11 million. Between 1904 and 1913, militia strength grew from 36,000 to 55,000. Efficiency, while less measurable, increased proportionately. When Canada assumed responsibility for the British fortress at Halifax, the permanent force expanded dramatically to take over new and highly technical responsibilities. An infusion of British officers and veteran non-commissioned officers helped.[36]

As the British army, particularly after 1906, reorganized for an increasingly probable role in continental Europe, integration of training and tactical doctrines throughout the British Empire spread new ideas to Canada. More Canadian officers were admitted to training courses in England and, in 1905, the first Canadian was admitted to the staff college at Camberley. Others soon followed. In 1907, colonial prime ministers hesitantly acceded to the notion of an 'Imperial General Staff' and, in 1909, agreed more whole-heartedly that their forces would adopt the manuals and follow the organization of the British home regular forces.[37]

Integration had to wrestle with Canadian self-confidence and autonomy. Thoughts about future overseas contingents had to be combined with dreams of defence against the Americans, particularly among those who responded in kind to President Theodore Roosevelt's bellicose threats. Such dreams could be fulfilled only by a nation in arms. Lord Dundonald, who commanded the militia from 1902 to 1904, preached the doctrine of a 'citizen army,' embodying more than a hundred thousand Canadians in a Swiss-style militia.[38] Dundonald's scheme languished when he was dismissed for openly denouncing the Liberal government for political meddling in the militia. The idea persisted, however, taking shape in the remarkable expansion of compulsory military training in Canadian schools after 1909.[39]

The South African experience underlined a long series of military lessons, most of which were taken to heart by the British army. It was obvious, for example, that military co-operation throughout the empire would be easier if weapons and equipment as well as tactical doctrines were held in common. It would also, of course, be beneficial to British manufacturers. Canadians, eager to spend their own money at home, disagreed. When the Birmingham Small Arms Co took no interest in opening a branch in Canada capable of producing the standard British Lee-Enfield rifle, Canadians looked elsewhere. Sir Frederick Borden, Laurier's minister of militia, was open to a beguiling offer from Sir Charles Ross, a Scottish sportsman with expansive dreams. To help evaluate Ross's rifle, Borden turned to Colonel Otter and to Colonel Sam Hughes, now the opposition's chief military critic. From the start Hughes became a passionate proponent of the Ross rifle. The tests at Rockcliffe Range in 1902 showed the weapon's excellence as a target rifle; they also reflected most of the faults that would plague the weapon on active service, particularly the stiffness of the bolt mechanism after rapid fire. Hughes, an expert marksman, rejected every criticism. When Sir Charles was discovered pouring oil on the rival Lee-Enfield before a trial in sandy conditions, the Scottish baronet might have been disqualified. Instead, the Liberal government adopted the Ross and financed Sir Charles's rifle factory in Laurier's Quebec East constituency. When the rifle came under bitter attack from the opposition, as it soon did, Sir Frederick Borden could depend on the Tories' own military critic, Colonel Sam Hughes, to rise as its most ferocious defender.[40]

The Ross rifle was the most costly and significant result of the congruence of Canadian military and economic nationalism in the pre-war years. Other items of Canadian uniform and equipment continued in use. The notorious Oliver leather harness, hated by Canadians in South Africa because of its discomfort and poor workmanship, was an example. It had, after all, been designed by a British army surgeon stationed in Halifax.[41]

Growing self-confidence, together with the long series of disputes that culminated in the removal of Lord Dundonald, persuaded many Canadians that they no longer needed a British officer at the head of the militia. Proposed amendments to the Militia Act in 1904 opened command of the force to a Canadian. Then, when the British replaced their hierarchy with an Army Council, the Laurier government amended its proposals by establishing a Militia Council. Although the senior position could now be held by a Canadian officer, the government proved faster in legislation than in action. The senior military position in the new council, the chief of general staff, was given to a British officer with long service in Canada, Brigadier-General Percy Lake. Only in 1908 was the post given to a Canadian, Brigadier-General Otter. Appointed inspector-general, Lake remained the senior officer.[42]

Through his long service and great influence, General Lake deserved credit for most of the military reforms of the Laurier years but, unlike other British officers, Lake never forgot that the real sponsor of militia improvements was Sir Frederick Borden. A Nova Scotia country doctor and businessman, Borden held his portfolio throughout the Laurier years. He was neither a power in the cabinet nor the bibulous mediocrity portrayed by critics. Longevity and a decent regard for political favours and patronage allowed Borden a free hand with his department. He used his freedom to promote medical, service, and other departmental corps, to encourage the training of permanent corps officers, and to ensure that Canada's defenders had their full share of the country's growing public revenue.[43]

Borden's Militia Council gave the minister access to a variety of departmental opinions and expertise, military and civil. Appointment of a chief of general staff encouraged a new emphasis on a badly neglected staff function: planning. Until 1896, despite British prodding, Canada had had no mobilization plan at all. Under the shadow of the Venezuela crisis, Captain Arthur Lee, an instructor at the Royal Military College and later Lord Lee of Fareham, hurriedly concocted a scheme to mobilize volunteer militia at key points on the border. In 1898, a commission of British officers, nominally under Canadian direction, improved on Lee's plan though its members secretly confessed to the War Office that their scheme was worthless without drastic reform of the militia. Most of the reforms of the Borden era followed, if at a cautious distance, the 1898 recommendations and 'Report No. 1' remained until 1920 the essence of Canada's mobilization plan in the unlikely event of a renewal of the War of 1812.[44]

It was not, of course, unimproved. In 1905, Lake had brought to Canada a remarkable former War Office subordinate, Lieutenant-Colonel Willoughby Gwatkin. A university-educated officer whose intellectual interests flowed into ethnology, ornithology, and, as a recreation, writing macaronic verse, Gwatkin was destined to spend most of the rest of his life at the Militia Department. In 1911, after a short staff appointment in England, he returned to Ottawa in the new appointment of general staff officer (mobilization).[45] Gwatkin's first task was to revise 'Report No. 1' to fit the six somewhat theoretical infantry divisions into which the militia had been organized; his major concern reflected the precedent set in 1899. As virtually his last major directive before the Liberals and he, himself, went down to defeat in the 1911 election, Sir Frederick Borden instructed Gwatkin to prepare an alternative mobilization plan in the eventuality that the government wished to dispatch another expeditionary force.[46]

It was a delicate task. The fate of Laurier's naval legislation at the hands of Bourassa and Quebec's *nationalistes* was sufficient warning. What would happen if word leaked out that one of Laurier's ministers had considered even the possibility that an infantry division and a cavalry brigade, about twenty-five thousand men in all, might be sent abroad to fight in one of Britain's wars? Gwatkin's plan decentralized much of the responsibility to the six divisional areas in eastern Canada and the three military districts in the west. Quotas were assigned on the basis of local militia strength. Once partial mobilization was completed at local 'places of assembly,' units would assemble at the huge new camp at Petawawa or, if winter intervened, they would head directly to ports of embarkation. The contingent would be prepared to fight in 'a civilized country' in 'a temperate climate.'[47]

Launched under Liberal direction, Gwatkin's plan was completed under very different auspices. Laurier's 1911 defeat seemed inevitable only after the event. The Tories swept into office on a wave of contradictory moods – isolationism in Quebec, imperialism and economic nationalism in Ontario, racial atavism in British Columbia. Now they were hungry for the fruits of office and quarrelsome about the spoils. In the traditional ordeal of forming a Canadian federal cabinet, the new prime minister regarded Sam Hughes as a major embarrassment.

Undoubtedly, as Borden later admitted in his memoirs, Hughes had earned promotion. Among Ontario's noisy Orangemen, Hughes would be a popular choice. In the backbench revolts against Robert Borden's leadership, Hughes had been a pillar of loyalty when other, more cerebral Tories had faltered. In 1904 Hughes had been the first to offer the defeated Borden his seat. Behind Hughes's often brutal, bullying manner was a large capacity for personal charm and generosity which has not easily been communicated to posterity. At the same time, his enemies in the Conservative party were numerous and influential. They included George Perley, a close confidant of the new prime minister, and Perley's future father-in-law, Thomas White, the ex-Liberal who would become Borden's minister of finance. No one who had sat in Parliament needed to be reminded of Sam Hughes's unbalanced enthusiasms or the manic ferocity with which he pursued his enemies. Besieged by advocates for Hughes, Robert Borden turned for advice to his cousin, the former minister of militia. Sir Frederick's advice was decisive: Sam Hughes should be given a chance. Overjoyed at his triumph, tearfully repentant for past indiscretions, Colonel Hughes promised to mend his habits. Borden, in turn, overcame the objections of the governor general, the Duke of Connaught.[48]

Voters presume that a change of government will produce a dramatic, if harmless, change of style. The flamboyant Hughes obliged. By tradition, ministers of militia had been discreet, even slightly apologetic, about their responsibilities. Hughes used his new status to preach the gospel of militarism to any audience that would listen to him. As a newspaperman, he had long been a virtuoso of self-advertisement; now he possessed a national organization to help him. Hughes found Canadians experiencing an unprecedented enthusiasm for military affairs. Even in Quebec he could find astonishing allies. Armand Lavergne might be a *nationaliste* even more ardent than Henri Bourassa but he was also a militia officer, prepared to preach the merits of compulsory military training – if only for home defence. Hughes secured Lavergne's early promotion to colonel by transferring his superior, Lieutenant-Colonel J.P. Landry, to the permanent staff.

Previous ministers of militia had fortified themselves behind the doctrine of separation of civil and military powers. Hughes joyfully ignored such barriers. Thanks to Fred Borden, Hughes had enjoyed a part-time appointment in the militia staff and had become the senior colonel in the force. Dutiful subordinates in the Militia Council lobbied the prime minister and the governor general to secure Hughes's promotion to major-general. At militia camps and troop concentrations at Petawawa, Hughes appeared in uniform, took charge of training, and issued commands, praise, and abuse in a stentorian voice. For the most part, militia officers were delighted. Summoned to Ottawa in the winter of 1912 for a conference, commanding officers discovered a minister who for once reflected their prejudices and ambitions. The drill hall, Hughes insisted, would become the school of the nation. Old grievances about drill pay, boots, armouries, and equipment would be remedied. After all, Hughes understood them as well as his audience. On only one issue was there bitter disagreement and Hughes silenced it with military firmness. Henceforth, he decreed, liquor and beer would be banished from militia camps. The women of Canada would know that their sons would be safe from alcoholic temptation. If Hughes could manage it, the two weeks under canvas with the county regiment would no longer be a boozy *rite de passage* for Canada's rural youth.[49]

If Hughes strained his popularity with militia officers by his hostility to liquor, he fully restored it by his disdain for the permanent force. It was constantly justified as a training cadre for the volunteer militia, but the staff officers and the officers and men of the tiny regular units across the country yearned for a higher role. Militia officers resented the fact that most of an inadequate defence budget was consumed by the staff and permanent corps. Politicians, especially those with militia connections, had long since discovered the benefits of dismissing the regulars as 'uniformed loafers' and 'mess room loungers.' Sam Hughes was no exception. As minister, he pursued his vendetta. Officers of the Halifax garrison, who had defied the minister's sensibilities by drinking during a mess dinner, were treated to a public tongue-lashing in the presence of a senior British officer.[50] Veteran staff officers who had incurred Hughes's displeasure were peremptorily retired or transferred. For replacements, Hughes looked to militia colonels like Colonel Landry or Lieutenant-Colonel E.A. Cruikshank, a competent amateur military historian of the Niagara frontier, whom Hughes posted to

Calgary. Old supporters, like the venerable Colonel Henry Smith, were resurrected and offered new appointments. Smith, at 75, became judge advocate-general.

Almost inevitably, such a minister would offend the more scrupulous of his military subordinates. The militia council system, adopted by Sir Frederick Borden to avoid the almost endemic quarrels between ministers and generals, became little more than an echo chamber for Hughes's ideas. General Lake's successor as the senior British officer was Major-General Colin Mackenzie, a conscientious if dour Scot who served as chief of the general staff. Mackenzie treated his political superior with a distant respect, performed his duty, and ignored Hughes's more outrageously political directives. Tory politicians, furious that plans for shifting camps to their constituencies or for winning favour for militia supporters were ignored, carried their grievances to the minister.[51]

Hughes later claimed that he had tried to make friends with Mackenzie and enlist his support for the minister's crusades. Relations rapidly soured and the Scottish general joined the long and growing list of men Hughes despised. Helpless to defend himself from the minister's abuse, Mackenzie sought support from the governor general, the Duke of Connaught, a fellow soldier. In Hughes's eyes, that compounded the offence. The prime minister, compelled to intervene and to wade through interminable memoranda of grievances compiled by both Hughes and Mackenzie, arranged for the general to resign. Though Borden interceded on his behalf with the War Office, Mackenzie was never employed again.[52] No other British general could be persuaded to take up a Canadian appointment in such circumstances. Instead, Colonel Gwatkin was obliged to abandon his mobilization planning to fill the vacancy. He became chief of the general staff on 1 November 1913 and held the post for seven critical years. Rarely have the virtues of a classical education been put to a harsher test.

The Mackenzie dispute was only one demonstration that Hughes, for all his tearful promises in 1911, had neither mended his ways nor curbed his temperament. A minister who had once been a popular asset to the new government rapidly became a liability. Hughes was not wholly responsible for the change. Harsh economic conditions, visible on the horizon during the later Laurier years, descended on Canada early in Borden's term. Rents and food prices rose dramatically. Wages lagged. As employment sagged and bankruptcies increased, investors grew cautious. The huge railway expansion authorized by the Laurier government could no longer be financed on the London bond market. Farmers, caught in a credit squeeze, lost homes and land to foreclosure and fled to join the urban unemployed. Public revenue declined dramatically.[53] 'Drill Hall Sam,' demanding yet vaster sums for his militia, boasting of new drill halls in every community, preaching imminent war with Germany, became the symbol of a Conservative government out of touch with reality and indifferent to human suffering. Liberal propagandists rejoiced when Hughes, his two female secretaries, and more than thirty senior militia officers and their wives set off on a highly publicized tour of the British, French, and Swiss manoeuvres in the summer of 1913. 'Hughes and his harem' were a delight for cartoonists.[54] Conservative strategists blamed Hughes for a disastrous showing in a South Bruce by-election on 30 October 1914. The minister's bellicose speeches had deeply offended the riding's German voters.[55]

While Canada's militia had reached unprecedented strength and efficiency on the eve of war, winning guarded praise from a visiting British inspector-general, Sir Ian Hamilton, Canada's brief flurry of military enthusiasm was long past. The Canadian Defence League, launched in 1910 to crusade for universal military training, quietly gave up the ghost in March 1914. The University of Toronto, whose leaders had been among the league's more fervent spokesmen, concluded in 1914 that the moment was inopportune to launch an officers' training corps. Maurice Hutton, principal of University College in the University of Toronto, who had earlier proclaimed that the empire could have too little militarism but never too much, now suggested that students had no time for military training.[56] When the newly knighted Borden set off for his summer holiday in July 1914, one of the problems he must have contemplated was the need to replace his troublesome minister of militia.

An unrepentant Hughes continued to add to the number of his enemies. Quebec's few remaining Conservatives were enraged when the minister forbade the Seventeenth Régiment de Lévis to provide a guard of honour for the newly consecrated Cardinal Begin. Only the Orangemen rejoiced. In June Hughes intervened again to prevent the Sixty-fifth Carabiniers Mont-Royal from bearing arms in Montreal's Corpus Christi celebration as it had for years. Regulations, the minister insisted, prohibited the carrying of weapons on a church parade. No exceptions would be made. Meanwhile, Colonel Hughes ranged the country in his private railway car, opening new armouries and preaching imminent war with Germany.[57]

In the circumstances, he might have been more concerned about Canada's readiness for such a conflict. Colonel Gwatkin's original plan had been distributed, on Sir Fred Borden's orders, to military commands and districts across Canada, to be kept in strict secrecy. Sam Hughes appears not to have become fully aware of the scheme until 5 May 1913, after a visit to Hamilton when he found a local militia regiment with its overseas contingent already selected. The fault lay less with Gwatkin than with General Mackenzie, who had dismissed the plan as a 'project' and whose frosty relations with Hughes had precluded any wide-ranging briefing.[58] The plan had been revised, reducing the infantry contribution from French-speaking Quebec and adding more divisional transport and a howitzer brigade. Hughes's own amendments were eminently sensible: the Canadian expeditionary force needed more medical and supply units on its lines of communications and it must have its own pay, postal, veterinary, and ordnance services. However, work on these changes was cancelled on the minister's orders and for more than a year the overseas mobilization plan lay in abeyance. On Friday, 31 July, 1914, word went out to all militia headquarters that the mobilization plan would be disregarded.[59]

Hughes's motives in scrapping the Gwatkin scheme remain impenetrable. Certainly the plan had defects. Through no fault of Gwatkin, mobilization stores needed for the plan had never been obtained or stockpiled. Arms and equipment, ordered as long ago as 1911, had never been delivered by Britain's inefficient armaments industry. Canada was desperately short of modern field artillery and could muster only a single battery of modern howitzers. Clothing, equipment, wagons, trucks, binoculars, even rifles and revolvers, would have to be ordered after war began. However, these were not Hughes's criticisms. In essence, he condemned the plan because it was not his personal creation, because its decentralized approach placed authority in the hands of staff officers he despised as incompetent, and because the plan offered him no major role. Instead, as George Stanley has observed, Hughes proceeded to improvise a mobilization which 'however spectacular, was neither economical nor efficient.'[60]

Hughes's own plan reflected a romantic view of war wholly characteristic of his time. On 6 August, an order-in-council put Hughes himself, the Militia Council, staff, permanent corps, details from sixty-two militia units engaged in local defence, and the whole of the British Columbia militia on active service.[61] The same cabinet meeting approved an overseas contingent 'composed of officers and men who are willing to volunteer for Overseas service under the British Crown ...'[62] That night, bypassing local staff officers, 226 lettergrams were sent to militia commanding officers, spelling out the conditions, from the height and weight and chest measurement to the priority for unmarried men. 'The force will be Imperial,' the telegram noted, 'and have the status of British regular troops.'[63] The order brought confusion only partially relieved by an ensuing flow of messages, orders, and counterorders. To Hughes and probably most Canadians, the mobilization was a marvel. Who could tell them it might have been possible in a more orderly and prosaic fashion? Even the existence of Gwatkin's plan remained a secret for years. Very few could challenge Hughes's version of the mobilization:

There was really a call to arms, like the fiery cross passing through the Highlands of Scotland or the mountains of Ireland in former days. In place of being forwarded to the district officers commanding, the word was wired to every officer commanding a unit in any part of Canada to buckle on his harness and get busy. The consequence was that in a short time we had the boys on the way for the first contingent, whereas it would have taken several weeks to have got the word around through the ordinary channels.[64]

Few paused to question whether local staff officers might have used the telegraph or the telephone at least as efficiently as the minister.

Gwatkin's plan had called for concentration of the contingent at Petawawa. Instead, Hughes decreed that volunteers would assemble at Valcartier, an area of trees and sandy flats sixteen miles north-west of Quebec City, already designated as a future camp for Quebec militia. In a much greater marvel than his mobilization, Hughes directed the creation of a huge tented camp, three-and-a-half miles of rifle ranges, water mains, sewers, and a few permanent huts.[65] The camp commander was Colonel Victor Williams, pulled from his responsibilities as adjutant-general, but the real authority at Valcartier was Hughes himself. On horseback, in full uniform, surrounded by aides, admirers, and favour-seekers, the minister was in his element. One of the few permanent buildings erected in camp was a castle-shaped structure to serve as the minister's residence and headquarters. Daily, Colonel Hughes rode forth to bring order out of the chaos he had created. Between 18 August and 8 September, a total of 32,665 men poured into the camp from every part of Canada. Only the minister held the ultimate authority to choose officers, organize units, and direct training and he guarded his prerogative jealously. Stories – some of them apocryphal – filtered across the camp. On parade, Hughes raged at one major as a 'pipsqueak' because his word of command was not loud enough. A junior officer was suddenly promoted when Hughes mistook him for a major and would not, of course, admit his error. A Humane Society official, protesting the maltreatment of horses, was ejected from the minister's quarters. So was the Anglican Bishop of Montreal, concerned about his denomination's share of chaplains.[66]

By the end of September, the organization of the contingent had taken shape. While the government had promised an infantry division of about twenty thousand men, with 10 per cent extra for casualties, Hughes found himself able to organize seventeen infantry battalions instead of the necessary twelve. In some cases, units had virtually organized themselves before coming to Valcartier. Toronto's two oldest militia regiments, the Queen's Own Rifles and the Tenth Royal Grenadiers, provided almost all the men for the Third Battalion. In Montreal, the Fifth Royal Highlanders sent thirty officers and 966 men to the contingent, virtually the whole of the new Thirteenth Battalion. The Fourteenth Battalion was organized from three other Montreal regiments, including the Sixty-fifth Carabiniers, one of French Canada's best units. Other battalions of the contingent were amalgamated from a large number of militia units. The Twelfth Battalion was formed from twenty-four different regiments from Quebec, New Brunswick, and Prince Edward Island. The smallest contribution came from the Régiment de Montmagny, four officers and two other ranks. In addition to infantry, the contingent included most of the varied units required for a British infantry division at war establishment, from field artillery to a hygiene section and a postal detachment. A major omission, because of equipment shortages, was two of the three batteries needed for the division's howitzer brigade.[67]

One of Hughes's chief responsibilities was the selection of senior officers for the contingent. The pattern of his mobilization left him enormous personal discretion. While a divisional commander was left to be chosen from the British army, four brigade commanders were nominated. They included Colonel Richard Turner VC, a South African veteran, a Quebec City timber and grain merchant, and a Conservative; Lieutenant-Colonel Arthur Currie, a Victoria real estate and insurance broker, a Liberal, but a friend and commanding officer of Hughes's son, Garnet; and Lieutenant-Colonel M.S. Mercer from the Queen's Own Rifles, a Toronto barrister. The fourth brigadier, Lieutenant-Colonel J.E. Cohoe, was a keen militiaman from Welland, a county court official with Liberal connections.[68]

Admirers could easily be persuaded that the contingent represented the finest of Canadian manhood and undoubtedly it was an impressive manifestation of a young nation. However, there were significant distortions. Only 30 per cent of the 34,500 other ranks had been born in Canada; the overwhelming majority, over 65 per cent, had been born in the United Kingdom. Gwatkin's original plan had proposed that virtually all the infantry come from eastern Canada's militia regiments. In fact, eight of the seventeen battalions came from the western provinces, six were from Ontario, two were composed predominantly of English-speaking Quebeckers, and one battalion mixed French-Canadians and Maritimers. The western predominance reflected not only fervent loyalty but also an economic depression which had fallen most heavily on the young men from Britain who had gone west to seek their fortunes. As in most wars, enlistment was often an escape from hunger and disappointment. By the same token, older parts of Canada were clearly under-represented. Despite fervent appeals to the prime minister, no battalion represented his native province of Nova Scotia. Far more serious for Canada's future war effort was the absence of any formal French-Canadian representation. From the French-speaking volunteers at Valcartier, a single, somewhat understrength battalion might have been formed. Sam Hughes did not reject the possibility; he ignored it. The oversight would prove unfortunate.[69]

If the Maritime provinces or French Canada were ill represented in the contingent, Hughes could argue, it was their fault for sending too few men. Few features of the contingent mattered more to him than the principle that it was composed entirely of volunteers. The few married men were even compelled to present their wives' permission to enlist. Meanwhile, the minister had enough to do to ignore local log-rolling and lobbying. Because militia stores held no reserves of clothing for mobilization, the wool for uniforms had still to be woven into cloth when the contracts were let on 10 August. The contingent's 853 wagons were assembled from eight different manufacturers. The 133 motor vehicles were of five different makes. Hughes's special contribution to the contingent was the 'shield-shovel,' patented in the name of his secretary, Ena MacAdam, from a device observed at the Swiss manoeuvres. The tool consisted of a heavy steel blade, with two loopholes and a tiny handle. Soldiers could presumably advance behind its protection, use the blade to dig a trench, and then gain added protection by adding the shield to the parapet. Hughes ordered 25,000 of them from a Philadelphia firm, at a price of $1.35 each.[70]

Canadians were enthralled by the phenomenon at Valcartier. Sir Robert Borden shared the general amazement when he visited the camp. Grumbles and criticisms were quickly dismissed. In the enthusiasm, the government was easily persuaded to send the entire assembly of volunteers to England. In addition to the infantry division, the two permanent cavalry regiments and the Royal Canadian Horse Artillery, on hand at Valcartier to help with administration, were authorized to recruit to full strength and form an extra cavalry brigade. The additional troops confused the already chaotic embarkation arrangements at the Quebec docks where William Price, a leading Quebec City businessman, wrestled with the unprecedented problems of loading the contingent on chartered ships.[71]

Somehow, by 1 October, thirty loaded transports had dropped down the river to assemble at Gaspé. Another vessel, with a British battalion from Bermuda, joined the convoy before it sailed. The Newfoundland contingent, in another ship, would join the convoy at Cape Race. Indignant at the Royal Navy escort of venerable light cruisers, Hughes insisted on naval reinforcements. Then, as the convoy was about to sail, the minister sailed up and down the lines of waiting ships, delivering copies of his farewell message:

Some may not return, and pray God they be few. – For such, not only will their memory ever be cherished by loved ones near and dear, and by a grateful country; but throughout the ages freemen of all lands will revere and honour the heroes who sacrificed themselves in preserving unimpaired the Priceless Gem of Liberty. But the soldier going down in the cause of freedom never dies – Immortality is his. What recks he whether his resting place be bedecked with the golden lilies of France or amid the vine-clad hills of the Rhine. The principles for which you strive are Eternal.[72]

The soldiers lined the railings and pelted the minister's launch with copies of his immortal words.[73]

2

Confusion

Every belligerent found it difficult to cope with the problems of the First World War. Such a massive, prolonged war effort tore apart familiar social and political institutions. To find the money, manpower, and material resources demanded by the struggle, governments turned to a piecemeal war socialism. Conscription, income taxes, rationing, and requisitioning became commonplace. On the battlefield, the machine gun and other forms of fire-power created a defensive dominance which military skill and technological ingenuity only slowly overcame. To sustain morale, wartime propaganda subverted both truth and traditional civilized values.

The man who had best foretold the nature of modern war was a Polish Jewish banker named Ivan Bloch. His prophecy that the combat would degenerate into a murderous stalemate between opposing lines of trenches inspired the Russian czar to sponsor peace conferences at the Hague but soldiers paid little heed. Bloch's race and occupation guaranteed that the aristocratic officers of Europe would dismiss his predictions.[1]

In consequence, by the time the Canadian contingent reached England, it was apparent that the war would not be over by Christmas. Instead, the remnants of the British Expeditionary Force had just begun a desperate battle around Ypres to keep the Germans from sweeping around the last open flank on the western front. When the battle dragged to a halt at the end of October, most of Britain's splendidly disciplined regular troops had fallen but the Allied line was complete. By the end of 1914, two trench systems ran north-east from the Swiss frontier to the sandy marshes where the Yser flowed into the English Channel. On both sides, soldiers burrowed into the ground to escape cold, rain, and enemy artillery. Behind the lines, generals and staff officers continued to insist that the breakthrough was still possible and that the war of manoeuvre would soon resume. Millions of men would die to prove them wrong. Ivan Bloch's nightmare had come true.[2]

With her amateur military organization and her negligible experience of war, Canada had no share in the tactical and strategic decisions of 1914. Indeed, even if the Borden government had been invited to contribute its views, most of its members would have modestly conceded that they had nothing to offer beyond loyal support for the military heroes who had suddenly blossomed as the empire's war leaders: the huge, taciturn Lord Kitchener at the War Office, the Irish cavalry hero, Field-Marshal Sir John French, in France. After all, Canadians had not meddled in the management of the South African War despite the conspicuous ineptitude of British generalship.

There was, of course, one Canadian minister who was superbly confident of his military expertise and correspondingly disdainful of a good many British generals. In South Africa, when Sam Hughes finally secured a number of staff appointments with smaller British columns, his performance was courageous and energetic. However, his pungent comments on the incompetence of Sir Charles Warren, published in Cape Town newspapers, led to his prompt, if discreet, removal and return to Canada.[3] Lord Roberts may well have regretted the discretion. Hughes never accepted the real explanation for his sudden departure but Warren and a number of other British generals joined Hutton on the list of his mortal enemies.[4] Not only did he pester anyone in authority, British or Canadian, for the overdue recognition of his role in South Africa, he was blunt beyond prudence in condemning British military leadership: 'The halos have been knocked off the heads of a lot of fellows, many a year ago, by me,' he boasted to Borden in 1914-15.[5]

Hughes's influence was all the greater because of another difference between Canadian participation in 1899 and in 1914. In the earlier conflict, the Laurier government had assumed no initial financial commitment beyond raising, equipping, and delivering the contingent to Cape Town. In 1914, in its pre-war offer of a contingent, the Borden government had pledged 'all necessary financial provision' for that contingent.[6] The Liberals offered no dissent. When Parliament met in special session in August, neither Laurier nor his backbenchers questioned the financial implications of the government's commitment even when the prime minister made it clear that the special war appropriation of $50,000,000 for seven months would only be a beginning.[7] If Parliament was the watchdog of the treasury, it never barked.

By paying her way, Canada acquired a practical influence over the management of her contingent and vital leverage in expanding both her control of her forces and her involvement in the over-all management of the war. Because Canada helped to pay for the music, the Borden government could criticize the orchestra and, more to the point, the British government was constrained to listen to the criticism. At the same time, Canadians were compelled to develop a more rational and orderly means of administering their forces and of exerting control than ever seemed necessary to Sam Hughes. The development proved difficult, expensive, and undignified.[8]

The representative of the Canadian government in Britain, the high commissioner for Canada, had occupied a somewhat ambiguous position ever since the first appointment was made in 1880. The British government communicated with its Canadian colony through the Colonial Office and the governor general; while Ottawa had always found it valuable to have a 'man of business' in London to handle its innumerable concerns, its official business returned through the governor general through the same channel. Certainly, Canada's representative in London had much to do in co-ordinating the activities of Canadian departments in London, encouraging Canadian businessmen in their search for markets and capital, and supervising the flow of emigration from Britain which, in the pre-war years, had become a flood.[9]

The influence and effectiveness of the Canadian high commissioner depended, like most such appointments, on the personality of the appointee. Sir Charles Tupper was Sir John A. Macdonald's abrasive but indispensable political lieutenant. Summoned to Canada when desperately needed for the political wars, he returned as soon as he could to the more congenial atmosphere of late Victorian England. His successor, Lord Strathcona, had been wealthy enough to contribute an entire regiment of Canadian mounted infantry to the South African War and to provide much of the financial incentive for the spread of the cadet movement in Canada, but he ignored the boring routine of his post. When he died in January 1914, at the age of 94, the office of high commissioner seemed to require a man of enormous wealth to perform a largely symbolic administrative role.[10]

Yet if the active and continual consultation implicit in Sir Robert Borden's view of the empire were to develop, it would have to occur in London: Canada's permanent representative there would become a key policy-making figure. In a world where it took at least a week for a Canadian prime minister to reach London and more than a month for premiers from Australia and New Zealand, the high commissioners of the self-governing dominions could not help becoming more significant. The Borden government found Strathcona's vacancy difficult to fill. Sir Robert Borden's solution was to dispatch his friend and ally, the Hon George Halsey Perley, minister without portfolio, to serve as acting high commissioner during the summer of 1914. The Harvard-educated son of a prominent Ottawa Valley lumbering family, Perley was wealthy, a leader in Ottawa and Montreal financial circles, and a man of social ambition. As MP for Argenteuil since 1904, he was one of Quebec's few remaining major figures in the Borden cabinet although formally he represented the province's English-speaking Protestants. As chief whip in opposition, he had won Borden's confidence by quelling a number of backbench revolts and, although he did not manage a department, the new prime minister placed Perley third in cabinet precedence.[11]

While Perley and his socially ambitious wife could look forward to the pleasures of an English summer, he took with him a number of official and unofficial chores. The order-in-council appointing him indicated that he would be responsible for investigating a new site for the commission offices and for negotiating some proposed amendments to the British North America Act. W.L. Griffiths, Strathcona's assistant and the faithful senior official of the commission, was warned that Perley would examine the organization of the office and the need to bring all Canadian government functions under its direct control. Lewis Harcourt, the colonial secretary, and Winston Churchill, First Lord of the Admiralty, were advised that Perley might be invited as Canada's representative at any meetings of the Committee of Imperial Defence held during his stay. 'His good judgement and discretion may be absolutely relied upon,' Borden assured the colonial secretary, 'and he has my complete confidence as to the policy which we shall pursue in the future ...'[12]

While Perley might reflect Borden's opinions on naval and defence matters, his judgment of the potential role of the high commissioner went far beyond the prime minister's views. The more Perley studied the office, the more he liked it. By July he had drafted a plan of reorganization which would bring all Canadian official activities in Great Britain firmly under the high commissioner's authority. In turn, the post would be elevated to cabinet rank. Only in that way could the high commissioner speak with the weight of the Canadian government behind him. It was a proposal Perley would argue without success for the next three years. In the meantime, the events of August changed a visit of a few months into a stay of eight years.[13]

War dramatically increased the work of the high commission. Canadians, stranded in Europe by the sudden outbreak, had to be helped. Businessmen, eager to profit from the crisis or desperate to rescue their affairs from disaster, besieged Perley for references and support. Since the Militia Department had always been among the most independent of the Canadian agencies in London, it was understandable that Hughes insisted on a direct link with the War Office. The Colonial Office grudgingly conceded that it could be by-passed on 'details of a military character relating to the contingents.'[14] None the less, Perley served as intermediary in the selection of a British general to command the Canadian contingent. Three possibilities, Canadian-born officers, were far away in India although one of them, Brigadier-General G.M. Kirkpatrick, the son of a former Conservative MP and lieutenant-governor of Ontario, might have been summoned in three weeks.[15]

The actual selection proved a complicated manoeuvre. In Ottawa, Hughes ignored the three junior but Canadian-born officers and reluctantly sacrificed his own ambition to command his 'boys' though, as he modestly conceded, 'I would get twice, if not three times as much out of them as anyone else ...'[16] Instead, he considered a list of three distinguished veterans of the South African War, rejected Lord Dundonald and Sir Reginald Pole-Carew, and judged Major-General Edwin Alderson the 'best qualified by far.'[17] As a mounted infantry colonel in South Africa, Alderson had not only commanded Canadians (under General Hutton), but he had also acquired a reputation that 'he would not get his troops into trouble.'[18] On 25 September Alderson was officially interviewed and appointed by Lord Kitchener and, on 14 October, when the Canadians reached Plymouth, he was promoted to lieutenant-general.[19] Hughes was satisfied: 'Canadian soldiers' ideal,' he wired Kitchener.[20]

Having overseen the departure of the contingent, Hughes himself sailed from New York on 7 October, reaching England several days before the convoy. Alarm at his coming was only partially allayed by Borden's reassurance: 'Hughes is going in unofficial capacity for a holiday and is not to assume any military command or interfere in military matters.'[21] In fact, Hughes arrived in a splendid mood, greeted the contingent at Plymouth, approved of the proposed camp on Salisbury Plain, soothed ruffled feathers among Canadian officers, for whom a costly messing contract had been arranged with the elegant firm of Harrod's, and supported Alderson's canteen policy against the criticism of fervent prohibitionists. Canadian soldiers, in trouble from the moment of landing with the more potent English beer, would be better protected by having their own drinking establishments.[22]

Underlying the minister's buoyant good spirits was news of his promotion to major-general. Ever since 1911, cronies on the Militia Council, led by Major-General Macdonald, the quartermaster-general, had lobbied for the promotion, insisting that Hughes was senior colonel in the force, to say nothing of his military attributes. The governor general had just as stubbornly opposed it, insisting with some justice that it would only encourage Hughes's confusion of his military and political roles. After the marvel of Valcartier, resistance collapsed. A delighted Hughes reported that he had had congratulatory cables and messages from thousands of well-wishers.[23]

In Hughes's absence, Borden had gradually become aware that there was another side to Valcartier. The outcry from aggrieved officers and contractors had been discounted. Now the Duke of Connaught confirmed that Hughes had been abusive and violent in handling officers and visitors alike. A general election was due in 1914 and within the Conservative cabinet debate raged whether the emergency would guarantee a government majority or whether it imposed a political truce. Hughes had been firmly instructed to keep his overseas visit brief so that he could return for the contest. As opinion divided over Hughes, admirers like Sir Clifford Sifton revelling in his toughness, cabinet opponents alarmed at the trouble he had caused, Sir Robert Borden began to feel that it might be as well if Hughes's ambition for active service were satisfied. 'In case Hughes should be desirous of going to the front,' Borden wired Perley, 'it would be advisable from political considerations to give him the opportunity ...'[24] Such a prospect found no support in England. 'Kitchener said could not be managed,' Perley cryptically reported, 'and in his opinion Hughes should return home to attend to work there.'[25]

By then Borden had finally decided not to hold elections. Perley, initially an enthusiast, had gradually come to the same conclusion. The Liberals would plainly use patriotic arguments against an unseemly political contest in wartime. The overseas contingent, disfranchised by distance, Perley warned, would contain a disproportionate number of Tory voters. Besides, he suggested, it would be a tragedy for the empire if the Borden government were defeated.[26]

Instead Hughes came home to the task of organizing a second contingent. Offered on 6 October as a force of twenty thousand men, the contingent was not formally accepted by Whitehall until 31 October when there had been a little time to assess Canada's first offering. On 7 November, the cabinet agreed to recruit thirty thousand men to provide a continuous stream of reinforcements, as well as to raise an extra 15,272 men who, with units already in England, could form a second Canadian division.[27] This time, with winter approaching, there could be no Valcartier. Indeed, with the balance of Canada's field guns shipped to Britain as a generous gesture, there were not even guns with which newly-recruited artillerymen could practise.

Back in Ottawa on 8 November, General Hughes ordered that units for the new contingent would be organized and trained at local headquarters. When the extra battalions of the First Contingent and three more battalions still in Canada had to be earmarked to provide replacements for the 1st Canadian Division, more infantry units were authorized until the contingent had its full twelve battalions.

This time, the gaps in representation in the First Contingent were filled. Nova Scotians could join the Twenty-fifth Battalion while a powerful delegation from Montreal and Quebec profited from Hughes's absence and gained authority for a 'French-Canadian contingent' which emerged as the Twenty-second Battalion. Although legend maintained that the unit rapidly filled its ranks, in fact, twelve days after the dramatic recruiting rally at Parc Sohmer, the battalion had mustered only 27 officers and 575 other ranks, not the nine hundred men claimed in the press. Thanks to drafts assembled from other battalions, the unit was eventually brought close to full strength before it left for England in May 1915.[28]

While Hughes devoted himself to raising the Second Contingent and to stirring fresh controversy in Canada, Canadians in England adjusted to their new commander, serious training, and a sudden change in climate. At first, almost everything went well. Hughes and Perley smoothed over their long-standing antagonism. The acting high commissioner reported after a long interview with General Alderson that he was a man 'with whom I feel sure that we are going to have very satisfactory relations.'[29] Unloading the contingent at Plymouth reproduced the chaos at Quebec. Equipment, stores, baggage, and vehicles had become hopelessly separated from their own units and, after a futile attempt to claim it at dockside, most of the material was simply collected and shipped to stations close to the camps on Salisbury Plain.[30] However, as warm, dry weather continued through October, the Canadians could rejoice in their tented camps and at the pleasure of turf underfoot in contrast to the sandhills of Valcartier.

The honeymoon lasted a week. On 21 October, a quarter of an inch of rain fell; rainfall continued for 89 of the next 123 days. Temperatures fell, often below freezing. The light summer tents offered little protection and storms on 11 November and 4 December flattened most of them. The turf underfoot proved to be a thin coating over limestone and rapidly turned into quagmire.[31] Serious training was hampered by the cold, sodden conditions, but the Canadians were soon busy with drill, physical training, route marches, and intensive efforts to emulate the skill and rapidity in rifle fire which had so impressed an advancing German army when it faced British regulars. Delighted to have an active command, Alderson worked hard, rediscovering the problems of serving two masters when the War Office sharply criticized his direct contacts with the Canadian authorities. After explanations, he was granted some latitude.[32]

There was certainly much to do. Sam Hughes could boast of the readiness of his contingent when it left Canada but, to professional soldiers, the contingent was woefully unready for active service. Few of the men in the ranks had even had prior militia experience while their officers had rarely known more of military life than summer camps and a few brief courses. Equipment, gathered with pride and at considerable cost, was inferior to British military issue. The hundreds of farm wagons purchased by Hughes were too light to carry heavy ammunition. A wide turning circle might be suitable for an Ontario or Manitoba farmyard but it was hopeless for a narrow French or English country road. Spare parts for the variety of wagons and motor vehicles were virtually unobtainable. In the appalling conditions on Salisbury Plain, the Canadian-made boots proved neither durable nor waterproof, leading to the rumour that they had been made from cardboard. The Oliver equipment, despite modifications, was as bad as ever.[33] However, the weakest feature of the contingent, as it had been in South Africa, was the officers. In a private letter to the Duke of Connaught, Alderson was scathing. Many officers, he complained, were ignorant of their duties, lacked the power of command, and some had been 'very drunk.' 'Officers seem to have been pitchforked about, often by word of mouth, in many cases claims to seniority and appointment are merely "the Minister told me to go and take it up."'[34]

The minister might be back in Canada but his presence lingered in the portly figure of Colonel John Wallace Carson. A highly successful Montreal businessman, president of the Crown Reserve Mining Company, general manager of the Crown Trust, and director of a prosperous array of banks, mining companies, and flour mills, Carson had also pursued an active militia career. For eight years he commanded the Fifth Royal Scots, the most exclusive of Montreal militia regiments. In 1910, to his considerable fury, Carson was retired but the victory of the Conservatives a year later gave him and several officers who had resigned with him a second chance. With warm encouragement from his good friend Sam Hughes, Carson set about reviving a once-distinguished regiment which had fallen on hard times, the First Prince of Wales Fusiliers. Transforming it into the Canadian Grenadier Guards, complete with British full-dress uniforms, was the kind of enormously costly enterprise only a man like Carson could afford. The reward was social standing and further favours from his friend, the minister of militia.[35]

At fifty, Carson was too old and too senior to join the contingent although he played a leading part in organizing the Fourteenth Battalion. As a reward, Hughes dispatched him as head of an advance party of administrative officers which left New York on 22 September. On arrival, Carson called on the acting high commissioner but, as Perley later explained to Borden, they discovered that 'neither of us knew exactly what he was supposed to do except that he had been asked to arrange so that things would be as comfortable as possible on the arrival of the troops.'[36] Carson took up residence at the White Hart hotel in Salisbury but he seems to have found little to occupy him. On 7 November, he was reported in contingent orders as 'representing the Canadian Government as regards certain financial and other questions in connection with the Canadian Contingent.'[37] Since Hughes did not take pains to explain to Carson or anyone else what such 'questions' might include, Carson assumed a wide mandate. On 14 November, in London to attend the Lord Mayor's Show as Canada's military representative, he took it upon himself to call on Lord Kitchener to inform him directly of the conditions of cold, wet, and mud prevailing in the Canadian camp. Shocked by Carson's revelations, the war secretary promptly offered to make room for the Canadians in huts by transferring British Territorial units to tents. He also summoned Alderson. Both Carson and Alderson rejected special favours for the Canadians. The general, on his return to Salisbury, summoned his senior officers and had them join him in denying that there had been serious grounds for complaint. Carson was furious at such a repudiation of his efforts; he was even more indignant when Lord Kitchener refused him any further interviews.[38] Understandably, Carson reported the situation to General Hughes. 'The conditions of camp life in England at this season of the year are simply appalling, and in my opinion are bound to have a serious effect on the health and morale of our troops.' It would be wiser, Carson suggested, to send the Canadians to train in Egypt where the outbreak of war with Turkey had led to an obvious need for troops.[39]

While a frustrated Carson returned to Canada in December, the men of the contingent accepted their fate with surprisingly good humour. Despite the conditions, health remained good and illness only spread when troops began to move into hastily constructed huts. An epidemic of meningitis, at first blamed on camp conditions, proved to have begun at Valcartier. It claimed twenty-eight lives. The most serious medical problem was venereal disease, with 1,249 cases. Had innocent young Canadians made contact with old world vice or had they brought both attitudes and experience with them? That debate would bubble discreetly through the war years. General Alderson, concerned to protect the good name of Canada, felt obliged to restrict an initially generous leave policy and to curb rowdy excursions to London. Most Canadians responded well: others, including ninety officers and 586 other ranks, went home to Canada as physically or mentally unfit or as undesirable members of the force.[40]

Back in Canada, Colonel Carson's report caused considerable concern to Borden and his colleagues. The prime minister was impressed by the Montreal executive, judging him in his diary a 'very competent and faithful man.'[41] He therefore gave full credence to Carson's further advice and information. Still seething at his treatment, Carson claimed that Alderson, while 'a perfect gentleman, a man for whom I have the greatest esteem and respect,' none the less lacked the ability to handle Canadians: 'he does not treat our men with a firm iron hand covered with the velvet glove, which their special temperaments require.' Moreover, on an issue which had already caused some concern to Hughes, he warned that the British were still contemplating the break-up of the Canadian division for service at the front.[42] Borden, impressed by his informant and kept almost completely in the dark by the British about the progress and problems of the imperial war effort, was shaken by Carson's information. Dispatching a copy of the report to Perley, the prime minister contrasted the achievement at Valcartier with the near-disaster at Salisbury Plain. In London, Perley was less impressed. He countered most of Carson's claims of British folly and mismanagement, recalled that Hughes had personally approved the campsite and suggested that if Carson had only brought his concerns to the high commission, Perley would have taken them to the War Office. Indeed, until he read Carson's report, he had been unaware that the colonel had ever visited the War Office.[43]

Even Perley agreed that part of Carson's problem was the vagueness of his assignment. Carson's own proposal was that he should be appointed assistant high commissioner under Perley. Instead, the prime minister directed Hughes to provide his agent with clearer terms of reference. The resulting order-in-council was not a great improvement. Carson would be: 'appointed during pleasure, to represent the Militia Department of Canada in the United Kingdom in connection with supplies and other requirements for the Canadian Overseas Expeditionary Force.' In addition, Carson would be: 'acting as the agent of the Minister of Militia in maintaining the depots of articles of equipment and other supplies necessary for the upkeep and subsistence of the Canadian Expeditionary Force both in the United Kingdom and at the seat of War.'[44] As a general staff officer, Carson would be paid twenty-three dollars a day plus travelling allowances.

Carson's role reflected the growing indignation of the Canadian government at what it now saw as the systematic rejection of Canadian equipment. In turn, this added immensely to the domestic political difficulties of the Conservatives. War had come as a further blow to a national economy already deep in recession, disrupting markets, tightening credit, and throwing thousands out of work. Canadian industrialists clamoured for military contracts and the contingent's equipment should have been a demonstration of Canada's productive potential. Instead, much of it was scrapped. To Borden's indignation, British purchasing agents headed to the United States, not Canada, even when, in a few cases, the work was actually subcontracted to Canadian industry. However vaguely it was set out, Carson's appointment was designed to regain control of equipment and supplies for at least the Canadian overseas contingent.[45]

Unfortunately, Carson himself was by no means satisfied with such important but pedestrian responsibilities. As soon as he learned the terms of the order-in-council, he warned that any restriction of his authority as the minister's personal representative in all military matters would restrict his *entrée* in London. The prime minister should send letters to Perley, Alderson, and the War Office announcing that Carson, as representative of the Department of Militia and Defence, would be at their disposal for consultation about any matter on which they might seek advice.[46] His suggestions were rejected. Borden believed that the order-in-council went far enough: 'I do not think it would be possible for me to control your relations with the War Office or with General Alderson. So far as Sir George Perley is concerned, he will, of course, be glad to have you consult with him at any time and I shall at once write to him accordingly. So far as other matters are concerned, your best course is to be governed by the terms of your Order-in-Council.'[47]

When Carson returned to England at the beginning of February, he found that the 1st Canadian Division was already on the move to France. Between 7 and 16 February the Canadians moved out of Salisbury and across to the French port of St-Nazaire on the Bay of Biscay. Behind them most units left an embarrassing litter of garbage and abandoned equipment. The extra units of the First Contingent also remained. On 1 February a Canadian cavalry brigade was formed from three permanent force units, the Royal Canadian Horse Artillery, Royal Canadian Dragoons, and Lord Strathcona's Horse, together with a British reserve unit, the Second King Edward's Horse, originally formed to train military enthusiasts in Britain from the dominions. One of the surplus infantry battalions, the Sixth Fort Garry Horse, was assigned as a reserve cavalry regiment and four other extra battalions moved into Tidworth Barracks near Salisbury to form the Canadian Training Depot. Another battalion, the Princess Patricia's Canadian Light Infantry, which had been raised on a contribution of $100,000 from A. Hamilton Gault and formed almost exclusively from British army reservists in Canada, had already joined the British 27th Division in France.[48]

Canadian military concerns in Britain had entered a new phase. Until the end of the war, they would embrace three functions: the training and dispatch of reinforcements to replace casualties, the organization, training, and dispatch of additional units and formations, and the rehabilitation of sick and wounded. They were the aspects of war in which the Canadians had least experience and for which they had made the least preparation, not entirely through oversight. General Gwatkin, as the architect of the Canadian plan, had presumed that the far larger British army would provide all the administrative support and management that was necessary. As he explained to Loring Christie, Sir Robert Borden's confidant on external policy: 'the closer we stand in with the Army, the better for the Army and a great deal better for ourselves.'[49] Even in the submissive mood of the early months of war, such an arrangement could not be completely acceptable. Lieutenant-Colonel W.R. Ward, the assistant paymaster general at Militia Headquarters, arrived early with orders to establish a pay and record office. Perley soon reported that Ward had been established with a growing staff at 36 Victoria St SW, not far from the offices of the high commission. By August 1915 the two offices, records and pay, were separated and by September 1916 the staffs of both offices, military and civilian, totalled 2,841 people. Another permanent force officer, Colonel Guy Carleton Jones, remained in England as director general of medical services for the CEF. He also established his office in London and presided over a growing collection of Canadian hospitals and convalescent facilities.[50]

Alderson had unquestionably commanded all Canadian troops in England. With his departure, the succession was in doubt. No available Canadian officer, in his view, was equal to the responsibility. Colonel Victor Williams, who had commanded the contingent during its ocean passage, had been relegated to camp commandant during the period on Salisbury Plain. Another senior permanent force officer, Colonel J.C. MacDougall, was due to accompany Alderson as his military secretary. Neither officer had impressed the general very favourably. Accordingly, the War Office dispatched Colonel W.R.W. James of the Royal Artillery to take command of the Canadian Training Depot at Tidworth. The Canadian Cavalry Brigade provided an ingenious solution to the problem of finding a position for Colonel J.E.B. Seely. Seely, a lively spirit who had led an adventurous life, had served briefly as secretary of state for war in the Asquith government until the Curragh incident, a near-mutiny of British officers in Ireland, forced his resignation in the spring of 1914. Both his rank, earned through service in a British yeomanry regiment, and his unfortunate experience as a Liberal politician made it difficult to place him in a British unit. The Canadian brigade provided a marvellous answer.

The Canadians were not pleased. Seely, later Lord Mottistone, may have been an excellent officer but his formal military experience was no greater than that of several of the Canadians under his command. By the time the Canadian government was informed, however, the deed was done and Perley recommended acquiescence. Borden consented but he warned that the next mounted corps he sent over would have a Canadian in command.[51]

Hughes had also taken belated steps to ensure that the Canadians would have their own senior officer in England. British insistence that a divisional headquarters had no vacancy for a military secretary compelled Alderson to leave MacDougall behind. On 9 February a telegram from the adjutant general in Ottawa notified MacDougall that he would have temporary command of all Canadians in England while another message to the War Office informed the British authorities that MacDougall would hold the rank of temporary and local brigadier-general while he held the appointment.[52]

Between Carson and his new instructions and MacDougall with his promotion and new authority, there should have been no grounds for conflict. It did not take long for misunderstanding to arise, however. On 15 February Major-General C.A. Altham, officer in charge of administration for the British army's Southern Command, wrote to Carson to ask whether any Canadian officer in the United Kingdom possessed the authority to return incompetent officers to Canada. Carson was immediately obliging: 'I am the only officer now serving in the country who would have that power,' he wrote, 'and I would not hesitate to act if the necessity were unfortunately to arise.'[53] While General Altham accepted this breathtaking assertion as fact, Carson soon sought to cover himself with the minister. In a letter to Hughes on 23 February he warned: 'from time to time other cases of undesirable officers are bound to arise and there is no authority now in England capable of dealing with them.'[54]

Even in early January, Borden had suspected that Carson would be dissatisfied with his restricted role. On the other hand, for all his presumed authority, General MacDougall found that he had very little to command. With James in charge at Tidworth and Seely commanding the cavalry at Uckfield, MacDougall's authority was restricted to a few Canadian hospitals and a growing ordnance depot at Ashford. In the circumstances MacDougall meekly turned to Colonel Carson to arrange that 'all matters concerning the command of the Canadians – including the Training Depot – should be under my thumb.'[55] After all, it was wise for a permanent officer to defer to one of the minister's favourites. For his part, Carson advised MacDougall to wait patiently until the minister had made up his mind. Next he wrote to Hughes to report the fragmentation of the Canadian organization in England and the need for a better command structure: 'Would it not be wise for you to consider the appointment of a senior Canadian Officer who would carry a rank not below that of Major-General, and put him in supreme central command of all the Canadian Troops who might be at any time in England and let him at his office, which could be in London or elsewhere, be the supreme authority on all matters of discipline etc., etc., without, of course, attempting to interfere with the, as it were, Head Office functions of the British War Office.'[56]

Within a week of Carson's letter, matters were changing of their own accord. Colonel James, offered an appointment on the lines of communication in France, left Tidworth on 2 March. On the same day, Carson reported to Hughes that the Canadians would be concentrated at Shorncliffe, a camp in Eastern Command close to Dover and Folkestone, and that MacDougall could take over the newly titled reserve brigade. By 10 March the move was complete and MacDougall's new command reported to Major-General J.M. Babington, general officer commanding the Shorncliffe district and also the 23d Division of Lord Kitchener's 'New Army.'[57] In Ottawa, Hughes had had a chance to consider Carson's suggestions. The result was a rebuff for Carson and a sharp rebuke for MacDougall. 'As Officer Commanding all Canadian troops in Great Britain,' the adjutant general cabled to MacDougall on 17 March, 'you are responsible to the Department of Militia and Defence, Canada, for all appointments to the forces and the training and discipline and all other matters pertaining to and including stores and equipment ...'[58] Hughes's message to MacDougall was characteristic: 'You will please remember that you are in command of the Canadian troops in England and will be held responsible for all appointments. You have a number of Canadian Officers yet there who must be utilized. You must assume your responsibilities.'[59]

Carson's message from Hughes came two days later. It was more polite: 'Regarding command of Canadians in Britain General MacDougall is in military command of all Canadian Units in Britain excepting those under General Seely. You will continue as authorized by order-in-council to represent the Defence Minister for Canada in Britain.'[60] With this flurry of telegrams, General Hughes might assume that all confusion was resolved. He was wrong. Part of the problem was, perhaps, that Carson really had very little to do. The War Office had undertaken to equip and feed all Canadians while any financial arrangements were made through the newly knighted Sir George Perley.[61] Ensconced in the Savoy hotel, in immediate contact with the War Office and the Canadian High Commission, Carson was in an ideal position to exercise influence. His letterhead, describing himself as part of the 'Canadian General Staff' and as 'Special Representative in the British Isles and at Seat of War' implied an almost limitless mandate. In contrast, isolated at Shorncliffe, MacDougall could turn only to Carson if he wished to appeal against his British superiors. At first sight, the series of messages had sustained MacDougall's authority: by not restating the essentially administrative responsibilities assigned to Carson, Hughes had failed to bar his overseas representative's bounding ambition. A shadow of authority was all that Carson needed.

Within a few days of receiving the telegrams, MacDougall had asked Carson to rescue him from subordination to the British 23d Division. Carson obliged and soon reported that the arrangement was temporary until MacDougall had organized his staff. However, he went on to explain that the British had not been satisfied by the standard of training achieved by the Canadians on Salisbury Plain and that, in this case, he could not refuse their help.[62] When MacDougall sought more staff officers from Canada, the request was channelled through Carson. So was Hughes's directive that all matters affecting the Second Contingent would be kept separate from Mac-Dougall's command.[63] By the end of April it was apparent that neither Mac-Dougall nor the minister still considered that Carson exercised narrowly administrative functions.

The arrival of the Second Contingent in May 1915 added a new element to the accumulation of Canadian military organizations in Britain. By now the Canadian government was determined that its forces would be led by Canadians. On the fervent insistence of his patron, Robert Rogers, the minister of public works, and as a sop to western feeling, command of the Second Contingent had been given to Major-General Sam Steele. A veteran whose mounted police career spanned the Fenian raids and the Red River expedition to the South African War, Steele had been hampered by injuries suffered in a painful fall from a horse but he was keen to serve.[64] The British, dubious of the competence of a sixty-six-year-old general from the colonies, insisted that 'very experienced generals' were needed. Hughes was indignant. Though he had himself rejected Steele for the 1st Division, he now claimed to Lord Kitchener that: 'I am convinced by my opinion based upon years of experience and observations, in war and on manoeuvres, that Steele and my brother Colonel John Hughes are each as qualified for a division as any officer in the British Service.' The minister eventually conceded that his 'splendid organizer and disciplinarian' might not go beyond England, but he went on to deliver an angry warning:

I know many of our Major-Generals, some good and capable but many the absolute reverse, far inferior for administration in office or capability in the field to Steele or a dozen of my officers. Have calmly and loyally remained aloof from Salisbury horror and disintegration of 1st Canadian Division but please do not ask that too much be borne. Claim no authority to manage Force in Field, but under Army Act Canada has absolute authority in respect to appointments. Further, offensiveness and contemptuousness of some Army Officers in 1st Division became almost intolerable. I look to see that courtesy and evenhanded justice and fair play are accorded to all my deserving officers.[65]

Carson took good care to welcome the politically-connected General Steele and to assure him of his good offices. The two men met for the first time on 27 May for a 'good, long confidential chat,' after which Carson arranged an interview with Kitchener. He also pressed his services on Steele's aide-de-camp, a son of Frank Cochrane, Borden's minister of railways and canals.[66] Next Carson explained to Steele why, at the behest of Eastern Command, his division and MacDougall's organization would be kept separate: 'MacDougall would have entire command of his Training Division and you would have entire command of your Second Division without possible conflict or question between you as to standing, seniority, or anything else.'[67] That was optimistic.

Carson's attempts to exert his influence were not limited to Britain. As a representative at the 'seat of war,' he was presumably justified in urging Hughes to grant a general promotion to all battalion commanders and brigade majors of the 1st Division for their part in the second battle of Ypres on 22-27 April. Alderson refused to take Carson's suggestion seriously and Hughes, after an initial interest, withheld his approval.[68] The project died, leaving Carson with a renewed sense of grievance against General Alderson. Later Carson claimed to Steele that, if he had had his way, there would have been a Canadian in command of the 1st Division.[69]

Carson's hostility was reflected in Ottawa where, in the view of at least General Gwatkin, 'he exercises over our Minister an evil influence.' If there was trouble between Canada and the War Office, Gwatkin suspected, 'he will be responsible to a large extent.'[70] In fact, Hughes was quite capable of developing his own prejudices. On 28 May he complained to Borden, perhaps on the basis of reports from his son, Garnet, Turner's brigade major during the battle at Ypres, that Alderson had failed disastrously in action. The Canadians, he claimed, had been left without artillery support and reinforcements and no one from the divisional staff had even visited Turner's headquarters during the long fight: 'I can see no hope with General Alderson in Command of our boys.'[71]

In fact, the handling of the raw Canadians in a confusing battle and under the world's first poison gas attack had showed Alderson's competence. When details of Hughes's charges reached him through the War Office, the divisional commander answered them in detail, extracting a written apology from General Turner for the allegation that his brigade had been neglected. 'I can only explain the strange lapse of memory to the awful pounding we received on the 25th April,' Turner sheepishly confessed.[72] Certainly Ypres had been a terrible shock for Canadians at home: losses of 208 officers and 5,828 other ranks appalled a nation wholly unprepared for the price of war.

The War Office *communiqué* provided some compensation: 'The Canadians had many casualties, but their gallantry and determination undoubtedly saved the situation.' That had not pacified Hughes nor had it protected Alderson. Aware of the minister's abusive criticism, Alderson sought help from his supposed friend, John Carson: 'I believe you to be an absolutely fair and square-minded man, and I think you will admit that, in all my dealings with you, I have been perfectly candid and open.' Carson simply forwarded Alderson's 'long epistle' to Hughes 'until I have had an opportunity of discussing the whole matter with your good self.'[73]

Units of Steele's division landed piecemeal in England during May and June. In training and equipment the Second Contingent was inferior to its predecessor. Not even the brigades had assembled before crossing the Atlantic. Only one of the three artillery brigades could be organized in Canada and months of winter training left little but a knowledge of drill. However, the troops had the advantage of a warm, dry summer in England and the services of a number of Canadian veterans from Ypres. A second Canadian division meant that a Canadian corps could soon be formed. It was sufficient justification for the minister of militia to set out on his second wartime visit to England. A considerable number of policy decisions awaited his arrival on 3 July 1915. The most important was the command of the 2d Division.[74]

Sir John French, the British commander-in-chief on the western front, had already decided that Alderson would have command of the new corps while Canadian officers would be allowed to command the two divisions. Although Steele continued to press his claim to take the 2d Division into action, the minister had made up his mind that the command would go to General Turner. Alderson, who did not consider Turner 'really fit' for the position and who had argued for Brigadier-General Arthur Currie, had to concede that 'Canadian politics have been too strong for all of us ...'[75] There was a further and in some respects more embarrassing battle over command of the division's three brigades. Of the acting brigadiers who had come from Canada, only Lieutenant-Colonel H.D.B. Ketchen, another of Bob Rogers's protégés, was confirmed and promoted. Colonel J.P. Landry, the first French-Canadian to secure senior rank in the CEF and the son of the Conservative speaker of the Senate, was displaced on grounds of inexperience and weakness in command.[76] Colonel Septimus Denison, a member of the prominent Toronto clan and a permanent force officer, was removed to make way for one of Hughes' protégés, Edward, Lord Brooke, eldest son of the Earl of Warwick. Hughes's Canadianism by no means excluded a certain snobbish fondness for aristocratic friends: Brooke, who owned ranching property in western Canada, had been invited to Canada in 1914 to command the militia camp at Petawawa. Even when Carson warned that Brooke was filling his brigade staff with British officers, the minister insisted that his friend must not be bothered. Landry's successor, Lieutenant-Colonel David Watson, was editor of the Conservative Quebec *Chronicle* and a loyal friend of Hughes but he had at least commanded his battalion at Ypres with considerable distinction.[77]

The British, undoubtedly relieved that Steele would not take his division to France, generously solved the problem of his future employment. General Babington had long since taken his 23d Division across the channel. His successor, Major-General P.S. Wilkinson, was returned to retirement and his place as commander of the Shorncliffe area was given to the elderly Canadian on 3 August. On 27 August, two days after he had been knighted as a KCB in the civil division, Sir Sam Hughes returned to Canada, delighted with his month's stay. His favourites had secured the senior appointments in the 2d Division, he had restored his own faith in Alderson, and he had revelled in the military atmosphere of wartime England and France.

Unfortunately, so far as Canadian command arrangements in England were concerned, confusion had been compounded. In Ottawa, General Gwatkin was convinced that MacDougall had been replaced by Steele as general officer commanding Canadians in England. Certainly he was the most senior officer overseas. Hughes himself had reported to Ottawa that Steele's Shorncliffe command extended to all Canadians in England.[78]

If this were so, it had not been made clear to those on the spot. A myth had developed in England that MacDougall owed his authority to a Canadian order-in-council and that his status would be unchanged until the cabinet revoked its decision. Steele himself believed in the existence of this fabled document, claiming later that he had been informed of it by the minister himself. Hughes had added, however, that the order had been passed without his knowledge or consent or, presumably, without his having ever seen a copy.[79] Carson also accepted the myth, perhaps encouraged in his credulity by a shrewd awareness that his own slender authority depended on ambiguity and ignorance. No sooner had Sir Sam left for Canada than Carson dispatched a lengthy memorandum to his fellow senior Canadians, asserting his claim to absolute military authority in the United Kingdom.

The memorandum, directed to Steele, conceded the elderly general's pre-eminence in all matters except training (controlled, in any case, by the War Office). At the same time, Carson indicated, Steele would exercise his command through Turner and MacDougall and MacDougall would also command detachments of Canadians scattered beyond the boundaries of Steele's

Shorncliffe district. Carson's key assertion was that he was 'the Minister's direct representative.' 'I naturally have very extended powers, and among others, the authority which is vested in the Minister, or acting Minister of the Crown, to correspond with anyone in Canada's employ and on any subject.'[80]

Did the memorandum, as Carson claimed, reflect Hughes's wishes expressed at the moment of his departure? Was it a grab for power by Carson at the moment that the minister was safely on the ocean? It would certainly have been characteristic of Hughes's erratic manner of administration to grant such authority to a trusted friend while guilefully neglecting to provide written confirmation. On the other hand, Carson's persistent pursuit of authority had demonstrated that he could cheerfully exaggerate his power. Widespread terror of the minister, particularly among permanent force officers like MacDougall and Steele, deterred questioning.

In either case, Sir Sam Hughes was responsible for the failure to ensure that his intentions for the Canadian command in England were made clear to all concerned, including the War Office and Sir George Perley. The stage was set for trouble.

3

John Wallace Carson

On 13 September an untried 2d Canadian Division entered the line near Wolverghem, on the left of the 1st Division, and General Alderson assumed command of the brand new Canadian Corps. Alderson's successor, a newly promoted Major-General Arthur Currie, had already proved himself the ablest brigadier in the division.[1]

From the creation of the Second Contingent, a Canadian army corps had been inevitable. Canadians were already envious of the conspicuous heroism of the Australian and New Zealand army corps at Gallipoli. Moreover, General Hughes would have regarded such a command as worthy of his talents. As early as 27 April Sir John French had moved to prevent that contingency, recommending that, if a Canadian corps were formed, General Alderson should have the command. Lord Kitchener cordially agreed. Sir Robert Borden, who also visited England and France in the summer of 1915, concurred. He had found Alderson to be honest, able, and generally popular with his men. Hughes's knighthood – pointedly in the civil branch of the Order of the Bath – would be a consolation prize.[2]

The role of the minister of militia was not to command soldiers in the field; for better or worse he was responsible for enlisting, training, and dispatching them to the front. He did the job badly. Once again, the South African experience could have provided a warning. During the Paardeberg campaign, Otter's battalion had wasted away to a few hundred men under the assaults of dysentery, typhoid, and Boer marksmanship. The only reinforcements had been a party of a hundred men, hurriedly recruited in mid-winter.[3] There was no better arrangement for the battalions of the CEF. The First Contingent had left Canada with five extra battalions. By the time losses on Salisbury Plain and the early weeks of fighting had been made up, few trained men remained to replace the casualties at Ypres. At Lord Kitchener's request, Seely's Canadian Cavalry Brigade volunteered unanimously to serve as infantry. On 4 May eighty-five officers and 1,427 other ranks crossed to France to serve with the division. Six other CEF battalions, sent to England in the spring, were dissolved to find men; other units still recruiting in Canada contributed drafts.[4]

The Militia Department might well have established depots for the existing CEF battalions. Hughes rejected any such dreary rationality. True to his romantic concept of war, concerned to enlist patriotism as well as men, he turned back to a venerable and discredited technique. Colonels would raise their own battalions, choosing their own officers, designing their own recruiting campaigns, and paying the bills. Businessmen, politicians, militia veterans, and some of Hughes's own friends would justify the minister's sublime faith in business acumen and amateur enthusiasm. In addition to battalions raised for the First and Second Contingents, 29 CEF battalions had been authorized by 13 June 1915 and a further 27 battalions were added during the summer. On 8 July an order-in-council raised the authorized limit on enlistment from 50,000 to 150,000 Canadians. By year's end Canada would be committed to recruiting half a million soldiers.[5]

There were some advantages to the Hughes approach. It was certainly cheap. By 1 April 1917 the federal government had spent only $26,571 to promote recruiting. County and municipal councils, fraternal orders, businesses, clergy, and women's organizations threw themselves into the recruiting effort, creating remorseless pressure on the country's young men, at least within the English-speaking community. The hidden costs included a duplication of effort, enlistment of thousands of unfit men, and harsh divisions within Canadian society, particularly between the French-speaking minority and an increasingly intolerant and passionate majority.[6]

Moreover, as the minister must have known, his recruiting policy was based on a confidence trick. The CEF colonels spent their money and delivered their brave speeches in the expectation that they would lead their battalions to glory and Berlin. Men enlisted on the assurance that they would share the dangers and hardships of war in the company of friends and neighbours. The CEF battalions were based on the affinities of men from Peel county or the Kootenays, of Scotsmen and Irish, of Methodists and sportsmen. One Toronto battalion accepted only 'bantams' – men who were too short for the official height limit. Yet, even at full strength, the Canadian Corps needed only forty-eight infantry battalions and four more of pioneers. Most of the hundreds of CEF battalions were destined for a melancholy and certain fate. Once in England they would be dissolved. Their subalterns and soldiers would be whirled into the lonely anonymity of a front line reinforcement. The remaining officers would have a legitimate and burning grievance.[7]

If there was an excuse for Hughes's policy, it was ignorance, inexperience, and a nagging fear that any less passionate means of recruiting might fail. In January 1915 the minister had proclaimed that he could raise 'three more contingents in three weeks if necessary' but he must have known that in rural Ontario recruiting quotas were already falling far short. The flow of patriotic and unemployed young Englishmen had dried up. In April news of the heroic tragedy of Ypres produced a dramatic increase in recruiting. So did the sinking of the *Lusitania* on 8 May. For the first time the native-born came forward in impressive numbers everywhere save in the French-speaking counties of Quebec. However, anxieties remained. The War Office had warned that maintaining two infantry divisions in the line demanded 148 officers and 4,825 other ranks each month. It might be all that a nation of seven million people could manage.[8]

By now the British government knew that the war would demand every man it could gather. Hughes was eager to oblige. Even as the Second Contingent was forming, he had ordered thirteen regiments of Canadian Mounted Rifles to be raised – officially for possible service against the Turks, in fact largely to meet the wishes of old friends from the militia cavalry.[9] Six of them were dispatched to England in June and July; a seventh provided a depot and cavalry for the 2d Division. On 24 June the War Office suggested that Canada consider offering a third division. The Canadian cabinet considered the manpower implications and balked. The issue was revived in September when Hughes, back in Canada, referred publicly to a third and even additional divisions. General Alderson could provide military arguments. An army corps on the western front, he explained, now included three divisions, with one of them normally out of the line.[10] The drain of casualties would be hardly greater than with two divisions. Borden, now persuaded that Canada's voice in strategy would be proportional to its effort, changed his mind. On 30 October 1915 the enlistment total was raised to 250,000. There would be a third division and a fourth.[11]

In the negotiations for these new formations, in the choice of their commanders, and in the growing reinforcement crisis in the Canadian Corps, the confused administrative structure of the CEF in England would be involved. From the end of August 1915 when Sir Sam Hughes left England until his return in the summer of 1916, the presiding figure amidst the confusion would be John Wallace Carson. Without any change in the modest status granted him in January 1915, Carson assumed an effective supremacy over Canadian military affairs in England.

The first evidence of Carson's growing importance was his promotion to the rank of major-general. Next, as the minister's representative, he intervened sharply to compel Alderson to reserve senior appointments in his new Corps staff for Canadians. Hughes, for example, had insisted that the commander of the Corps artillery must be Brigadier-General Harry Burstall. The British General Headquarters insisted that he had too little experience. Carson pressed the point: 'the Canadian Government will, to say the least, be very much put out if other than Canadian Officers are chosen for these posts ...' Alderson obediently transmitted the message and Burstall was appointed. So was another junior Canadian, Lieutenant-Colonel C.J. Armstrong, who became chief engineer for the Corps. Both appointments proved quite successful.[12]

It had not taken Hughes long to resent his exclusion from influence over the Canadians in France. Indeed, by the time Borden visited England, he and most of his colleagues had become much more concerned about the management of a war in which Canada was being spurred to ever greater efforts. During his summer visit the Canadian prime minister became increasingly disturbed by what he saw of the quality of Britain's wartime leadership. His indignation was undoubtedly fed by David Lloyd George, the new minister of munitions in the Asquith government but Borden's mood was also shaped by visits to wounded Canadians and to units of the Corps in France. If Hughes wished to challenge British military leadership, Borden's overseas visit had made the prime minister a sympathetic, if discreet, ally.[13]

Hughes's attempt to establish a link with the British commander-in-chief, Sir John French, were anything but discreet. At the outset of the war, the British had solved the problem of press information with stark simplicity: there would be no war correspondents with the British Expeditionary Force. An official *communiqué*, later embellished by slightly more colourful prose from an official 'eye-witness,' gave the press their entire diet of information. In turn, that was all the news Sir Robert Borden, Hughes, or anyone else was offered from the seat of the war. General Hughes's solution was characteristic; he turned to a crony. John J. Carrick was American-born, a Quaker in religion, and one of Port Arthur's most flamboyant land speculators and politicians. Five years after he landed in the city, he was mayor and its provincial representative; eight years later, he was its member of parliament. For Hughes, almost any self-made promoter was a fellow spirit. When war came, Carrick found himself adorned with the rank of honorary colonel and dispatched by Hughes to France with the title of 'Official Recorder, Canadians.'[14]

Like Carson and other Hughes appointments, Carrick's instructions were vague, his responsibilities overlapped with others, and the minister made no attempt to clarify the situation. 'There is no record in this office of any Colonel Carrick ...,' complained the newly opened Canadian records section at Rouen, 'Could you inform me who this officer is, please?'[15] While Carson could intimidate fellow Canadians with the fear of Sam Hughes, Carrick's only real asset was a junior business associate he had brought with him from Port Arthur. Captain R.F. Manly Sims had earned the Distinguished Service Order with the British army in South Africa and he had also completed staff college before resigning his commission to seek his fortune in Canada. Not even Sims could establish Carrick's status at General Headquarters or even with General Carson in London, however. 'If I have been asked once, I have been asked a dozen times both in the War Office and during my visits to France – "Who is Colonel Carrick?"' Carson complained.[16] To Sir George Perley, who had reluctantly used his influence to get Hughes's appointee to France, Carrick was simply 'the last straw.'[17]

Carrick's inglorious career ended when Hughes returned to Canada at the end of August 1915. The Port Arthur promoter was posted to Headquarters staff in Ottawa, promoted to colonel, and compensated for his services at the rate for a member of parliament, fifteen dollars a day. Manly Sims remained, as did Carrick's business partner, Major Donald Hogarth, the Conservative MLA for Port Arthur. Both would play major roles in the CEF's overseas administration: Carrick would not. The downfall of the ambitious promoter came at the hands of an even more ambitious, agile, and influential friend of the minister of militia, Sir Max Aitken.[18]

The New Brunswick-born financier had capped a youthful triumph in Canadian corporate mergers by moving most of his fortune and his energy to Britain. Ownership of the mass-circulation *Daily Express*, a seat in Parliament as the Conservative member for Ashton-under-Lyme, and a knighthood were among the marks of his progress. Aitken still planned to return to Canadian politics and, even more than Carrick's, his entrepreneurial genius and energy captivated Sam Hughes. The war gave both men a chance to reward each other. Aitken would be Canada's own 'eye witness,' collecting records of Canadian service overseas and issuing daily cables to Canada. In return, he would enjoy the rank and uniform of a Canadian lieutenant-colonel and easy access to the war zone, a privilege no other newspaper proprietor or correspondent could boast. Inevitably, Aitken's work overlapped with the embarrassing Colonel Carrick. In July, Hughes promoted his friend to colonel and, once Carrick had left, Aitken was awarded the title of 'General Representative for Canada at the front.'[19]

Aitken was hardly more compatible with the British high command than Carrick. It was easier to batter one's way into British society than to be accepted as an equal and the upstart Canadian nursed a lifelong grudge against the complacent networks of the governing classes. Much later, he would recall to Sir Robert Borden that, 'The Trade Union of the Regulars – within which was another closer ring the P.S.C., or "passed Staff College" man – was more exclusive even than the Doctors or the Bricklayers Union here today.'[20] It was a viewpoint entirely shared by Aitken's official master, Sir Sam Hughes. It guaranteed that when new appointments were made in the expanding Canadian Corps, Hughes's preferences for his own friends and dependents would have an energetic and agile advocate at General Headquarters.

Military logic might have dictated that the minister of militia appoint a single officer to command all Canadians in England. That was approximately what the Australians did for their base units in Egypt. Both the British and the Canadians would have been able to identify a clear line of authority over complex and expanding Canadian activities. There was certainly no evidence that the British would have resisted the idea. At the same time, such a rational arrangement would have been objectionable to Sir Sam Hughes. If he had confirmed the authority of MacDougall, he would have added to the prestige of a member of a group he had hated throughout his own militia career, the permanent force officers. If General Steele, a more senior officer, were given full authority in England, Hughes would have rewarded a protégé of his cabinet rival, the minister of public works. Even if he had recognized his own favourite, John Wallace Carson, Hughes's capacity to meddle in day-to-day CEF matters would have been reduced. By deliberately creating confusion among the Canadian commanders in England, the minister guaranteed that his own will would remain paramount.

Nothing gave Hughes more pleasure than giving senior appointments to his friends. One reason for sending the six regiments of Canadian Mounted Rifles overseas was to justify the formation of two brigades, one commanded by Colonel Maynard Rogers, the other by Colonel Charles A. Smart, a Montreal manufacturer and Conservative member of the Quebec Legislative Council. When the brigades dissolved, an additional training brigade was put together at Shorncliffe to provide Rogers with a suitable appointment.[21]

The training situation was soon further complicated. On his return to Canada, Hughes determined to dispatch a further twelve CEF battalions to England. The men's enthusiasm had been dulled by months of training in Canada; both it and any efficiency would vanish during a long Canadian winter. Hughes had not, of course, consulted the British. Short of winter accommodation and mindful of Canadian discontent over the previous winter's suffering on Salisbury Plain, the War Office protested. The minister was unmoved, and once Steele agreed to find room for 5,000 at Shorncliffe, the

British promised to locate the balance at Aldershot. Unfortunately, no one bothered to advise Carson. Early on 11 October Carson was awakened by a telephone call advising him that a thousand Canadians had arrived unexpectedly at Bramshott, fourteen miles from Aldershot. No one had met them nor were any facilities available for them.[22]

The unexpected arrival was the inauspicious opening of the big Canadian camp at Bramshott. The British had mistaken the draft for the first of the twelve new Canadian battalions: in fact the men belonged to a collection of small parties properly destined for Shorncliffe. More troops followed. Carson's first major task was to find an appropriate commander for the new camp. The solution proved unexpectedly easy. A month in the trenches had persuaded General Turner that Lord Brooke was unsuited to command a brigade. The risks of removing one of Hughes's favourite protégés would be reduced if Brooke could at once be promised an important new command in England. Carson was delighted to help. So was Aitken and even Garnet Hughes was enlisted to help ease the transition. On 19 November Brooke formally assumed command of the new Canadian camp.[23] Under Brooke, there would be two training brigades which Carson hurriedly assigned to Colonel Rogers and Colonel Smart. The minister's good friends had been well served.[24]

If the Canadian command structure in England had so far been merely confused, Lord Brooke's position at Bramshott added wild absurdity. From a British standpoint, MacDougall's Canadian Training Division was under the authority of Shorncliffe district in Eastern Command. Lord Brooke's training division at Bramshott came under Aldershot Command. On matters of Canadian concern, MacDougall could deal with Ottawa through Carson. If, as was widely believed, MacDougall exercised authority over all Canadians in England, then he must also be responsible for Lord Brooke and the Canadians at Bramshott. Thanks to Hughes, MacDougall's authority was vague while, in terms of military rank, it was Major-General Steele who was far and away the senior Canadian officer in England. However, his appointment was now purely British and Steele could claim absolutely no authority over Brooke or the Canadians in Aldershot Command or even over Brigadier-General Mac-Dougall when that officer functioned in a Canadian role.[25] Carson, who had no formal authority at all, had manoeuvred himself into the key role of go-between, not only with Sir Sam Hughes but with the War Office as well.

Well aware of potential explosions if two elderly and rank-conscious officers began quarrelling over their authority, Carson set out to find a solution. To the War Office, he proposed that Bramshott camp might be transferred for the time being to Shorncliffe area. There was no response. Next he suggested to Steele that he might accept the appointment of inspector-general of the Canadian troops in England, with the promise of visits to France. 'You are,' he wrote to the old veteran, 'and I say it without trying to throw away bouquets, a master hand on matters of inspection and the handling of men ...'[26] When Steele did not object, Carson tried out the proposal on Hughes in Ottawa:

There is no question of friction between these two distinguished officers, and yet I do know that the only thing that prevents friction is the common sense displayed by both of them, and perhaps I should also say the presence of myself here always ready to throw oil on the troubled waters at a moment's notice, and the thought has struck me, and struck me only today, could we not make much better use of General Steele's services by getting him an appointment similar to that which he held in Canada and make him Inspector-General of all our forces in England? He could then give up the Shorncliffe command which is a fifth wheel to the coach in any case, have his Headquarters in London or elsewhere, wherever best suited to his position, and spend his time in inspecting from camp to camp, hospital to hospital, convalescent home to convalescent home, etc ...[27]

When neither the War Office nor his minister replied to Carson's proposals, the problems of Bramshott continued. Were the battalions being sent from Canada to be used to build a third division or were they to be broken up for reinforcements? For the units involved, the question was far from academic. A British inspector of infantry, Major-General Howard, inserted his firm opinion that all Canadian reinforcement units should be under a single command, Shorncliffe. Howard's recommendation undoubtedly moved the War Office to a belated response. On 12 December an official message informed the general officer commanding-in-chief at Aldershot that henceforth Major-General Steele would be 'entirely responsible for the training of the Canadians in your command.'[28]

Steele felt both delighted and vindicated and concluded that Carson was his benefactor. The minister's representative responded with appropriate congratulations: 'this is very pleasing news to me indeed, and I know the Canadians will benefit by your long and useful military experience.'[29] MacDougall was indignant and he could remind Carson that the War Office's proposed arrangement was contrary to Canadian policy as expressed by Carson himself. It was, after all, MacDougall, not Steele, whom the minister had put in charge of training. General Carson found himself obliged to return to the War Office and to secure assurances that nothing had been done to

weaken MacDougall's authority. Finally, on 9 January 1916, Carson offered
Steele his analysis of the current Canadian command structure:

The position of affairs today is that General MacDougall remains in the position to
which he was appointed by the Canadian Government, and approved of by the British Authorities, namely, General Officer Commanding Canadians in England.

Brigadier-General Lord Brooke is commanding in Bramshott and serving directly
under General MacDougall, and subject to his orders and directions, and the same
syllabus of training carried out in Shorncliffe is to be carried out in Bramshott. You
remain in your command of General Officer Commanding the Shorncliffe area, and
in addition to that your supervision authority has been extended to also take in our
troops in Bramshott which was the exact thing that I asked the War Office to approve
of many months ago.[30]

Steele was no fool. Carson's bland assurances meant nothing. If MacDougall was responsible for Canadian training and discipline, 'supervision authority' from Shorncliffe was a mirage. Even more serious was the marked decline
in good feeling among senior Canadian officers in England by the end of
1915. Carson developed his own grievance when he discovered that Colonel
Frank Reid, appointed by Hughes to be director of organization, was under
the impression that General MacDougall's authority extended to the growing array of administrative organizations of the CEF in England. In a sharp
memo, Carson warned MacDougall that the minister had given him full
control of the 'entire business end of the proposition' always excepting discipline 'which is in all respects under your good self.'[31] Even discipline was
involved when Carson passed both MacDougall and Brooke a sharp rebuke
from a British assistant provost marshal in London about the state of Canadian discipline.[32] Carson was personally most offended when MacDougall, in
the course of establishing a seniority list for all the officers of the CEF,
insisted that the minister's representative had never been a member of the
force. MacDougall was almost certainly correct. For all his militia rank, Carson never had been formally gazetted to the CEF. Yet MacDougall's insistence on the point, backed by his senior staff officer, Lieutenant-Colonel H.
Kemmis-Betty, would have undermined Carson's military authority and
prestige. Challenged and aggrieved, Carson demanded that the minister of
militia clarify his status:

MacDougall's ideas and mine do not coincide and I want this understanding of my
powers, responsibility etc., to be thoroughly straightened out. I claim that I have full

authority over and charge of all directorates and that they are my administrative staff, MacDougall's duties being restricted in so far as directorates are concerned, to discipline only ... My claim is that I am a member of the C.E.F. and that as your representative here I am senior to all ... I don't claim military seniority over Steele. That common-sense officer recognizes my position and standing, so does the War Office and everyone else including MacDougall when it suits him and at all times he is ready to shove responsibility on to my shoulders but when a gradation list is being made up which will be a permanent record, why he wants chief place at the feast.[33]

Hughes's reply was prompt, abusive, and not particularly constructive. It was also a fair reflection of his notorious prejudice against officers of the pre-war permanent force:

Have had many complaints from several sources concerning MacDougall's lack of attention to his proper training duties, but have not asked you to investigate them hoping he would give attention to the detailed training and development of his officers and men. However, I have thus far refused to recall him. If he would centre his efforts on developing the soldiers of all grades under him it would be well. There is too much time wasted over petty trifles and personal aggrandizement. I had to point out several times in England his lack of supervision in detail in each corps. He is not there simply as a figure-head to work out ideas. Please show him this.[34]

MacDougall was both angered and frightened by this rebuke. Without in the slightest clarifying Carson's authority or responsibilities, Hughes had confirmed that Carson was the channel for ministerial communications. Desperate for allies, MacDougall poured out his feelings to Sir Max Aitken – who promptly sent the letter on to Carson. With a mixture of charm and discreet warning, the minister's representative promptly assured the unhappy MacDougall that he had never, in any way, proposed his recall. A few days later he added: 'I think you must know that I have had and still have the warmest personal regard for you ...'[35]

Having put MacDougall firmly in his place, Carson next set off on a more difficult errand: getting recognition of his status from the minister. 'The trouble is,' he reported to Hughes, 'that there is not one solitary soul on this side of the Atlantic Ocean authorized to say "This shall be or this shall not be" and the time is rapidly coming when we must have authority to act on any or every matter on this side of the water.'[36] On 15 December he went farther, proposing a duplicate of the Militia Department structure in Ottawa. He would himself become 'practically acting Minister of Militia' and he would need branches for an adjutant general, quartermaster-general, and inspector-general. Hughes could come over to see the situation for himself. Otherwise, 'the sooner authority is given me by mail or otherwise to make these changes the better for our organization over here.' On 27 December, Carson pleaded for a 'sub-militia council' as the only way to cope with such problems as the growing surplus of senior Canadian officers in England.[37]

Carson's concern about the structure of authority was well founded. One aspect was the confusion about the proper routing of messages and directives from Ottawa. Militia Headquarters dealt without evident pattern with Carson, Steele, the War Office, MacDougall or anyone else in charge of Canadian records, medical services, or supplies. From France General Alderson complained that he received communications directly from Steele, MacDougall, Lord Brooke, Carson, and even from Sir George Perley and Sir Max Aitken.[38] One consequence was that when King Edward's Horse was removed from the Canadian Cavalry Brigade to make room for a third Canadian regiment, two separate units were ordered to prepare themselves to fill the vacancy. Under orders from the War Office, MacDougall re-created the Fort Garry Horse from the Canadian cavalry depot at Shorncliffe. Under identical orders, General Steele directed Lord Brooke at Bramshott to form a regiment from battalions of the Canadian Mounted Rifles. It was a situation made to order for Carson to claim supremacy over the Canadian administration in England. 'Now is this not an absurd condition of affairs,' he complained to Sir Reginald Brade, the under-secretary of state for war: 'and this absurd condition of affairs and every other absurd condition of a like nature could be overcome and overcome in one way only, and that is by these official instructions of the War Office coming to me as the representative of the Department of Militia and Defence, Canada, and to me alone, and I would see that prompt action is taken at all times and no mistake made.'[39]

Another way to reduce the confusion was to eliminate some of the competing figures. In October 1915 Carson believed that he might have persuaded Aitken, a wholly unmilitary figure, to train himself to fill Lord Brooke's vacancy at the front. 'Max would make a success of this as he is wonderfully smart,' Carson assured the minister of militia, 'he is ready to take off his coat and work like the devil with this object in view, and I believe that he would have a great deal of practical and theoretical knowledge in the back of his head after six months work.'[40] Aitken's ardor cooled when Sir Sam insisted that his friend revert to the rank of provisional captain and learn soldiering under Brooke or MacDougall. Carson also changed his mind, recalling, doubtless at Aitken's prompting, that 'At the present time he is the centre around which the political forces of the Coalition Government seem to be gravitating ...' Aitken's health was another problem and 'his physical frame and physical condition were not equal to the hardships of even soldiering in England.'[41]

General Steele also had a try at ridding himself of his rival, MacDougall, urging him, with suspicious generosity, as a suitable commander for the new 3d Canadian Division when it was formed in December.[42] Instead, the new formation was built from the growing collection of units grouped as 'corps troops.' The command went to the third of the original 1st Division brigadiers, Major-General M.S. Mercer. Princess Patricia's Canadian Light Infantry returned from a British division where it had gained great distinction and Canada's only permanent force infantry unit, the Royal Canadian Regiment, was rescued from the humiliating garrison duty in Bermuda to which Hughes had consigned it. Another brigade was formed from the six regiments of Canadian Mounted Rifles and, despite some heartburning, the command went to Colonel Victor Williams of the detested permanent corps. A third brigade, formed from four infantry battalions in England, joined the division in February but the lack of Canadian artillery meant that Mercer's division depended on the guns of the 3d (Lahore) Division until the summer of 1916.[43]

Carson had tried and failed to persuade Alderson to organize a special brigade of Montreal units for the new division, partly to celebrate the contribution of that city's English-speaking militia, partly to justify the promotion of his friend and business partner, Colonel Frank S. Meighen, president of Lake of the Woods Milling Co.[44] However, Carson had more serious worries as 1915 came to an end: Canadian reinforcements were drying up.

Although Sir Sam Hughes blithely ignored the problem, promising a fourth and even fifth and sixth Canadian divisions, the supply of young Canadians willing to enlist was limited. In the summer of 1915 a cautious General Gwatkin had warned a friend that maintaining 50,000 Canadians at the front might be all the country could manage.[45] Carson had resisted the formation of a third division, needed to complete the Canadian Corps to the usual strength of British army corps at the front, until he was reassured by Alderson that one of the three divisions would normally be out of the line.[46]

The problems of recruiting might be beyond the direct influence of the military authorities. They were also not responsible for the expansion of munition-making under the Shell committee and later the Imperial Munitions Board. The war increased farm prices, encouraging farmers to keep their sons at home to expand production. Complaints about military management of recruiting in Quebec were largely unfounded, comfortable alibis for the real reluctance of French-speaking Quebeckers to join in the national crusade. However, Hughes and the Militia Department were much more culpable when their system of raising complete battalions held recruits in Canada under inexperienced and often incompetent leaders, waiting for additional men to volunteer. When Canadian soldiers reached England, after as much as a year in uniform, the British authorities judged them no better trained than recruits in their third week. Since the War Office had no desire to keep fighting men from the trenches, it may have been a fair assessment of the Canadian training system.[47]

Training in England may have done much for efficiency but there was a deep and perhaps inevitable schism between the battle-hardened officers and men of the Corps and the officers of the Canadian Training Divisions at Bramshott and Shorncliffe. Most of the latter had never seen fighting service or, like Lord Brooke, had been found wanting. Whatever Hughes's fondness for 'the boys,' it was hardly reciprocated by most soldiers at the front and it was notorious that senior officers in England like Smart, Rogers, and Meighen owed their appointments to political favour. The shortage of qualified reinforcements made matters worse. In December Lieutenant-Colonel Edward Hilliam visited Shorncliffe from France to find some experienced officers for his badly demoralized Nova Scotia battalion. Colonel R. Burritt, MacDougall's chief staff officer, curtly refused assistance for such an unusual search and a furious Hilliam returned alone to France.[48] Another officer who finally asked Carson for help in finding trained machine gunners was advised that only the British could approve his request. General Currie, who had endorsed the appeal, was indignant: 'I almost feel as if it is no further use making complaints because the position is almost hopeless. Apparently Shorncliffe has got its back up and does not intend to help.'[49] By early February 1916 Alderson was so desperate for reinforcements for his depleted ranks that he passed his complaint through British channels. Though 25,000 Canadians were reported to be training in England, only a thousand reinforcements were apparently available. It would be better, Alderson argued, for semi-trained soldiers to come to France to complete their training in the field. Carson, under attack, blamed the discrepancy on a lack of training facilities.[50] MacDougall demanded a court of inquiry to investigate the sneers and insults which officers in the Corps freely directed at the training organization. Major-General Mercer had publicly described Shorncliffe as a joke. 'The statements,' complained MacDougall, 'are just the limit and are the first more or less specific statements that I could take hold of. They reflect upon us all.'[51]

As serious as the reinforcement shortage was the problem of surplus officers. When CEF battalions arrived in England, only subaltern officers and the other ranks were needed to replace the sick, wounded, and dead of the

Corps. Newly-fledged colonels, majors, and captains remained in England. To return to Canada so soon after a glorious departure would mean certain humiliation; to remain overseas meant idleness and frustration; to go to France, for those fit enough to be accepted, meant a loss of rank, pay, and prestige. The surplus of officers, once battalions were broken up, contributed a little to the burgeoning number of Canadians who served with the Royal Flying Corps or its successor, the Royal Air Force; most were too senior or elderly to relish transfer to the new arm.[52] Many officers did sacrifice rank, forfeiting income on which their families depended, rather than appear to be shirking danger. Others, because they were too old or because they were so inclined, used every shred of political or personal influence to find themselves a suitable appointment in the expanding Canadian organization in England.

For Hughes, the problem, like any, could be solved. 'You must insist on Steele, MacDougall and every acting brigadier weeding out every weak officer from brigadiers and colonels down,' he commanded Carson in October. 'See that these two senior officers actually test out day after day all officers and make sure all are able to think and act like lightning. Deliberately mix them up so as to test them and get rid of those not thoroughly fit.'[53] By year's end, Steele's list had only seven names, most of them French-Canadian. A few weeks later, when he asked what had happened to even these few, Carson discovered that some of them had actually been sent to France. Carson's own investigation was equally suspect. In January 1916 he reported that all the officers of the Canadian Training Division at Shorncliffe were poor with one impressive exception. Captain Byron Greene, staff captain with the Twelfth Brigade, was 'hard working, always on the job, popular with his men and a decided success.' Greene also happened to be Sir Sam Hughes's son-in-law.[54]

It was easy for Carson to deliver sweeping condemnations; it was left to Steele to name the inefficient. He preferred the charitable view that none of the officers were really soldiers and that all were studying their temporary profession as hard as they could. For some time Steele had urged that senior officers might be more willing to go back to Canada if they had a short visit to the front line. Ostensibly designed to give them practical experience to take back for training duties in Canada, the trips would serve as a modest bribe and a face-saver. In addition, some of the more enterprising officers, once in France, would find themselves an appointment. An intermittent series of two-week visits, derisively termed 'Cook's Tours,' continued until September 1916, when the War Office asked that they be ended.[55]

Perhaps the real problem with surplus officers was not a lack of military authority but an absence of political strength in England sufficient to guarantee immunity when such officers took their acute sense of grievance home to Canada. The minister had ingeniously avoided any direct blame by sending over complete units. Writing half a century after the event, Leslie Frost blamed the break-up of his beloved Simcoe battalion on Canadian authorities in England, not on his hero, Sam Hughes.[56]

It was in that light as much as in his yearning for power and titles that General Carson's efforts to expand his authority may be understood. In early November, when Aitken had abandoned his military ambitions, the two of them hatched a new scheme for the minister of militia. Carson would claim the title of 'Commissioner of War for Canada' while Aitken, already deeply engaged in plotting the downfall of the Asquith government, would be content to be 'Assistant Commissioner.' The two 'should join forces and gravitate from a common centre, and,' Carson added, 'I think, even if I say it myself, that we should make a strong team and capable of doing the very best of work in Canada's interests ...' Otherwise, Carson painted a glowing picture of influence and good order:

The condition of affairs now, as against November, 1914, are (*sic*) as different as day is from night. Now every door is open to me and every official generally helpful, kindly and very much at my disposal. A year ago every door that could be was kept shut and kindness and consideration were very much the exception. If I do say it myself, I consider that we have a very good organization here. Changes are being made from time to time but they are all helpful. I am arranging to have weekly meetings with all our Chief Officials, one week here, one week at Shorncliffe, where we can have a sort of board meeting and thresh out difficulties and decide on policies as occasion presents itself.[57]

Hughes's response to this bland bid for power was a demand for a complete report on all the Canadian organizations in England: 'I wish a neat, concise, yet clear framework of all under you.'[58] Armed with this authority, Carson ordered senior Canadians from Steele and MacDougall to Lieutenant-Colonel A.D. McRae, director of supplies and transport at Sandgate, Kent, to report on training, chains of command, pay, ordnance systems, remounts, and much more within the week. A number of officers pleaded for extensions and some, like Colonel W.J. Neill, director of veterinary services, clearly did not know very much about their own operations.[59] One officer, Colonel W.R. Ward of the Pay Office, went rather farther, using the occasion to propose to Carson an entire headquarters organization which would pull together the growing number of Canadian authorities, from the Training Division to a brand new director of chaplain's services. Understandably, such a structure would have a more significant role for Ward himself as 'director of financial services and accounts' but the over-all commander would be Major-General John Wallace Carson.[60] The scheme was transmitted with the rest of the reports, bearing Carson's warm endorsement: 'We have got to, in my judgement, carry on this organization on this side of the Atlantic Ocean until we have almost a duplicate of your complete organization in Ottawa.'[61]

Hughes did not acknowledge Carson's proposal or his invitation to come to England to put it in place. Instead, it was the War Office which provoked a response by enquiring through the Colonial Office whether the powers assigned to Carson in the order-in-council of 21 January 1915 had been extended and whether, as he claimed, he was to be the sole channel of communication. The cable passed through the governor general's and the prime minister's offices to reach Militia Headquarters. As usual, the minister was away, and General Gwatkin had a long overdue opportunity to offer his own opinions. He bore Carson little good will. Almost a year earlier he had warned Loring Christie that the Montrealer 'exercises over our Minister an evil influence ... His presence in England is productive, I fear, of more harm than good.'[62] Nothing had changed Gwatkin's mind. In a memorandum to the deputy minister of militia, Surgeon-General Eugène Fiset, Gwatkin noted that while Carson's business ability might be unquestioned, 'in military matters he had gradually acquired an influence which is viewed with alarm on both sides of the Atlantic.' Gwatkin's solution resembled Carson's – a replica in England of the militia under a representative of the minister. However, Carson was explicitly excluded from that role when Gwatkin proposed that he should represent the quartermaster-general while General Steele would represent the chief of the general staff. Lieutenant-Colonel Kemmis-Betty, a permanent force officer, would represent the adjutant general while Colonel Ward would be finance member.[63]

Confessing in advance that his proposals would generate a sharp debate, particularly as they affected Carson, Gwatkin sent a copy of his proposal to Loring Christie, the prime minister's legal adviser. He added that his views were shared by Fiset, Colonel Ward, and the adjutant general, Major-General W.E. Hodgins. He had not consulted the quartermaster-general, Major-General Macdonald, who could be expected to echo the minister's views.[64] In fact, Hughes may have been no better pleased than Gwatkin by Carson's bid for power. That was the message Sir Robert Borden took to the governor-general: 'The Minister of Militia informs me that Major-General Carson conceived an extravagant idea of his jurisdiction which the Minister took occasion to correct in the month of November last.'[65] The official Canadian reply certainly added nothing to Carson's powers: 'Carson's original functions have not been extended. It is considered appropriate that War Office should communicate with him touching matters for which he was appointed or any matters incidental thereto. Militia Department will, if necessary, communicate more fully with War Office on this subject. Minister of Militia hopes to visit Great Britain soon as opportunity offers and will then take up fully the situation in this regard.'[66]

Hughes had a number of reasons to be annoyed about the management of affairs in England since his departure. During his absence an order-in-council, probably drafted by General Gwatkin, had finally clarified the authority for promoting officers in the CEF. Henceforth, officers in Europe would be recommended by the Corps commander while promotions in England would be approved by Steele as general officer commanding, Shorncliffe, in both cases without the need to secure approval in Canada.[67] Hughes always insisted that the order had been passed without his knowledge or consent. A number of ambitious Canadian officers also complained that their prospects had been blighted because their advancement now depended on General Alderson and the British officers who held the key positions in the Corps and divisional staffs. Hughes responded to their indignation, particularly when rumours reached him through Aitken that the Corps commander regarded Garnet Hughes's dramatic rise from major to brigadier-general as politically motivated. The minister exploded in a letter to Sir Max: 'It is discreditable to have British Officers run the Army Corps and Divisions positions. It would be insulting to have them brought into the Brigades ... it is the general opinion that scores of our officers can teach the British Officers for many moons to come ... There is altogether too much staff college paternalism and espionage abroad.'[68]

Hughes's indignation was infectious. Sir Robert Borden had surprised Canadians by a New Year's announcement that Canada would now be committed to raising half a million men for the war. Doubling the national contribution was more a bid for influence in what appeared to him to be a dreadfully mismanaged British war effort than a cool assessment of Canada's manpower resources. After hearing accounts of British generals sending troops to attack machine guns across unbroken barbed wire and listening to the claim by David Lloyd George that officers of another British department 'could not have acted differently if they had been traitors,' the prime minister was in no mood to surrender any Canadian authority.[69] On 23 February

1916 the cabinet scrapped its previous order: in future, promotions in the CEF would be recommended by the War Office and, in active theatres, by the field marshal commanding-in-chief, but they must also be supported by the minister of militia and approved by the governor-in-council.[70] Such a procedure, repatriating a responsibility long given to the British and opening, in British eyes, the prospect of more of Hughes's colonels, provoked a long and acrid correspondence with the War Office.

Hughes also became concerned that his cherished Ross rifle was in danger of joining other Canadian-designed equipment on the scrapheap. There could be no clearer challenge to Hughes's reputation as a military expert or to the minister's claim that he had given 'the boys' better equipment than the British.[71] In fact, even on Salisbury Plain, men of the CEF had grumbled about the Ross; battle experience at Ypres had persuaded the men of the 1st Division to rearm themselves from dead British soldiers with the shorter, lighter, and far more robust Lee-Enfield. The most alarming problem with the Ross was its breech mechanism. Mud easily clogged the rifle and the heat of rapid firing soon made it impossible to extract expended cartridges. For soldiers facing a massed German attack that was a daunting problem. During the summer of 1915 an elaborate programme to ream out the chamber of the Ross rifles was authorized by Hughes but, increasingly, loyalty to the Ross was the ultimate test of loyalty to Hughes. Garnet Hughes and Brigadier-General David Watson cheerfully passed the test; Arthur Currie, General Mercer, and a growing number of senior officers in the Corps would not. Hughes insisted on a propaganda campaign to inform Canadian soldiers that the Lee-Enfield was inferior to the Ross. Despite rechambering and threats of harsh disciplinary measures, troops continued to switch the Ross for British rifles. Reports continued of jammed rifles, bayonets falling off, and soldiers' inability to use the Ross's complicated sights.[72]

The political climax came when Gwatkin invited General Alderson to comment on a letter from an American citizen serving with the Canadian Ordnance Corps commenting on the relative merits of the Ross and Lee-Enfield. Alderson replied with passion and detail, spelling out ten reasons why 85 per cent of his men did not like Hughes's favourite rifle. He rejected the argument, beloved by Hughes and his allies, that the fault lay with the ammunition, protesting that he had done his utmost to speak well of the weapon but leaving no doubt why 'the men, who are good judges in these matters, should prefer the Lee-Enfield.'[73] Hughes was furious. Nothing more was needed to convince him that Alderson was untrustworthy, biased, and incompetent. In a long, savage letter, he used his old weapon of innuendo to imply that General Alderson was utterly ignorant of rifles, had engaged in a long-standing conspiracy, and had been criminal in allowing bad ammunition to get into Canadian hands. Referring to Alderson's conclusion that he would not be fit for his duties if he ignored anything that endangered his men's lives, the minister concluded sarcastically: 'Your emphatic energy concerning what your intentions are, if you will pardon me, might be better directed to having your officers in every grade responsible in the premises make sure that none of the defective ammunition again finds its way into the Canadian ranks.'[74] Next the minister commanded that copies of the letter would be sent to every CEF officer down to the rank of battalion commander, 281 in all.

On 9 March, two days after he wrote his stinging letter to the Canadian Corps commander, Hughes left for his third wartime visit to England. He left behind as acting minister the Hon A.E. Kemp, a prominent Toronto manufacturer and chairman of the War Purchasing Commission, while Sir Robert Borden faced a parliamentary session in which allegations of military mismanagement and gross corruption in munitions contracts would certainly be issues. Hughes justified his mission to a reluctant prime minister on the grounds that he must investigate the state of training in England and probably dismiss both MacDougall and Brooke for incompetence. The minister also needed a rest and a change. His heart was giving him trouble, he suffered from insomnia, and his temper was even more explosive than usual.[75] After some misgivings, Borden approved the visit but took the precaution of warning his friend, Sir George Perley: 'In case his impetuous temperament should lead him into any difficulties, I earnestly hope you will send me a secret message so that I may get in touch with him by cable.'[76] Hughes was also urged to be cautious: 'In case any difference should arise between your Department and War Office with regards to matters affecting the conduct of the War, I hope you will have them disposed of with a minimum of friction.'[77]

If Hughes was looking for problems, they awaited him. In early January MacDougall had sent a senior staff officer, Colonel Burritt, to London to explain some of the problems at Shorncliffe. Carson had used the opportunity to sit down with Burritt and consider each of the officers in the Canadian Training Division. MacDougall was indignant. Carson was wholly unrepentant: 'as the Minister's representative here, and in fact as what might be called the Acting Minister here, I have got the perfect right, and I have every intention of exercising that right, of keeping myself in the closest possible touch and getting any information that I think is necessary that I should know through the medium of any officer of the Canadian Expeditionary Force.'[78] MacDougall collapsed before the onslaught, blaming Burritt and

Steele, who had also asked Burritt for a report. 'As to your position "as representative of the Minister,"' MacDougall conceded, 'I have understood it all along and am aware that the way you carry out your duties is a matter between you and the Minister and that, even if I had the slightest desire to interfere, which I have not, it is none of my business.'[79] By March, however, when the minister was on the ocean, conflict again arose, this time about the control of various Canadian military directorates in England. Once again Carson insisted on his full authority.[80]

Within a week of his arrival, Sir Sam Hughes was certain that he had grasped the entire problem. He had met with sixteen senior Canadians and discovered that the fault lay with General MacDougall. He had shown 'petty, childish jealousy.' He was not 'broad enough or big enough.' He had been nasty to Carson and Steele. The minister also concluded that officers' wives, who had followed their husbands to England in considerable numbers, were a major source of gossip and conflict. To resolve problems, Hughes solemnly gathered more than two hundred Canadian officers in a theatre at Shorncliffe and lectured them at length. However, in Hughes's mind, even worse than MacDougall was Alderson, with his hostility to the Ross rifle and to Canadian appointments. Reporting to Borden, Hughes preferred some serious charges:

Alderson – I have proof of this – has deliberately been playing double with Turner, with Brooke, with Garnet, with Watson and with others. He has sent the now famous report of the Ross Rifle everywhere ... I have the evidence to show that he plays men so far as they suit his purpose and then throws them away; to show that he is insistent on trying to ruin Turner and from the time the second contingent crossed over under General Turner, and Lord Brooke stood by General Turner, he has never ceased trying to ruin Lord Brooke. He did his best to prevent Garnet becoming a Brigadier-General, although he, at first, voluntarily recommended him and he has, without any let-up, been picking on every officer known to be a friend of mine in the entire force.[81]

In his search for evidence against Alderson, Hughes felt no need for judicial impartiality. Although the Corps commander had written strong recommendations that General Carson be put in charge of the Canadian organization in England, this was interpreted by Hughes as no more than a bid to make room for one of Alderson's friends. Another British officer, a Colonel Harrington, had advised Hughes that 'it was impossible for any self-respecting man to remain with Alderson.' 'Haig despises him,' Hughes informed Borden, 'Earl Kitchener, with whom I had the honour of lunching today, it is asserted, has no use for him ... The result is that to-day General Turner, Garnet and General Watson stand far ahead of General Alderson in the opinion of the greatest men at the Front and in England. They are recognized as practical soldiers and giants while poor General Alderson is regarded as a pigmy and an intriguer.'[82]

If MacDougall and Alderson were the real problems, it is surprising that Hughes found any reorganization necessary. However, in the same lengthy letter to the prime minister he explained that he had summoned Brigadier-General Watson back from France to become inspector-general to 'knock the whole thing into shape.' Next, he decided to appoint Watson, a fellow newspaperman and Quebec Tory, as the chief Canadian military commander in England. Sir Max Aitken was to help Watson build 'an informal Council or Committee to handle overseas affairs.' Watson, promoted to major-general, would be chairman; Carson would still represent the minister, Colonel George Murphy, another of Hughes's Ottawa friends, would be quarter-master-general and, if Watson wished, MacDougall could be adjutant-general. Watson was to meet his officers weekly and the director-general of medical services, Major-General Guy Carleton Jones, would be invited. 'In matters concerning any question other than military, the Council will be good enough to call in for consultation, Colonel the Honorable Sir George Perley, K.C.M.G., the Canadian High Commissioner.'[83]

Hughes was delighted with himself and his arrangements. The visit to England, the chance to be among soldiers and to bask in the approval of his supporters improved his health and his temper. Perley, no admirer, confessed to the prime minister that the visit had gone very well and that he wished that it had been longer. So did Hughes. However, Borden's fears had been well founded. The political truce of the outset of the war was long since dead. The Liberals had come to the 1916 session certain of victory in any general election and loaded with evidence of government mismanagement. The biggest targets were in Hughes's department and in the minister's relations with a fast-moving promoter named J. Wesley Allison. Thanks to sharp detective work, a Cape Breton Liberal, George W. Kyte, had convincing evidence that Allison, one of Hughes's honorary colonels and an admired friend of the minister, had helped an American syndicate pose as fuse and shell manufacturers. On 3 April, Sir Robert Borden insisted on his colleague's instant return. A reluctant Hughes abandoned his parades, inspections, and demonstrations of bayonet-fighting and hurried back to Canada.[84]

4

The Acting Council

By the beginning of 1916 most of the illusions about the First World War had vanished. Among the last to go was the belief that the war could be ended swiftly by some master-stroke of strategy. The failure of the British strike at the Dardanelles, for all the incredible heroism of the British, Australians, and New Zealanders at Gallipoli, doomed Winston Churchill's dreams of an eastern strategy and confirmed the fate of czarist Russia. On the western front, the flower of the British army perished hopelessly in the Loos offensive. An autumn of fruitless assaults had cost the British 60,000 men, the French almost 200,000, and the Germans 150,000. They also cost Field-Marshal Sir John French his job. On 19 December, Sir Douglas Haig of the First British Army became commander-in-chief of the British Expeditionary Force and French was transferred to command the forces in Britain.

Eighteen months of war had drained a good deal of the confidence which many Canadians had freely given to British leadership, whether in the higher strategy of the war or in the detailed business of tactics and military administration. In the field, Canadians had proved themselves as fighting soldiers; behind the lines, however, Canadians could blame only themselves for the failings of reinforcement camps, training depots, and administrative organizations. Since the war was now fated to last for years, not months, reorganization had become essential.

In the absence of any directing hand, Canadian administrative units had simply proliferated in England. Although by 1916 virtually all equipment and supplies were procured through British channels, a large and growing ordnance depot flourished at Ashford in Kent, largely to look after discarded Canadian-made equipment. Pay, records, a supply and transport organization thrived and added staff under mandates from the minister that were quite as vague as those which guided Carson, Steele, and MacDougall. The medical organization, under Major-General Guy Carleton Jones, was only a little more coherent than the rest of the Canadian administration. From his own headquarters in London, Jones and a small staff managed a number of general and stationary hospitals in England and France, staffed by an erratic flow of doctors and nurses from Canada and aided by a distinguished team of senior medical consultants ranging from the famous Sir William Osler to Colonel John McCrae, the author of 'In Flanders Fields.' However, as Sir Andrew Macphail later complained, personnel decisions were complicated when the transfer of even a captain depended on the personal authority of the minister. Medical doctors, uncomfortable in the unfamiliar constraints of military discipline, were all too prone to challenge unpopular decisions through political channels. Hughes's authority and his contempt for permanent force veterans like General Jones gave encouragement to malcontents throughout the CEF in England.[1]

In France, almost a month before Hughes's visit, General Alderson had appealed for change. Carson, he suggested, should be put in charge. Both MacDougall and Brooke must be replaced by experienced British officers, immune to the kind of political pressures both of them had accepted. Well aware of the political minefield he crossed by offering any such suggestions to Sir Sam Hughes, Alderson had sought Carson's support: 'The rank & file of the Corps & also the bulk of the officers are so splendid that I cannot & will not sit still and see anything done that will, judging from my nearly 40 years experience of soldiering, in any way handicap them ...' It was Carson, he claimed who had: 'impressed in me most that you are, as I am, playing for the side & for the side only.'[2]

Unfortunately for him, Alderson's faith in Carson's friendship was wholly misplaced. Carson's loyalty was to himself and to the minister. Like Aitken, he echoed and amplified Hughes's resentment and suspicion of British senior officers. A year earlier, Carson had concluded that Alderson was 'too soft' on Canadian troops; repeatedly he complained that he was too harsh about Canadian officers, and suspiciously eager to put British officers in their place. Late in 1915 a bitter dispute broke out when Alderson displaced a Canadian, Major J.F. Homer-Dixon, from a key staff position in the 2d Division, replacing him with a staff-trained British officer.[3] Alderson was forced to explain that Dixon was one of several Canadian officers sent home from Salisbury Plain for 'drinking to excess' and that he had willingly given him another chance when he returned with the Second Contingent.[4] Aitken was aroused again by the appointment of Lieutenant-Colonel Edward Hilliam to command the troubled Twenty-fifth Battalion, a Nova Scotia unit. Though Hilliam had joined the CEF from western Canada, Aitken noted a little scornfully that part of his reputation was based on rising to the rank of sergeant-major in the Seventeenth Lancers, a famous British cavalry regiment.[5]

Hughes's nationalism was often a cover for croneyism. Canadian appointments were distributed to well-connected British friends like Lord Brooke or Lieutenant-Colonel Claude Lowther, a British MP whom Hughes made 'consultative assistant' early in 1915.[6] However, the minister's contempt for the British high command gradually infected his cabinet colleagues. The prime minister shared his concerns with the stoutly anglophile Sir George Perley, seeking his advice and intervention in relations between the War Office and the CEF. It had been Perley who was the reluctant messenger of the appointment of General Seely to command the Canadian Cavalry Brigade. He had also transmitted War Office displeasure at shady Canadian promoters like J. Wesley Allison, only to find out that Allison carried Hughes's full endorsement.

Although Borden must have known of the strained relations between Hughes and Perley, he continued to use the acting high commissioner as a source of advice on letters from disgruntled members of the CEF. In October 1915 Perley was invited to comment on the serviceability of the Ross rifle, a delicate task he delegated to Aitken, Alderson, and General Carson.[7] At the end of November Perley was invited to make discreet enquiries about how the troops would react to the refusal of Sir Wilfrid Laurier to enter a wartime coalition.[8] In December he was directed to press the War Office for more staff vacancies for Canadian officers, a task made no easier when Perley discovered that British censors had intercepted a vitriolic letter on the subject from Hughes to Aitken.[9]

The plain fact, in Perley's eyes, was that Hughes was damaging Canada's reputation in England, whatever his success or failure as a military administrator. 'Everyone expects that this war will bring great changes in Empire relations,' Perley suggested to Borden in May 1915, '& it is especially necessary that we should just now impress on the people here that we are both sane and capable in the management of our own affairs ...'[10] That was certainly not possible if Canada was to be personified by the absurd figure of Sam Hughes. Throughout 1915 and particularly during the prime minister's summer visit, Perley pressed for the transformation of the high commissioner into a regular cabinet portfolio, responsible for all Canadian affairs in Britain. Increasingly resentful of his 'acting' title, he proposed to Aitken that he be called 'Member of the Canadian Government in charge of the Office of the High Commissioner in London.'[11] To Borden, Perley insisted that elevation of the office would be 'a natural step in the development of imperial relations.'[12] The prime minister was not persuaded. In fact, imperial relations were not developing in that direction at all.

For Borden, one obvious step was to make sure that Perley was in closer contact with both Carson and Aitken. Indeed, Hughes assured the prime minister that both men had been instructed to consult the acting high commissioner before any matter was taken up with either the War Office or the Colonial Office. This was simply not true. As Perley promptly reported, his relations with Carson were personally cordial but Hughes's representative came only when he was invited and, while Aitken came more frequently and discussed matters much more freely, both agreed that they had no instructions whatever from Hughes to involve the High Commission. 'In fact,' Borden was advised, 'Aitken feels as strongly as I do that the full influence of Canada over here can only be brought into play if the Office is used in all official matters ...'[13]

Reluctant to add to Perley's stature and so to provoke a certain outburst from Hughes, Sir Robert Borden used the turbulent minister's absence to consult officials in the Militia Department. On 11 March, two days after Hughes's departure, Gwatkin and Fiset were summoned to a cabinet meeting to explain why, when there were 240,000 Canadians in uniform, only 60,000 of them were in France. It was an opportunity for Gwatkin to speak bluntly in the absence of his political superior and he took it. The problem, he suggested, lay largely with MacDougall and Brooke, who were inexperienced and unable to co-operate with Alderson. Using Carson to co-ordinate the work of the two training division commanders had failed. 'General Carson exceeds his proper functions and there is friction.'[14] During the weeks of Hughes's absence, Gwatkin and Fiset prepared a further memorandum for the prime minister emphasizing and amplifying their criticism: 'By Orders-in-Council dated January 15, 1915, certain duties were assigned to Carson. He exceeded those duties and on January 11th, 1916, Mr. Bonar Law asked questions on the subject. The questions were evaded. General Carson meanwhile continued to perform functions beyond the scope assigned to him by Order-in-Council. There is friction, misunderstanding, extravagance; and the War Office, not without reason, stands aloof.'[15]

Both men reiterated Gwatkin's earlier recommendation of a local council. This time, Major-General François Lessard, the inspector-general for eastern Canada, a fifty-six-year-old permanent force officer and a frequent butt of Hughes's prejudices, was substituted for Steele as senior military member. Three associate members were proposed, one each from the artillery and engineers, and Surgeon-General Guy Carleton Jones from the medical services. In a covering letter, Gwatkin suggested Fiset as president of the council if Sir George Perley were too busy.[16] Borden endorsed the proposal with a few changes. Perley would be president of the proposed 'Canadian Overseas Council' with Fiset as vice-president. Lessard, Kemmis-Betty, Carson, and Ward would all be members. In the cabinet, ministers added a fourth associate member to be named by the War Office and proposed as secretary A.B. Goldwyer-Lewis, an engineer then acting as secretary to the small arms committee. The proposed council would make promotions and appointments in the CEF, approve purchases and requisitions, and, with the agreement of the British Army Council, suspend any officer pending approval by Ottawa.[17]

It was a good indication of the relations between Sir Sam Hughes and the rest of the cabinet that these arrangements should have come so close to final approval without even a warning to Hughes. Indeed, General Lessard, then completing a three-month tour of England and France, was kept in England. Sir George Perley managed to catch the astonished general at Liverpool on the point of embarkation. When Lessard demanded an explanation, Borden authorized the cautious intimation that he was contemplating forming a subcommittee of the Militia Council and that more information would soon be forthcoming.[18]

It was not. Hughes returned to Ottawa on 16 April brimming with self-congratulation, proclaiming perfection in every department of the overseas administration. Borden was caught. If the prime minister insisted on his own proposal, he would not only provoke a storm but he could obviously offer no proof that Hughes's arrangement would not work. Indeed, the inclusion of both Watson and Aitken in the 'informal council' gave it legitimacy in Borden's eyes. Sir Robert was also reluctant to appear to undermine a colleague about to face both an angry Liberal opposition and a Royal Commission of Inquiry. In the 'Shell scandal,' Hughes carried the reputation of the entire Conservative government. The 'Canadian Overseas Council' was gently shelved.[19]

There remained only one embarrassing proof of its existence: the stranded Lessard. A suspicious Hughes demanded to know why the elderly French-Canadian soldier had not come home on schedule. After hurried explanations, Lessard was given the face-saving chore of inspecting the two Canadian Training Divisions. Fortunately, Perley had had the discretion not to tell Lessard about the important role proposed for him.[20]

Although Borden might believe that the key role in Hughes's new arrangement would be played by Watson or Aitken, it was Carson who summoned the first meeting. On 5 April, the day the minister left London, Carson, Brooke, Colonel G.P. Murphy, the acting quartermaster-general in the new arrangement, and Brigadier-General Watson met for the first time. The first decision was to announce to the War Office that Watson was Hughes's choice to command the new 4th Canadian Division, assembling at Bramshott. Watson would be in temporary command of all Canadians in England and 'immediate steps would be taken, through the friendly influence of Colonel Sir Max Aitken, to have Brigadier General J.C. MacDougall C.M.G. attached to the Canadian Army Corps Headquarters in France for instructional purposes for an indefinite time.'[21]

Once he was confirmed in command of the newest Canadian division, Watson washed his hands of the 'unofficial' council. Until both MacDougall and Steele were removed, he wanted nothing to do with the chaotic, politics-ridden Canadian organization in England. Neither Steele nor MacDougall would co-operate. As soon as MacDougall realized that his posting to France was no more than a subterfuge to get rid of him, he refused to go without an appointment suitable to his seniority.[22] Steele, who could claim the patronage of both Hughes and the minister of public works, Robert Rogers, was even more obdurate.[23] Watson could feel justified in turning his attention back to the task of building a division from the tangle of CEF battalions in the Canadian camps.

Aitken took no interest whatever in the 'council,' attended neither of its two meetings, and coolly reported its collapse to Hughes on 10 May 1916. In fact, the only effect of Hughes's arrangement was to place power more firmly in Carson's hands while still denying him any official confirmation. The absence of Aitken and Watson allowed Carson to set up his own secretariat under G.D. Oulster, a former secretary to the Canadian Northern Railway. Another assistant, Sergeant-Major Pinkney, was commissioned and put in charge of the new council's minutes because he had done the same work for 'sixteen of the Mackenzie-Mann interests.' Oulster was full of advice for Carson. The filing system would be revised and put in order so that the Opposition could find nothing to criticize at the end of the war. General Steele should be made inspector-general and ordered to dig out financial waste. 'I think General Steele would jump at this job and co-operate with you to the last ditch,' Oulster argued, 'because he would be doing a great service to the Canadian public and the present party by saving their money, and therefore get a certain amount of individual advertising. He gets nothing from his present job.'[24]

Oulster's judgment of Steele's motivation may have been shrewd but one able secretary could not save the council. At its only other meeting, on 20 April, only Carson, Murphy, Brooke, and Surgeon-General Jones appeared. Although they chose Carson as chairman and approved a title for the organization – 'Headquarters, Canadian Expeditionary Forces, London, England' – other business was held over for Watson. Two successive dates were set but no meetings were held.[25]

In addition to Gwatkin and Hughes, Sir George Perley had also given thought to the Canadian organization in England. His pretext was a critical letter from a CEF officer in France, referred by the prime minister, denouncing the Canadian organization in London and alleging widespread corruption in the Pay Office. While Perley suggested that the criticism might be exaggerated, there was no doubt that 'the senior officials here have been working a good deal at cross purposes.' The Pay and Record Offices had 'become an immense institution but I have no idea as to whether the percentage of expense in maintaining them is greater than it ought to be.'[26] Pressed further, Perley offered more detailed advice. There should, he suggested, be a small committee under strong, capable leadership, with clearly defined powers that the War Office would recognize. Even Perley could see that that was not the situation Hughes had left behind: 'The story is that Steele and MacDougall are far from happy together at Shorncliffe and that Carson has attempted to exercise his military authority over them, which they are not willing that he should do. Then the situation between MacDougall and Brooke is not very clear, and I am told that it leads to a great deal of duplication of work.' The truth, in Perley's eyes, was that only a clean sweep of the senior Canadians could produce an improvement. They might be doing their best, he advised Borden, but 'most of them might be improved upon for members of the proposed Committee.'[27]

By the time he received Perley's lengthy letter and Aitken's warning that the 'unofficial' council had ceased to function, Sir Robert Borden would have had ample reason to intervene. He did not. Once again he was the prisoner of Sir Sam Hughes's troubles. To undermine Hughes's overseas arrangements at the denouement of the Shell inquiry might have struck loyal Conservatives as unforgivable. Even when Hughes added to his own troubles, the prime minister seemed helpless. Enraged at a critical article in the Ottawa *Journal*, a Conservative paper edited by the highly respected P.D. Ross, Hughes let the parliamentary press gallery know that Colonel J.G. Ross, chief paymaster overseas and the editor's brother, would be recalled. The reasons were hardly obscure and one of Hughes's aides, John Bassett, boasted 'I'll bring that son of a bitch, P.D. Ross, to his milk.' Fortunately for the minister, old friends in the gallery suppressed the report but the damage was done.[28]

Hughes's spiteful attempt to destroy the reputation of a highly respected and politically influential financial official pointed directly to problems in the

Canadian pay offices overseas. J.W. Borden, the accountant and paymaster general, had been appointed by the Liberals but he was both the prime minister's brother and closely trusted. Within the Pay Office in London a power struggle had developed between Borden's officers from the Militia Department, led by Colonel Ward, and a newer group, led by Colonel Ross and the general auditor, Major J.W. Dowie, brought in from civil life. Borden could cite an inspection report from a Mr H. Dunn, alleging deep dissensions, suspicious connections between Dowie and a firm of English contractors, and the undoubted fact that 500 officers were collecting $3,000 a day while obviously surplus to the CEF's establishment. Like almost everyone else but the minister, Dunn had concluded that strong leadership was a necessity: 'It seems to be a recognized fact that appointments have been made wholesale by General Hughes, General Carson and General MacDougall without consulting each other, and it would appear that the appointment of a strong man as Adjutant-General to act in London is very essential.'[29] Once again, the prime minister consulted Perley but this time the acting high commissioner protested that he knew little save from rumour and hearsay.[30] Sir Robert Borden's anxieties were not allayed but he could hardly expect Perley to undertake a personal audit without granting him a clear mandate.

While the prime minister, Perley, Gwatkin, and even Sir Sam Hughes himself may have wished to curb Carson's increasing power in England, none had done so. Accordingly, Carson continued to act as though he were the minister's full representative in England. When he learned of a meeting at the War Office, in which Steele, MacDougall, and Colonel Edmund Ironside, a staff officer at Bramshott, had discussed the use of Canadian manpower, Carson demanded a full report. Steele was directed to explain the large number of Canadians apparently diverted from training into various duties around Shorncliffe. Instead, Steele should form battalions of convalescents to provide guards and to fill noncombatant jobs.[31] Henceforth, Carson advised Major-General Whigham, deputy chief of the imperial general staff, he would be the only person empowered to speak on questions of policy for the Canadian Militia Department and he should be present at all such meetings.[32] Whatever the British reservations about Carson, they undoubtedly welcomed the simplification and Carson was present when a further meeting was held on 28 April.[33] Early in May, Carson approved the transfer of all troops at Bramshott to Watson's command and away from MacDougall, a decision made easier when, under further pressure from Hughes, Lord Brooke was given command of a brigade in the 4th Division. A fortnight later, MacDougall was scolded for appointing the commander of a training brigade without waiting for approval from Carson and the minister.

It was an act of *lèse-majesté* which Carson would be obliged to report to Sir Sam.[34]

MacDougall could easily be browbeaten. Steele was both more sensitive and better connected. On 12 June, when Carson commanded MacDougall to parade his four best battalions so that he, Watson, and Ironside could select one for the 4th Division, Steele wrote twelve querulous, repetitive pages of protest at the indignity. A small sample may be cited:

I do not think for one moment that you intend to slight me, it would be very strange if you would, but nevertheless the slight has been put upon me. There is no short circuit in such things and I think that when you wanted a regiment selected for General Watson you might at least have let me do it. I would as *you know* have given fair play to Watson or any other man. I have the confidence of the Minister and I want yours. The Minister's cable when I was appointed here is proof that he sought something of me, and as I have always done my duty without favour or affection I trust that I cannot in the future feel that there is any slight meant and that as G.O.C. troops I get fair play. I may as well say that men, who if they were in Canada dare not open their mouths about me talk of me in this town as if I were *side tracked*. It has been common talk for a month past. I reported it to the Minister and he was furious about it.[35]

A month earlier Steele had made his own bid for command of all Canadians, appealing for the intervention of his friend, the minister of public works. Rogers, he urged, 'should press this matter to the utmost extent.' So much for favour and affection.[36]

Meanwhile Carson had faced a far more serious crisis than the damaged egos of elderly colleagues. On 27 March, after mines were exploded to devastate the German front line near St Eloi, soldiers of the British 3d Division had fought a desperate battle to gain a few hundred yards of Flanders mud. Exhausted and decimated, the British were replaced by Canadians. Pelted by rain and German artillery, the landscape dissolved into a featureless bog as the Canadians struggled to rebuild the defences. On 6 April, a pre-dawn German assault recaptured most of the costly British gains. Efforts by Brigadier-General H.D.B. Ketchen's 6th Infantry Brigade to throw back the Germans failed. By 16 April, when General Headquarters ordered the battle to stop, the 2d Division had lost 1,373 men. German casualties were 483.

It was the first and worst Canadian setback of the war. Quite apart from the appalling battlefield conditions, the acute shortage of artillery ammunition, and the impossibility of constructing solid defences in the shattered earth, it soon became apparent that the Canadian forward positions had not been where senior officers believed them to be and that, in consequence, even the artillery support available had been misdirected. While aerial photography had been limited by bad weather, sufficient photos existed to suggest that generals could have used them to locate the troops instead of insisting that some of the mine craters were occupied when it was obvious that they were not. As Corps commander, General Alderson came to an unpleasant and inevitable conclusion. General Ketchen, whose brigade had borne the brunt of the disaster, must be replaced. When Turner refused to endorse the criticism of Ketchen, Alderson added him to the list of those to be removed.[37]

A first-class crisis had developed. At issue was not competence but nationality. Moreover, the battle had been the 2d Division's first real one. If, unlike the 1st Division, it had failed its first test, it was not for lack of courage or energy. If Canadian generals were to be punished for inexperience, where were better Canadian replacements to be found? While the commander of the Second Army, General Sir Hubert Plumer, demanded removal of both Turner and Ketchen, Sir Douglas Haig was not convinced. An officer of some political shrewdness, he could appreciate the arguments which Sir Max Aitken now poured in on him.[38] At the very least, Aitken warned, other Canadian senior officers would resign if Turner and Ketchen were made scapegoats. Canadian opinion would be outraged and enthusiasm for the war effort would be affected. Haig needed no further persuasion. Even before Aitken arrived he had judged that a 'serious feud' was more dangerous than the 'retention of a couple of incompetent commanders.'[39]

If Ketchen and Turner stayed, Alderson would have to go. That was obvious to Haig. To Aitken and certainly to Hughes and Carson, it was also welcome. To Sir Sam, Alderson had been the single-handed influence in disparaging the Ross rifle, Garnet Hughes, Turner, and almost every other Hughes appointee. However, the British commander-in-chief had a price. Alderson must be offered a significant appointment by the Canadians, preferably as inspector-general. Aitken agreed. Faced with an ultimatum to take the post or return to half-pay, Alderson accepted the inevitable. On 28 May Canadians learned that their new Corps commander would be Lieutenant-General Sir Julian Byng, a cavalry officer who had so far commanded the Cavalry Corps in France, the IX Corps in the Dardanelles, and, since February 1916, the XVII Corps on the western front.[40]

While there were undoubtedly Canadians who might have insisted that the command go to a Canadian, even Hughes was satisfied by getting rid of Alderson. Turner, as the senior major-general in the Corps, was under a cloud; to promote Currie, the next senior, would have been to raise dangerous questions about Turner's competence.[41] Meanwhile there were enough political difficulties in creating the post of inspector-general. To Haig the position would be of considerable significance, relieving the Canadian Corps commander from direct involvement in Canadian military politics.[42] Aitken, on the other hand, had made it clear to the War Office that the post would be nominal.[43]

No one troubled to explain the confusion to Alderson. Within days he had set out to establish his headquarters in Shorncliffe, demanding clerks, orderlies, and cars to fulfil his new duties. Steele was indignant. 'This is no place for Alderson,' he complained to Carson, 'his place is in London with you and if he is here I shall consider it a direct affront.'[44] Carson was hardly better pleased with the arrangement since it threatened to add yet another participant to the overcrowded Canadian hierarchy and it was by no means clear whether Alderson owed his allegiance to the British or the Canadians. In answer to an inquiry from General Watson, Carson would only explain that Alderson would report to Lord French, commander-in-chief of Home Forces, that he had a sort of roving commission and that it was impossible to predict where he might go.[45] In fact, the British had no more interest in Alderson than the Canadians. In July, after Alderson had contributed some embarrassing memoranda on the plethora of Canadian officers, Carson asked the War Office, through Aitken, to remind the inspector-general that he was a Canadian appointment.[46] Even that was questioned by Ottawa, where no official record of the arrangement could be found. The unfortunate General Alderson, who had in fact served his Canadian masters with courage, integrity, and ability, was rescued from his humiliating plight on 26 September by a War Office appointment as an inspector of infantry.

Alderson's removal was not the only change among senior Canadian commanders in the spring of 1916. Early on 2 June the Germans launched a massive artillery barrage and infantry assault on troops of the 3d Canadian Division guarding Mont Sorrel a few miles from Ypres. In minutes the defending troops were annihilated in a tornado of fire. Among the casualties were Brigadier-General Victor Williams, wounded and captured, and Major-General M.S. Mercer, eardrums shattered, leg broken, and finally killed by shrapnel. Hughes's response to the news was immediate. Brigadier-General G.J. Farmar, one of Byng's senior staff officers deciphered the message; 'Give Garnet 3rd Division, Sam.' Farmar assumed it was a code; Byng understood the message well enough and ignored it. The man for the job was Brigadier-General Lipsett, a British officer on pre-war loan to Canada. He had commanded the Eighth Battalion with great skill through the long battle at Ypres and, at the head of the 2d Brigade, had helped recapture Mont Sorrel. On 16 June the appointment was made.[47]

By the summer of 1916 both the Allies and the Canadian Corps had reached a new pitch of fighting effectiveness. The lack of munitions which had affected the Canadians as late as the battle of the St Eloi craters had largely been overcome and henceforth the Germans would be at a material disadvantage. One consequence was that Canadians could finally abandon the Ross rifle and their American-made Colt machine guns for Lee-Enfields and the legendary Vickers. All three Canadian divisions in the line had proved themselves in battle, learned from bitter experience, and begun to acquire the practical efficiency which would eventually characterize the Canadian Corps. During the two summer months of 1916, while much of the rest of the British army was sacrificed in a futile series of assaults along the Somme, the Canadians guarded Ypres, rebuilt their strength, and waited.

The contrast between the growing efficiency of the Corps and the quarrelsome confusion of the Canadian administration in England developed steadily. In near desperation, the War Office tried to interpret the Canadian command system to Lord French. MacDougall, it explained, was supposed to be in command of all Canadians but his position had been 'modified' by the arrival of Steele. As a result, Steele now commanded all Canadians at Shorncliffe while MacDougall commanded the Canadian Training Division. At Bramshott, Watson was independent of both Steele and MacDougall. Though Carson was supposed to be responsible only for stores and supplies, his office had become the channel for dealing with all Canadian matters. When drafts were needed for France, the adjutant general at the War Office ordered them from either Bramshott or Shorncliffe. Alderson, as inspector-general, could inspect either camp.[48] Even then, the War Office oversimplified. Steele had never renounced authority over Watson. MacDougall refused to admit that he was subordinate to Steele. Carson plainly did more than channel correspondence.

Early in July Sir George Perley returned to Canada for the first time since the war began. He had much to do, from restoring his business affairs to reassuring the neglected voters of Argenteuil-Two Mountains, but the problems of Canadian military administration in England were bound to take high priority. 'From what I hear,' he warned Borden shortly before his departure, 'I should judge that there is a good deal of difference of opinion as [to] relative rank and powers ...' On his first day in Ottawa, Perley met Hughes and the prime minister to recommend reorganization of the Canadian administrative structure overseas.[49]

Restless by nature and eager to get close to the fighting front, Hughes needed no urging to get back to England. The Shell inquiry was over and Sir Sam had been generously exonerated by the Royal Commission. His troubles, however, had not ceased. By now, many of his responsibilities had been transferred to others. Purchasing was being managed by Sir Edward Kemp. The creation of hospitals and medical services for returning sick and wounded was the work of a commission headed by Senator James Lougheed. Hughes's coterie of manufacturers in the Shell committee was supplanted by the Imperial Munitions Board under the firm business management of Joseph Flavelle. In Canada, Hughes's responsibilities were limited to recruiting and training soldiers for the CEF. Those tasks were probably as mismanaged as the rest but Canadian civilians had no inkling of trouble until July when riots broke out at Camp Borden among troops protesting the dust, the lack of drinking water, and the ban on smoking.[50]

The minister took personal credit for the creation of the huge new camp on the Angus Plains near Barrie but he blamed the trouble on his staff officers, ill-conceived attempts to harden the troops, and the spirits of 'a few brats of boys.'[51] Other Canadians were less tolerant. Though military censors did their utmost to prevent reports, details leaked into the Toronto *Telegram* and *Star*, newspapers that disagreed on everything but their dislike of Hughes. The truth was that Hughes was congenitally unable to settle down to systematic administration. His admiring biographer recalled how Sir Sam would fill important meetings with long accounts of his South African experiences. 'To see a bevy of staff officers of high rank, each with urgent and important matters to discuss, forced to forget their current worries for half an hour while the Minister held the floor with some side-splitting story ... was amusing in the extreme.'[52]

It would have been sensible on many grounds to end Hughes's ministerial career that July. His exoneration had hardly done credit to his judgment in dealing with shady operators like J. Wesley Allison but at least he could have retired with honour.[53] The prime minister could have had no illusions about his military or administrative competence. Overseas administration was a mess and Camp Borden was public proof that all was not well at home.[54] However, Hughes remained a formidable figure in the prime minister's eyes, with a poweful network of supporters across the country and in the halls of the Loyal Orange Lodge. Like other war leaders, propaganda had helped build Hughes to heroic stature and it was not yet easy to admit that heroes could be replaced. Borden had no zest for the furious controversy that would accompany any forced resignation. Instead, he agreed that his old friend would once again cross the Atlantic 'to reorganize our forces in England and assist in getting things in better shape for the Front.'[55] The appointment of F.B. McCurdy, a Halifax lawyer and financier, as parliamentary secretary to the minister of militia was some assurance that departmental business would not languish in Hughes's absence.[56]

Hughes set off in a buoyant mood on the evening of 18 July. Next day at New York he boasted to Borden that he had spent his time arranging shipments of lumber to Britain before embarking. During the voyage he devoted himself to composing a violent diatribe against his cabinet colleagues, Perley and Sir Thomas White. The latter he accused of condemning the Ross rifle and of inspiring newspaper assaults on him. 'It has long been recognized that White is possessed of a sort of mental epilepsy or rather that mental epilepsy controls him.' It was Borden's duty 'to confine Sir Thomas and Sir George each to his proper function in his department ...'[57]

Sir Sam reached England in such a combative frame of mind that he virtually ignored the polite message from the prime minister which awaited him: 'When you have reached conclusion respecting your proposals for the reorganization, please cable them fully as they should be definitely embodied in Order-in-Council and it would be desirable to consider them before they are actually put into operation.' Other messages followed. What about the report from Colonel J.G. Ross that there were 214 surplus officers in England, drawing $1,064 a day in pay? There were not fifteen unemployed officers in England, Hughes promptly retorted. 'Carson informs me we are short several hundred.' Soon there were more questions from Ottawa. What were the names of officers not on official establishments? Why had so many non-effective troops accumulated in England? Were Canadian boots, bicycles, and motor vehicles used at the front? Why were soldiers from Canada considered fit only for the third week of the War Office training syllabus?[58]

Hughes ignored the questions. Instead, on 15 August, bubbling with martial enthusiasm, Hughes urged the prime minister to raise four more divisions and to dispatch fifty to eighty thousand more troops at once. 'Big drive expected,' Hughes explained, 'and great desire that Canadians should be first in Berlin.' It was a fanciful interpretation of the Somme offensive which would eventually cost the Allies 623,907 casualties, including 24,029 young Canadians. On 16 August Hughes left for France, announcing that he would discuss his plans with Sir Douglas Haig.[59]

In Ottawa, Borden could only conclude that Sir Sam had forgotten the rather mundane responsibilities he had taken to England. In a lengthy telegram he attempted to bring the minister back to the job at hand. There was, he noted, an apparent lack of system and control in the Canadian organization, and an absence of co-ordination with Canada. Each branch in Canada should have its counterpart across the Atlantic. 'I regard this as one of the most important objects of your visit,' Borden concluded, 'and hope you will be able to give prompt and effective consideration thereto.'[60]

Hughes paid no apparent attention. As Borden knew from the newspapers, the minister was having a joyous military holiday in England, inspecting troops, visiting camps, demonstrating how bayonet-fighting and other exotic skills should be taught. In uniform as a major-general, a stout but aggressive figure, he could rejoice in the respect of subordinates and the attention of the British public. On the same day that Borden pleaded for attention to administrative reform, Hughes sent him a chatty cable embodying random thoughts on the efficiency of Lloyd George, the shortage of timber in England, and the possibility of supplying Canadian soldiers with Canadian fish. Almost as an afterthought, he concluded: 'Will submit detailed organization on return.'[61]

Borden was suspicious. So was Perley. Was it possible that Hughes would set up his new arrangements without consulting his colleagues? By now neither man trusted Hughes. On 24 August the prime minister again cabled Hughes, urging him to report progress. A covering letter explained that no report had been received.[62]

In fact, Hughes had not neglected the main purpose of his visit. There were, of course, many other concerns. Carson had insisted on holding over a bundle of decisions, particularly on appointments. To Carson's alarm, Steele and the brigadiers at Shorncliffe insisted on an interview with the minister as soon as he arrived. Carson was relieved to learn that the meeting was intended to denounce all critics of the Canadian Training Division.[63] Plans for a grand review of Canadians at Bramshott had to be completed. On 4 August, Canadian officers were crowded into a theatre to hear Hughes promise that four additional divisions would absorb the officer surplus.[64] In March Hughes had come to England determined that heads would roll; in August his euphoria persuaded him that all of his chosen officers were excellent. The only problem was the system of communications, particularly with the War Office and British General Headquarters in France. A visit to France, in which he attempted to browbeat Byng for failing to promote his son, also ended in surprising good feeling. He liked Byng, who stood up to him, and there would be other divisions and perhaps even another Canadian corps for Garnet to command. Meanwhile, Sir Sam would create another council, this time to be called a 'Sub-Militia Council.' Recalling the prime minister's directive that no permanent arrangements were to be made without cabinet approval, Hughes politely attached the prefix 'Acting' to his title. On 5 September a first meeting was held and on the following day Hughes sent a somewhat enigmatic progress report to Ottawa: 'After carefully considering from every viewpoint plan for organization here after consultation with War Office and our officers at front and General Headquarters have a system practically ready. Fault is not with training so much as disorganization and irritation through cases mentioned previously. Hope to have full report

based on most mature consideration from every viewpoint ready to mail by the end of week. Meantime everything going splendidly.'[65]
Things were not going so well in Ottawa. By the time Borden received Hughes's message, he had had four days to digest reports in the Ottawa *Journal*, repeated in other newspapers, telling him far more than Hughes had been prepared to reveal. The *Journal* headline was representative:

MILITARY COUNCIL FORMED IN LONDON TO SOLVE
TROUBLES IN HIGH COMMAND
SEVEN MEMBERS, LATER TEN UNDER MAJOR-GENERAL
WILL IMPERIAL AUTHORITIES APPROVE
THE ONLY QUESTION

The *Journal's* London correspondent was certainly flattering. 'It is thought generally in military circles that Sir Sam Hughes has shown the military judgement of a Solomon in this solution and that the existing unpleasant overlapping among various Canadian Major-Generals, which certainly has caused friction in the past, will be ended by the council.'[66] On 7 September the Canadian Associated Press added that Carson, Steele, MacDougall, Brigadier-General Frank Meighen, Colonel Murphy, and Colonel Frank Reid, the director of records, had all been included. The prime minister was furious, and his anger permeated the telegram he promptly dispatched to his errant colleague:

Extraordinary press reports appeared last evening giving details of arrangements which you are said to have made with respect to the control of our forces in Great Britain. Please note my cable of thirty first July on this subject. In my judgement more effective and definite arrangements must be made for control of overseas expenditure and for direction of overseas forces. Such arrangements must be put in definite shape and embodied in an Order-in-Council. It is most undesirable that proposal contemplated should be announced in advance of consideration by Council.[67]

Hughes's reply was lame: he had given 'positive orders' that nothing was to be said about the proposals until they were approved in Canada and he was investigating the leak.[68] Borden was unimpressed. 'Greatly surprised that composition of proposed Overseas Council is announced in press this morning,' he cabled on the eighth, 'Hope you can return immediately.'[69] Hughes still did nothing to pacify his leader: 'Know nothing whatever about our own composition of proposed Council and cannot understand your peculiar message. Report on proposed Council mailed you. Question of salary or rank never once raised by an officer. Absolutely understand nothing settled until approved by Order-in-Council.' Far from coming back to Canada at once, Hughes was off to Scotland for a week to inspect Canadian Forestry Corps camps.[70]

It was left to Sir Max Aitken to mollify the prime minister. Having helped in the arrangements, he set out on 11 September to explain both details and personnel. As Borden had wished, the proposed overseas sub-militia council would be modelled on the Militia Council in Ottawa. Carson would act as chairman and agent of the minister; Lord Brooke would be Canadian representative at the front while Brigadier-General R.G.E. Leckie, a former brigade commander in France, would serve as chief of staff. Aitken had a kind word for these and other members, noting that Brooke seemed better suited to diplomatic duties than a field command. If there were press leaks, Aitken explained, it was not Hughes's fault: 'Minister has not made any statement to Press but members of proposed Council are talking freely.' A second cable recalled Borden's own instructions to Aitken to use his best efforts to get effective results:

I have urged Minister to adopt line suggested in your telegram and it appears to me that scheme cabled today is very good. Principal weakness in England lies in training and although Leckie is not best man available he had long experience and good record at front and Minister has selected him on my strong recommendation. Understand Leckie will select his staff from officers at front. This will do much to crush criticism of training in England. Lord Brooke has difficult task to keep balance between Minister, Staff Officers at General Headquarters and General Byng but Geary appears to be good assistant. Council would be strengthened by substitution of one or two officers with experience in France of recognized reputation. If you object to any names on Council suggest you communicate your views to Sir Sam and advise me at same time as Minister is disposed to accept suggestions.[71]

The 'full explanation' from Hughes consisted of a long and effusive letter, boasting that he had been 'testing the matter out in every available way,' that he had consulted both British and Canadian officers and that his chosen appointments were excellent in every way. Choosing Brooke to channel communications between Carson and the field was a master stroke and if Brooke might be suspect, his assistant, Major G.R. Geary, a former mayor of Toronto, would give reassurance. Colonel A.D. McRae, another leading Conservative and prominent Vancouver businessman, would be 'a sort of Deputy Minister.' He had, Hughes insisted, proved himself 'a marvellous manager.' Leckie, still convalescing from wounds, was 'the best available man' while Colonel Reid was 'a perfect master of organization and getting things on a system.' Murphy was 'a splendid officer as you know' and, if Borden was still worried about financial control, such matters were to be confided to the well-connected Colonel Ross. Other members would include Steele, MacDougall, Colonel Neill of the veterinary service, and Brigadier-General Frank Meighen, who would replace Brooke at Bramshott. Hughes's concluding paragraphs poured out the customary pleasure in his own handiwork:

I do not think there is an officer or man in the service at the Front or in Britain but will agree that we have the best possible organization obtainable here. The men have all proven themselves big and strong. MacDougall had a vile job, every organization and detail was unloaded on his command, they would be with him a few days or weeks and half of them would be taken away and new men brought in. The unfit ones were always remaining and becoming more numerous. I think his staff might be strengthened, but I will not touch that until a committee which I have appointed to examine both camps reports.

Poor old Steele, I fear, is pretty well run down, still, out of compliment to him, we put him on the committee. In many ways he is a good man although I fear his race is nearly run. I saw him yesterday near Folkestone, and really he should have been in hospital.

Frank Meighen shows up as one of the greatest men I have ever met, thorough organizer in every sense, McRae and Neill have already earned everything that a Government could confer on men. Both are regarded as great men in business and economy. Indeed, the British Adjutant General, General McCready [sic], wished, to me, the other day that they could model in everything after our systems here, but he said their system, built on in patches, could not now be altered materially in this war; they had not the men with big enough grasp to handle it, and they well envied the splendid system we have established and are establishing.[72]

Hughes's delight in his creation was doubtless shared by Carson who could now look forward to be confirmed in the position he had virtually created for himself. However, it was the minister who was the real winner. With its twelve members, the council was too large and disparate to offer Hughes any effective challenge. Most of its members, certainly Carson, Brooke, MacDougall, Murphy, Reid, and Meighen, owed their positions entirely to the minister's favour. As he had explained, perhaps a little too cryptically, to Borden, Hughes had in fact spent most of September ensuring that his Sub-Militia Council would work to his satisfaction. One sample of his influence was the choice of secretary. Carson had assumed that Oulster, now promoted to major, would be the automatic choice. Instead, the minister insisted that his son-in-law, Major Byron M. Greene, must have the job. It was so arranged.

For the first full meeting of the council on 8 September, eight of the members were present: Carson, MacDougall, Meighen, Murphy, Reid, McRae, Ross, and Neill. Oulster, not yet displaced, took the minutes. Sir Sam launched the meeting and dominated discussion. There must be an investigation of unemployed and inefficient officers at Shorncliffe and Bramshott. Why were unfit and unsuitable soldiers still being sent from Canada? Colonel Reid must discover why the British press gave larger headings to Australian than to Canadian casualty reports. In the afternoon, with Hughes absent, discussion was, if possible, even more banal. The meeting solemnly approved a request from the Red Cross that a blanket be issued to each Canadian prisoner of war in Germany. The meeting ended after a motion by Carson, seconded by MacDougall, that the minister be asked to found a Canadian order of chivalry to be known as the 'Order of the Beaver and Maple Leaf' or, alternately, as the 'Star of Canada.'[74]

Hughes was still in Scotland when the second meeting was convened on 15 September and his absence obviously paralysed discussion. Nothing more important was suggested than the creation of a Canadian army pay corps. By the third meeting, a pattern was beginning to emerge. Lord Brooke, wounded a few days after his 12th Brigade entered the line, never took his seat in the council. His place was taken by Colonel E.C. Ashton, a politically active physician-soldier who had been given command of a training brigade at Shorncliffe without ever serving in France. On 22 September Hughes was present to introduce both Ashton and his son-in-law and to issue his own regulations for the body. The Acting Sub-Militia Council, he explained, was 'an advisory body, advising generally with respect to the Canadian Expeditionary Force.' It might meet weekly and more often if necessary. Members must give the secretary forty-eight hours notice of any matter to be raised. Each member would have equal voice and all votes were to be recorded. Minutes would be sent in triplicate to the minister in Ottawa.[75] On 29 September Hughes was present for the last time, granting Colonel Murphy special permission to return to Canada to care for a sick father. Hughes himself left England on 1 October.

Sir Sam may have believed that he had done all that was asked of him. Certainly Carson, as 'Minister's Representative and Chairman of the Council,' McRae as 'Overseas Deputy Minister,' and Leckie as 'Chief of the General Staff' had powerful-sounding titles. However, if the minister had explained each officer's responsibilities, he left no written record. Nor did he settle the relative status of MacDougall and Steele, a recurring dispute of more than a year's duration.[76] Few, if any, of the council members commanded prestige or respect in the Canadian Corps or elsewhere. Hughes's main concern seems to have been to guarantee his own continuing daily influence, not least by ensuring that his loyal son-in-law would watch over proceedings.

Left to itself, however, the council probably did represent significant progress in at least defining major problems in Canadian overseas administration. It debated the need for adequate dental services, the replacement of soldiers by civilians in the London offices, and the introduction of 'working pay' to match British pay regulations. After learning that 522 graves had been registered by the end of September 1916, the council authorized Colonel Kemmis-Betty to create a graves registration section and to investigate the cost of procuring a standard cross. However, the minutes of the council's nine meetings hint strongly at ineffectiveness. Members spent hours discussing the design of a badge for CEF veterans discharged in England. Matters apparently settled reappeared again and again.[77]

Above all, council work was crippled by constant reminders that it was still the creature of an increasingly erratic Sam Hughes. The minister had barely reached Ottawa before he cabled the council that all its reports 'must be carefully prepared and must be endorsed from here before final adoption.'[78] On 13 October Carson informed the sixth meeting that Hughes rejected the title 'Canadian Imperial Forces' which the council had proposed for the CEF. Shortly after, when members responded to the appalling casualty toll of the Canadian Corps in the Somme offensive, Hughes countermanded proposals to break up units intended for a fifth and sixth division.[79] Since only 7,800 other infantry reinforcements were available to replace more than twenty thousand casualties, the council persuaded McRae to appeal to Hughes to change his mind. Presumably he was regarded as the man with the greatest store of influence. However, at the meeting on 27 October, criticism of one of Hughes's impromptu promotions led McRae to move that: 'it would be presumptuous on the part of the Council to criticize such action of the Minister.' The motion passed unanimously.[80]

The problem was not the institution; it was the minister of militia.

5

The Overseas Ministry

Whether or not, as Sir Sam boasted, the Sub-Militia Council really inspired British admiration, whether it was wise or foolish, it was doomed. The minister of militia may never have realized the fact but when he left for England at the end of July, he was on probation. Sir Robert Borden's insistence that any reorganization overseas must have prior cabinet approval was as clear a warning as he could give. Hughes would no longer be the unfettered master of his department.[1]

With Sir George Perley back in Canada, Borden believed that finally he had a trustworthy source of advice about the state of affairs in England. Perley had suffered too long from Hughes's methods to cloak his feelings. During August, while Perley busied himself with personal and constituency concerns, the prime minister kept him in touch with his frustrating attempts to get answers from Hughes. Early in September a Militia Department proposal for channelling CEF promotions served as an invitation to Perley to return to a familiar theme: the need for a strong, overseas-based control organization. On the same day that Ottawa papers reported Hughes's Sub-Militia Council scheme, Perley submitted an argument for a small council of three or four members, headed by a civilian, with a first-class military officer to exercise executive command. In place of the unsatisfactory, unofficial basis on which Carson and Aitken managed their relations with the War Office and General Headquarters, such a council must be firmly based on an order-in-council, with authority to 'manage our military affairs across the seas in a businesslike way ...'[2]

Borden needed no further persuasion. Ever the cautious lawyer, he turned to E.L. Newcombe, the deputy minister of justice, to establish first that Canada had the right to exercise effective legal control over her overseas contingents. Newcombe was equal to the task. Certainly the Canadian cabinet in 1914 had done everything in its power to push authority over to the British. Fortunately, he argued, the British had been equally persistent in pushing responsibility back to Canada. The CEF, Newcombe suggested, was neither militia in the original sense of the Militia Act nor was it a colonial force raised on the authority of the Army Act. 'Being neither, they must be seen as a force of militia sent abroad to defend their country.' A crucial feature was that appointments and promotions in the CEF were made on the authority of the governor-in-council and its bills were paid by Canadian parliamentary appropriation. Having ingeniously recast a little history, Newcombe followed with a logical (and perhaps inspired) suggestion:

Details affecting matters of discipline should perhaps be suggested and considered in consultation with the military advisers of the Government, but if I may venture to suggest, I should think that the executive or administrative requirements of the case would be best satisfied by the establishment of a Canadian Ministry of War in London charged with the administration of the Overseas forces, to be held by a member of this Cabinet, assisted if thought advisable by a council of competent experts, whose advice would be considered by the Minister in submitting his recommendations to the Governor General-in-Council for approval.[3]

It was a further measure of Newcombe's ingenuity and of the status ministers had achieved in the Canadian constitution that he could propose that a cabinet member could function on the far side of the Atlantic. It was a suggestion Borden swiftly embraced since it was the most plausible means of cutting Hughes away from functions which he had plainly mishandled. By 22 September he had in his hands a draft order that would create a ministry of the overseas military forces of Canada. The accompanying report emphasized both the magnitude of the overseas administration and the enormous training responsibilities that would remain in Canada with the Militia Department. The proposed department would have responsibility for the personnel, property, and expenditures of the Canadian forces in Britain and on the continent. The minister would normally reside in London and, on matters requiring the approval of the governor-in-council, he might proceed on his own when urgency dictated. On all matters affecting the overseas forces, the minister would be responsible for negotiations with the British government. To assist him, he was authorized to create an organization and to appoint officers and clerks, none of whom would be subject to the civil service examination. He was also authorized to form an advisory council, although its members were to be appointed by order-in-council. The minister would report to the cabinet through the prime minister and he would receive no pay for the post.[4]

A few days after the preparation of the draft ordinance, on 28 September, Perley sailed from Halifax for England. His ship probably passed Hughes's in mid-Atlantic. Perley, having been in Canada when Borden had reached his conclusions, almost certainly knew of Borden's intentions. Throughout his summer in Canada, Perley had been closely consulted on military matters and it was his suggestion that the chief authority in England should be given to a civilian, not a general. The proposal that the minister remain unpaid was tailor-made for him for Perley was wealthy enough to manage without a salary. Under the Independence of Parliament Act, a member of parliament who entered the cabinet was obliged to seek re-election unless the position – as with ministers without portfolio – was unpaid. As acting high commissioner, Perley had avoided the nuisance of a by-election by refusing a salary; now he could continue. His mixed French-English constituency of Argenteuil had not only been badly neglected in his absence, but would also reflect the rising French-Canadian resentment at Conservative war policies.

By 7 October Sir Sam Hughes was back in Ottawa and Perley had reached London. Soon the prime minister began to hear contrasting versions of the minister's summer sojourn in England. Hughes rhapsodized about his new organization. His appointees had done marvels, saving millions of dollars. Through his own system, Hughes had found more than five thousand soldiers idling in England and sent them to France. Only the medical services had earned Hughes's disfavour and, in one of the more dramatic measures of his summer visit, the minister had taken steps to put them right. His chosen instrument, Colonel Herbert A. Bruce, was professor of surgery at the University of Toronto and the creator of the new Wellesley Hospital, already a byword in up-to-date, systematic surgical techniques. Bruce was also a man with a grievance. During earlier service in France, he had tangled with his military superiors. When he went back to Canada, Surgeon-General Jones accused him of taking government-owned X-ray plates to use in his lectures. Bruce immediately appealed to the minister and established himself as a man ready to do battle with entrenched military professionals and red tape.[5] Hughes brought Bruce with him to England, appointed him 'Special Inspector-General' and was rewarded, before his return to Canada, with a devastating critique of Jones's medical organization, a healthy whiff of scandal from the Duchess of Connaught's Red Cross hospital at Taplow, and proposals for a 'top-to-bottom' reorganization of the entire Canadian medical system. One of the first acts of the Sub-Militia Council after Hughes's departure was to strip General Jones of his position and give it to Colonel Bruce. Who better would carry out the work of reform?[6]

Perley, who reached England on 6 October, was outraged at the Bruce report and indignant at Jones's treatment. So were many others. However, the target of his anger was Hughes's so-called 'acting' council. On 11 October he notified Borden: 'Understood you instructed Minister Militia not arrange any organization here until Council had approved of same. Stop. Although designated as acting and technically not yet official new organization is completed and in saddle. Stop. Regret much outspoken criticism Minister here. Among others two Conservative Canadian Members of Parliament have told me very unpopular among officers and men.'[7]

In Ottawa, Borden was still busy quietly mustering support for his reorganization plan. He could certainly count on Sir Thomas White, Hughes's worst enemy in the cabinet. Even in August White had argued for an overseas war purchasing board under Perley to trim Hughes's powers. Now, as minister responsible for overseas expenditures totalling more than Canada's entire federal spending in 1914, White demanded a change. 'For myself, I feel that the matter is vital and I cannot assume responsibility for the acts of officials not directly under the immediate supervision and control of a Member of the Government.'[8]

Only on 18 October, almost two weeks after Hughes's return to Ottawa, did the prime minister dare break the news that he had adopted a contrary approach to overseas administration. Choosing the day when Sir Sam's promotion to honorary lieutenant-general in the British army was announced, Borden sent the old minister a copy of the draft order-in-council and a long explanatory note: 'It is apparent that we should have a more efficient organization in Great Britain. Your recommendations as to an Overseas Militia Council are based on that view, as I understand. I am not criticizing your suggestions as to the personnel of the proposed Overseas Council, but I am of opinion that the direction of a member of the Government resident in London is both desirable and essential.' Borden can hardly have hoped to pacify Hughes with the assurance that the proposal was not 'intended as a reflexion upon your efforts or your administration.'[9]

By now Hughes knew perfectly well what Borden had in mind. If there was any doubt, the Montreal *Gazette* reported on 19 October that the government planned to put military affairs in England in the hands of a resident minister. The minister was in a fighting mood. He was also tired and ill. Borden had noted his haggard appearance on 7 October. During a visit home to Lindsay on the Thanksgiving week-end, his wife, daughter, and grandchildren had been involved in a serious car accident. Hughes was badly upset. On 13 October, when he inspected Camp Borden, young Leslie Frost noted his pallor.[10] Still, he fought back, pleading that he would be humiliated if his proposal were rejected. On 23 October Hughes presented his own draft order-in-council for his Sub-Militia Council and seven long, angry, and often disjointed pages of argument against any overseas minister: 'There is no more necessity for a resident Minister in Britain than there is for a resident Minister in our camps in British Columbia, Calgary, Camp Hughes, Camp Borden, Valcartier &c. Indeed, there is less need in Britain because where formerly General Carson was alone the representative, he is now surrounded by a Sub-Militia Council composed of the ablest officers to be found ...' Instead, Hughes insisted, Borden's arrangement would lead only to increased subservience to the British. Perley, he claimed, was a toady to the British authorities and a proven bungler. Under his own system Hughes boasted, 'it is impossible to lay a finger on any part of our service that is not better and more economically administered than the British and infinitely better than anything that ever occurred before.'[11]

Hughes's rebuttal, full of unsubstantiated claims and accusations, made no impact on the prime minister. Neither did supporting letters from Major-General E.W. Wilson, the insurance agent who had taken command of the Montreal military district, or C.C. Ballantyne, managing director of Sherwin-Williams in Montreal, who insisted that Hughes must retain supreme control.[12] Borden was more impressed by advice from Colonel G.H. Bradbury, a Conservative MP serving in France, who insisted that Hughes was a major liability among the troops.[13] Doubtless aware that he was now writing for the public record, the prime minister replied on 26 October insisting that a minister was needed for close control on the spot in England and that the only motive was efficiency and economy.[14]

On the same day, Hughes suddenly switched tactics. On re-reading the papers, he informed the prime minister, he had noticed that no one was actually named as minister though he had only assumed that it would be Perley. Since his only real concern was to 'prevent humiliation and insult to our mutual friend, Sir Max Aitken,' a solution was easy. 'Therefore, please fill in his name, let the office be attached to him instead of him to the office, and you have my exact wish.'[15] Sir Robert refused the gambit. The minister would be appointed, he advised Hughes, only after the department was established.[16] Aitken also disappointed his patron. When Hughes hurriedly cabled his friend to accept the post, Sir Max politely declined. He was not qualified.[17] On 27 October the cabinet met, ignored Hughes's angry protests and endorsed the draft of 22 September without significant amendment. At once, Borden notified Perley: 'Order-in-Council signed today creating Ministry Overseas Forces, Hughes greatly excited and may resign. Order will not be made public until Monday. This message therefore confidential in meantime.'[18]

By 30 October Hughes was beaten. Further almost pathetic appeals to the prime minister not to humiliate him by appointing Perley were unheeded. Another cabinet enemy, George E. Foster, the minister of trade and commerce, sardonically noted in his diary: 'Hughes raged but did not resign.'[19] In vain, Sir Sam pleaded for any arrangements that would exclude Perley. Even with Aitken's rejection staring him in the face, Hughes insisted that his old friend would serve as 'Canadian Representative there for War Purposes under me.' In a final, desperate concession, Hughes even agreed that Perley could serve as head of the Sub-Militia Council provided that Hughes remained the sole authority for promotions and appointments.[20]

For once, under pressure, Borden remained resolute. His patience long since exhausted, the prime minister had finally concluded that Hughes was not only a needless embarrassment to the government but that his substantial personal support had been dissipated. 'I have read your letter with care,' he informed Hughes on 31 October, 'and it does not seem to me that the proposals which you outline are practicable; thus I regret that I cannot concur in them.'[21] Next day Sir George Perley was formally appointed Minister of the Overseas Military Forces of Canada. His secretary at the High Commission, W.L. Griffiths, was given special authority to swear him in.[22]

Hughes now knew himself bereft of power. Everywhere enemies had triumphed at his expense. Joseph Flavelle, who despised Hughes as a bungling ally of shady promoters, now exercised an autocratic control of munitions-making. Sir Albert Edward Kemp, archetype of the Toronto Tories with whom Hughes had often tangled, was chairman of the War Purchasing Board. R.B. Bennett, chairman of the National Service Boards, had a special responsibility for manpower. F.B. McCurdy, parliamentary secretary of the Militia Department, could manage day-to-day administration. The appointment of Perley excluded Hughes from the responsibilities he most enjoyed. Now he proceeded to burn his bridges in yet another violent letter to the prime minister. He had not, he insisted, ignored cabinet authority by proceeding with his acting council, but had merely tested it: 'Permit me to draw to your attention nearly every Commission which has been formed. They look beautiful on paper, but few if any one of them have been anything like perfect in practice.' If he had tried to run the CEF by order-in-council, he insisted, the 1st Division would never have left Valcartier. The tirade might have been endured but there was a charge in Hughes's concluding paragraph which Sir Robert could not ignore:

One other point and I am through. It might be implied from your memorandum that my failing to secure authority by Order-in-Council impelled you to the course you are now pursuing with regard to Sir George Perley. May I be permitted to say that both you and I know to the contrary. I knew early in August that Sir George Perley had planned something along these very lines. You have, also, admitted that as early as the first week of September you had this matter under consideration by you and Perley earlier. You incidentally remarked yesterday that you had not consulted any of your colleagues. Of course, when I drew attention to the statement, you corrected yourself.[23]

Quite apart from the insulting, if largely accurate, charge of lack of frankness on the part of the prime minister, Hughes had made it clear that there would be no co-operation between the Militia Department and the Overseas Ministry as long as he held office. It was not a comfortable decision for Borden to demand a colleague's resignation and the prime minister spent almost a week sounding out colleagues and even consulting the parliamentary librarian about British precedents and procedures. Perley was warned that Borden had received a letter 'which demands most serious consideration at my hands.'[24] Correspondence with Conservatives across the country was studied to assess the likely impact. Finally, on 9 November, Borden delivered his reply:

Under conditions which at times were very trying and which gave me great concern, I have done my utmost to support you in the administration of your Department. This has been very difficult by reason of your strong tendency to assume powers which you do not possess and which can only be exercised by the Governor in Council. My time and energies, although urgently needed for more important duties, have been very frequently employed in removing difficulties thus unnecessarily created. You seemed actuated by a desire and even an intention to administer your Department as if it were a separate and distinct Government in itself. On many occasions, but without much result, I have cautioned you against this course which has frequently led to well founded protests from your Colleagues as well as detriment to the public interest ...[25]

For Borden, the last straw had long since been Hughes's disregard of a cabinet directive; Hughes's letter was a legitimate pretext for dismissal. Avoiding any attempt to meet his colleague's charges, the prime minister merely concluded: 'You must surely realize that I cannot retain in the Government a colleague who has addressed to me such a communication. I regret that you have thus imposed upon me the disagreeable duty of requesting your resignation as Minister of Militia and Defence.'

According to Fiset, Hughes 'almost collapsed' when he received Borden's letter of dismissal. Over a long career as editor, politician, and soldier, he had issued such a wealth of hectoring, abusive letters that perhaps he no longer believed that one could ever bounce back to hurt him. He also failed to realize that he had forced Borden's hand. Hughes spent a week touring camps, lecturing officers and delivering speeches designed to warn his colleagues that he might be a vocal and dangerous enemy. At Toronto, he had hinted broadly at the shocking contents of the Bruce report and he had also indicated that conscription might well be necessary. On Saturday, his spirits restored, he returned to Ottawa and composed his letter of resignation. It was a lengthy recital of abuse and innuendo, culminating in the charge that Borden had been plotting to retire to the Supreme Court of Canada.[26] On Monday, 13 November, the news was made public and two days later Hughes handed over the keys to his office, spoke briefly to his assembled staff, and departed. 'I leave with regret,' he wrote Borden, 'not on account of the office, or anything special, outside of friendships which will last – but for the welfare of the soldiers. However a kindly watchful eye will be kept over them by your humble servant.'[27]

The next day Hughes left Ottawa for the southern United States to recover his strength, await the resumption of Parliament, and, as he explained to Aitken, explore his political options. 'Just at the moment,' he boasted, 'I control the situation.'[28] In fact, as dismissed politicians soon discover, those who live by flattery perish in neglect. Hughes's dependents sought to save themselves; the victims of his abuse or favouritism expected revenge. When the lengthy and vituperative resignation correspondence was tabled on 16 November, potential sympathizers among the Conservatives immediately closed ranks against a man so clearly intent on embarrassing their government. Only the Liberals could possibly take comfort from the ex-minister's allegations and revelations and they were unlikely to share the proceeds with Hughes. The Ottawa *Free Press* spoke for other opposition papers when it admitted that 'it was Sir Sam Hughes himself who piled the faggots on the fire that ultimately consumed him,' while also insisting that Borden's loyalty to his minister bore 'a striking likeness to the loyalty of Sir Sam to that unpleasant shadow John Wesley Allison.'[29]

It is hard, even with the passage of time, to find much to praise in Hughes's service as minister of militia. His bellicose trumpeting of the imminence of war and his bullying tactics on cabinet colleagues ensured that Canada's militia was better prepared in 1914 than it might have been although the basic lines of its development had been established under his predecessor, Sir Frederick Borden. Hughes's preference allowed advancement for some of the ablest senior officers in the Canadian Corps, including Sir

Arthur Currie and Major-General David Watson; it also left a poisonous climate of suspicion and favouritism. His proud Canadianism was never proof against Hughes's own predilection for aristocratic titles, such as Lord Brooke.

Any minister of militia, given the unprecedented circumstances of the First World War and the unpreparedness of most Canadians, would almost certainly have made serious errors of judgment. It was Canada's misfortune that Sir Sam Hughes defended wisdom or folly with undiscriminating zeal and often bitter consequences. Whether it was the Ross rifle, his recruiting policies, or the defence of worthless friends like Allison, Hughes was immovable in his self-confidence and inflexible in his determination to make every decision himself. Unfortunately, the ignorance and timidity of his colleagues, including the prime minister, allowed Hughes to hang on to powers which were far beyond his competence for half the period of the war. By then much of the damage, particularly in recruiting policy, was past repair.

Though there was some pressure for Borden to strengthen his feeble Quebec wing by replacing Hughes with Major-General F.L. Lessard, the prime minister preferred P.D. Ross's advice to appoint a man 'who could fight the battles of the Conservative Party.'[30] Horatio Hocken, editor of the Orange *Sentinel* was entirely mollified by the appointment of Edward Kemp. Both Protestantism and Conservatism would be safely defended by the MP for Toronto East and the proprietor of the Kemp Manufacturing Company.[31] Kemp himself was instructed by the prime minister to 'hint to our press in Toronto and Western Ontario that discreet silence is advisable with regard to Hughes unless he attacks Government or Ministers.'[32] Like most political excitements, the Hughes resignation passed with unexpected speed.

For all his faults, however, Hughes has always found defenders in every generation, from his own to the present. His outrageous statements speak to frustrated nationalists and to those who resent the painful disciplines of professionalism. A national yearning for colourful characters has made us undiscriminating about their basic qualities. To his own age and ours, Sam Hughes offers an uncomplicated clarity of opinion. His contemporaries often found him charming as well as infuriating. Why shouldn't we?

Although Perley was fully informed of developments, he was too busy to follow the game. Against powerful inclinations and for the first time, he had been saddled with a major administrative responsibility. To Borden's dismay, his friend showed no pleasure or enthusiasm over the honour thrust upon him, conceding only that he would 'try for a while and do my best.'[33] To Perley, being high commissioner held far higher status in the eyes of his

British hosts than becoming a colonial cabinet minister in London. When Borden offered to send another cabinet minister to look after High Commission business for four or five months, Perley hastened to make his own preferences clear: 'Much prefer work High Commissioner to being Minister Overseas Forces. If it should transpire later that I cannot do both will advise you so that you can send over another Minister to take charge of Overseas Forces.'[34]

The prime minister was dismayed. Having precipitated a crisis with Hughes, he would be in an impossible position if his chosen instrument proved defective. By fortunate coincidence, Sir Thomas White was in London in November and he was pressed to ensure that his good friend and son-in-law fully grasped the importance of his new responsibilities. White reported on 6 November that Perley really did understand the relative significance of the two posts but that the two were so closely connected that he might continue in both of them.[35] An anxious Borden acquiesced.

If Perley felt daunted by his task, he was justified. Later he confessed to Borden that, if he had known what was involved, he would never have accepted the portfolio. In the month after his return from Canada he had begun to appreciate that almost every branch of the Canadian overseas administration harboured some major problem of personnel or policy. As dozens of new CEF battalions unloaded their men in the reinforcement camps, the host of aggrieved surplus officers grew larger. So did the army of convalescents, fatiguemen, orderlies, clerks, soldier-servants, permanent picquets and 'details' who somehow never seemed available for service at the front. More than thirty-five hundred Canadians were employed on clerical duties in London alone. General Lessard's report on Shorncliffe, submitted in June, claimed that out of 19,500 in the camp, only 11,560 were available for training and a fourth of each training brigade spent its time on odd jobs. Brass and bugle bands absorbed 1,200 of the soldiers.[36]

The 4th Division had finally gone to France in August 1916 after a number of angry battles over the choice of brigadiers and battalions. After a considerable delay, Sir Sam Hughes had imposed his own choices, Lord Brooke and his younger brother, William St Pierre Hughes, allowing Watson to include a Winnipeg Liberal, Lieutenant-Colonel Victor Odlum.[37] The expansion of the Canadian Corps meant a corresponding need for growth in the Canadian training and reinforcement organization in England. The prime minister's commitment of half a million men had not altered recruiting methods though it had markedly lowered standards for acceptance and drawn even more questionable individuals into the responsibilities of organizing units. The consequences were painfully apparent in England by the autumn of 1916. When the 136th Battalion arrived in England after months of recruiting in central Ontario, it mustered only 472 men, less than half the authorized strength. Almost a third of the men (144) were unfit for service. Half were either over- or under-age.[38] With such recruits, the Overseas Ministry's most urgent task – sustaining the ranks of the Canadian Corps with trained reinforcements – was already almost impossible.

One aspect of the Canadian manpower problem touched Perley directly and immediately: the growing conflict which Colonel Bruce and his report had aroused in the ranks of the Canadian Army Medical Corps. Bruce's report, with its thirteen recommendations, was probably a much better document than anyone at the time was prepared to concede. However, it was marred by sweeping condemnations of Jones and his hardworking subordinates who had wrestled with problems largely overcome by 1916. Faced with huge casualties and at least the potential for better medical care than any previous war had seen, the British had developed twenty different kinds of specialized hospitals. They had encouraged a host of Voluntary Aid Detachment hospitals, often staffed by local doctors and inexperienced women volunteers, to cope with convalescents. Prominent Canadian ladies in England, Lady Perley among them, had devoted time, energy, and money to these hospitals and they were stung by Bruce's sweeping condemnation of their administration and effectiveness. General Jones had allowed the complete integration of Canadian hospital and medical resources with British medical installations and Bruce had no trouble proving that the great majority of Canadians, given a choice, would far prefer to be in their own Canadian hospitals. However, the supreme example of 'toadying' to the British had been Jones's agreement to send several Canadian hospitals to the Mediterranean to help British troops in the disease-ridden Salonika theatre. Bruce recommended segregation of Canadian casualties in Canadian facilities, prompt return of the Canadian hospitals in Salonika, elimination of the VAD hospitals, far more ruthless treatment of venereal disease sufferers, and a programme designed to get the sick and wounded back to the trenches as fast as science and hard-headed administration could manage.[39]

Bruce's views had delighted Hughes. Though General Jones had accepted most of Bruce's suggestions, he and his former assistant, Colonel Lorne Drum, had plainly been found wanting. Hughes's contempt for permanent force officers had fresh confirmation. However, Bruce's report, flecked with colourful invective, pilloried other Canadian medical officers as well. Operations, Bruce claimed, were 'poorly performed' or done as 'a private hobby.' He had found Canadian soldiers 'asking and begging' to be transferred from British hospitals. Worst of all, both for medical men overseas and for anxious families in Canada, was Bruce's vague claim that 'many of the officers who have been given commissions are drug fiends or addicted to alcoholism.' Moreover, Bruce had made no allowance for past difficulties or short-run expedients. In 1915 there had been no alternative to the improvised VAD hospitals. Segregation of Canadians in Canadian hospitals made no sense when casualty loads varied unpredictably with the state of operations along the western front. As the Hughes-appointed head of the Canadian medical services, Colonel Bruce faced wholesale non-co-operation. The venerable and revered Sir William Osler promptly resigned his consulting appointment to the Canadian military hospitals and notified Sir Robert Borden that he would denounce Bruce's report to the entire Canadian medical profession. As president of the Canadian Red Cross and patroness of the Taplow hospital, the Duchess of Connaught sailed into the dispute. She was utterly opposed to segregating Canadians in their own hospitals.[40]

Sir George Perley needed little persuasion. As minister, his first act was to launch a thorough investigation of the Bruce report. To lend prestige and experience to the inquiry, the War Office offered the former director of medical services in India and in the Mediterranean, Sir William Babtie. To be fair to Bruce, Perley included Colonel E.C. Ashton, a doctor and a friend of Sam Hughes. Three respected medical officers from France, Colonel J.T. Fotheringham, Colonel A.E. Ross, and Colonel J.M. Elder, would bring experience and prestige to a difficult task. In the first hours of his new responsibility, Perley had launched the bitterest controversy of his political career.[41]

A more obvious problem was the fate of the acting Sub-Militia Council and its Hughes-appointed members. From the outset Perley understood that his only hope of escaping from the routine administration of the new department was, in contrast to Hughes, to appoint the strongest and most self-reliant officials he could find. Moreover, only with new faces could he hope to alter the tawdry image of the Canadian military administration. So long as Hughes's future remained in question, Perley proceeded cautiously. No one could tell him how his influence in the distant cabinet would compare with that of the minister of militia. On 3 November he sought official guidance about what to do with the members of the existing Sub-Militia Council.[42] On the next day, he attended his first meeting of the council and left a pointed reminder with Carson that the word 'acting' must still be used. On the afternoon of 6 November Perley finally visited Argyll House, the main headquarters building for the council, and inspected previous minutes. In the wake of his visit, a long list of council decisions was compiled and Major Greene was directed to report on follow-up action.[43] It was soon apparent that poor Greene had never considered this a part of his responsibilities nor had other members taken much interest in turning collective decisions into action.[44] After a few more inquiries Perley needed no more convincing that the Sub-Militia Council was a failure. The problem was to replace it.

On 6 November Perley also had had his reply from Ottawa. In a lengthy cable, followed by an even longer letter, the prime minister offered detailed advice and a clear warning. Colonel A.D. McRae, for example, must go. The western cabinet ministers, Perley learned 'do not highly regard his reputation and they say that his conduct and demeanour in the purchase of horses ... rendered him extremely unpopular in the Western Provinces.' They also suspected him of being a strong Liberal. On the other hand, both Fiset and Gwatkin were eagerly available. 'Fiset is of course excitable and pours forth torrents of words on occasion,' Borden noted, 'but he has a wonderful grasp of his Department.' As for Gwatkin, the strain of working with Hughes had finally broken even his spirit and he had actually submitted his resignation. Both men would help ensure a close relationship between the Militia Department in Ottawa and the Overseas Ministry.[45]

The relationship certainly had to be clarified. How far was a 'ministry' subordinate to a 'department'? From 3 November cables to and from Canada were funnelled through Perley and an exchange of telegrams on 6 November established that all matters of ordinary administration would pass through the Militia Department in Ottawa. Draft recommendations to the council from Perley would be sent in duplicate to the prime minister so that a copy might be given to the department.[46] On 10 November, the Militia Council in Ottawa, meeting without Hughes, agreed that questions of policy affecting more than one branch of Militia Headquarters would be dealt with at a ministerial level. In essence, the two organizations would be equal.[47]

Perley was not eager to bring Fiset and Gwatkin from Canada and, in any case, Hughes's removal persuaded the two senior officials of the Militia Department to soldier on. Nor was the new minister any more enthusiastic about the pressure for advancement and recognition which promptly developed from officers in England. First in line was General Steele, deluging Perley with recitals of old grievances, the promise of a medical certificate, denunciations of rivals like Colonel Frank Reid and Colonel A.D. McRae, and a confidential plan of reorganization which he also sent to one of his influential patrons, Lord Shaughnessy of the CPR.[48] Others were less persistent but equally clamorous. Brigadier-General H.D.B. Ketchen, frustrated in an earlier bid for the 4th Division, staked his claim to be chief of the general staff in the new organization. Colonel Reid contributed a neat diagram of the adjutant general's responsibilities together with his own bid to retain the position. Only Colonel Ward from the Pay Office seems to have impressed

Perley by offering advice, not a demand for advancement: 'One of the great failures in connection with the previous administration of the Forces in England has been due to the fact that the people who have been responsible for it have not had a professional knowledge of the subject and consequently to obtain any results in remedying complaints, the panacea for such cases has been experimental. Experiment has followed experiment and very often has resulted in confusion worse confounded.'[49]

Experience, Perley concluded, could best be found in France. The test of battle had weeded out failures and developed the only leaders who possessed the confidence of the CEF. By that standard, the Sub-Militia Council was again a failure. On 9 November both Perley and White attended its weekly meeting but nothing was settled beyond a decision to send troops earmarked for the 5th Canadian Division to France as reinforcements. On 16 November White and Perley went to France, leaving instructions that the council must discuss only routine matters. Instead, on Colonel Ross's suggestion, members debated submitting their resignations. With Hughes out of office, they would have to make peace with the new régime. Carson reported that he had discussed resignation with Perley and that the new minister had declared that it 'would be a gracious act on their part.' The motion passed without dissent.[50]

White and Perley spent three days in France, meeting senior Canadian officers down to the rank of brigadier-general. On their return, Perley met with Major-General Currie who had been on leave in England. After three weeks the two ministers agreed about what the new department needed. On 22 November Perley notified Borden that he wanted a first-class officer to take command of Canadian troops in England, with the backing of a full military staff. He would need a deputy minister for civil matters, including pay and record offices and possibly the chaplain's and medical departments. With two good men in these positions, there would be no need of a council.[51] The first and biggest problem was finding the right soldier. In a separate and confidential telegram, Perley bluntly outlined his difficulties:

For G.O.C. Canadians England Currie is generally preferred by officers at front but objections might very likely be raised in some quarters. He says he used to work on Liberal side but got disgusted with politics and now takes no interest. Turner much beloved by everyone but perhaps not quite so firm or forceful as others. Believe he is a Liberal of neutral tint but exceedingly fine and reasonable. We like Lipsett who is splendid soldier very good at training but is regular English officer and might not be considered Canadian. Watson fine chap but is junior and still gaining much experience by remaining at front. White and I think Currie most capable for position but Turner would be more popular with our following.[52]

On 24 November, in response to an urgent telegram, Borden dispatched a cable designed to persuade either of the reluctant generals to take up the command in England. The reluctance was understandable. Ambitious soldiers knew that the only real advancement would come in battle. Whatever the title, return to England would be regarded as a relegation to the rear. Currie, pressed hard by Perley to take the appointment, characteristically suspected a political intrigue to end his military career and exploit his reputation.[53] Only later did he realize that the minister's praise of his abilities was sincere. Rebuffed and annoyed, Perley redirected his pressure to General Turner. The Quebec-born soldier was severely squeezed. As the senior Canadian major-general, Turner knew that he could well be in line to command the Canadian Corps. On the other hand, his sense of duty, the prime minister's message, and a very firm shove from General Byng convinced him to accept Perley's appeal. Having sought to safeguard his right to eventual command of the Corps, Turner consented.[54]

The rest of the ministry staff could now be chosen. It proved much harder than either Turner or Perley had expected. In his original plan, Perley had suggested that he could dispose of two of the senior Canadians in England by making Major-General MacDougall the new adjutant general while Steele was appointed to a new post of inspector-general.[55] Neither was even remotely acceptable to Turner. Consequently, Perley asked that the (mythical) order-in-council originally appointing MacDougall as GOC Canadians be cancelled and that he be recalled.[56] On 19 December MacDougall was summoned back to Canada. Steele's expectations ended abruptly when Perley learned of his backstairs efforts through Lord Shaughnessy.[57] Instead of MacDougall, Turner's choice for adjutant general was a staff-college-trained permanent force officer from his own division, Colonel P.E. Thacker. A much more difficult problem was finding a suitable quartermaster-general. Hughes's nominee in the Sub-Militia Council, Colonel Murphy, was rejected as too easy-going. In Ottawa Borden eagerly offered the services of Major-General D.A. Macdonald, a superannuated ally of the former minister. Perley politely suggested that he might not be 'forceful enough' to set matters right.[58] The embarrassing fact was that only one man apparently possessed the energy, business ability, and experience to sort out the problems of a troubled and extravagant branch: Colonel A.D. McRae. Despite the warnings of his western colleagues, Rogers, Lougheed, and Arthur Meighen, Perley had retained McRae as chief executive officer throughout December. However, with Turner pressing for a quartermaster-general and McRae eager to remain in uniform, Perley won grudging consent for the appointment.[59]

With McRae placed, Perley still needed a strong assistant on the civil side, 'a strong business man' and someone 'with whom he could consult freely.' Moreover, in a staff beginning to have too many Quebeckers, the position would have to go to someone from Ontario or the west. Though White and other ministers urged the claims of Thomas Gibson, a lawyer from Sault Ste-Marie, the choice fell on Major Walter Gow, a partner in the eminent Toronto law firm of Blake, Cassels. Unlike McRae, Gow preferred to become a civilian and assumed the more conventional title of deputy minister. Gibson became assistant deputy minister.[60]

With Gow's appointment on 23 March (with effect from 29 January 1917), the senior appointments in the Overseas Ministry were complete. Perley had chosen carefully, with little pressure from colleagues or the prime minister. When Robert Rogers, the most notorious pork-barrel politician in the cabinet, intervened to demand more jobs for the west, Borden forwarded his telegram with the weary comment: 'There are continual complaints, of course, from all parts of Canada of unfair treatment and it will be so to the end.'[61] Borden himself was not immune. It would be convenient, he suggested, if Senator J.S. McLennan could assist in the duties of the high commissioner. A senate vacancy for Cape Breton would have been very useful. Perley, determined as ever to safeguard his favourite job, replied that it seemed 'hardly feasible.'[62]

On 5 December 1916 the headquarters of the General Officer Commanding Canadian Forces in the United Kingdom formally came into existence. The War Office was advised that henceforth the chain of command would extend through General Turner at his headquarters in Cleveland House.[63] The previous day Perley had notified Major Greene that he had accepted the resignations of the members of the Acting Sub-Militia Council. On the same day, Brigadier-General Leckie, Colonel Reid, and Colonel Neill of the veterinary service all learned that their appointments had been ended.[64]

Perley was no happy warrior. The situation, he warned Borden, 'is much worse than even I thought. The difficulty in the medical branch would be enough in itself to keep one busy for some time.' Complaints about the dental services, the chaplains, and the Forestry Corps would simply have to wait. Almost every difficult problem, from surplus officers to the treatment of venereal cases, had been shelved or ignored or aggravated by controversy. 'If there had been a proper organization here, like one of the regular government departments,' he complained, 'it would have been easier to come in and take up the problems which need decision and settlement. If on the other hand everything had been working smoothly, there would not have been any great difficulty in arranging some proper organization.'[65]

Like other new brooms, Perley may have been reluctant to admit that the techniques of sweeping rarely change. His response to the problem of surplus officers repeated a policy General Steele had inaugurated nine months earlier. Once again the more senior surplus officers were granted a few weeks at the front as a reward for their services. For the first time, however, Perley extended his concern to surplus senior non-commissioned officers who also lost pay and status when compelled to revert to the ranks.

On both sides of the Atlantic, it was apparent that Perley's political honeymoon in his new appointment would be brief. Hughes and his allies had utterly failed to arouse an immediate crusade on their behalf in 1916. Colonel J.J. Creelman was probably typical of many Canadian officers when he noted in his dairy: 'I do not like to kick a man when he is down but I am willing to break nine toes in kicking Sam.'[66] However, the former minister would be itching to attack his old enemy as soon as he could and he would do so with an insider's knowledge. Perley attempted to conciliate Hughes's chief lieutenant overseas by putting Carson in charge of a committee to plan demobilization. Carson refused. A more effective pacifier was a knighthood, arranged for March 1917. The ex-representative was allowed to remain in England on full pay for more than a year until 31 January 1918, when finally he was retired from the CEF.[67]

An even more effective way of neutralizing the ex-minister's formidable threat would be through his son, Garnet. No sooner had General Turner accepted the appointment in England than the prime minister proposed that the younger Hughes should be his successor. Such a shrewd, if cynical, political stroke had been forestalled when Sir Julian Byng had offered the 2d Division to Major-General Burstall of the Corps artillery. Perley refused to launch his new career by gross and politically-motivated interference. The prime minister was bitterly disappointed: 'I have no knowledge of military matters but with respect to personal ability, I have no doubt that man selected by Byng is much inferior to other mentioned ... I would strongly advise you to have capable representative at Front who can keep you informed.'[68] Borden's annoyance persisted for several weeks but it would have been difficult to justify overruling both the Corps commander and the new minister. Instead, the prime minister approved a new order-in-council of 19 December on the vexed subject of promotions. Henceforth, all CEF promotions outside Canada would be approved by the War Office, authorized by the overseas minister, and published in the London *Gazette*. There would no longer be a channel for Ottawa interference.[69]

By the beginning of 1917 recruiting in Canada had changed from a serious problem into a national crisis. In the summer of 1916, when Australia had put five divisions into the line, knowledgeable Canadians wondered whether their own four divisions might not be too much. Despite increasingly frenzied and sometimes foolish efforts, enlistment totals sagged monthly until December 1916 when only 5,279 joined, the lowest total since the war began. As recruiting flagged, employers and editors complained that haphazard recruiting had swept irreplaceable skilled workers into uniform. Farmers complained that food production would be cut if they lost their sons. Canada edged closer to conscription while the government tried out every alternative it could conceive, from launching still more colonels to organizing a national registration. Even Sir Robert Borden got involved, using his prestige and that of Lady Borden to help recruit a Highland battalion in Nova Scotia.[70]

If Perley had any primary role, it was to make better use of Canada's uniformed manpower. His first task was to assess his resources. In November 1916 he learned that there were 120,000 Canadians in England, 40,000 of them unfit for active service. That left a balance of about 20,000 men for each of the divisions at the front, hardly enough to meet a year's losses.[71] Yet Canada was pressed to do at least as much as Australia. In August Hughes had ordered that a fifth and then a sixth division be organized. For politicians and battalion commanders (sometimes identical) it was a last chance to save units from dissolution but by now it was obvious to both Perley and the new minister of militia that Canada could maintain an additional division in France for barely a year. It seemed wiser, despite the insistence of the War Office, not even to try. On 17 January 1917 Perley advised Sir Edward Kemp of his compromise: the 5th Division would be recruited to full strength but it would, for the time being, serve only as a home-defence formation in England. It also served as a suitable command for a newly promoted Major-General Garnet Hughes.[72]

To house the growing number of Canadians held in England and the increasing variety of training establishments and schools, the original concentrations at Shorncliffe and Bramshott had spread across southern England during the summer of 1916. Witley, south of Guildford, with space for 24,000 men, became the base for the new 5th Division. Smaller Canadian camps opened at Shoreham, Seaford, and Crowborough.[73] At Hastings a school for officer candidates opened to meet the appalling toll among junior officers. The new Canadian administration found elements of more than seventy CEF battalions in England, ranging from full units to skeletal remnants. In a major reorganization, fifty-seven battalions were compressed into twenty-six reserve battalions. By March, battalions at the front and reserve battalions in England had been grouped by territorial association into regiments, corresponding to the newly defined military districts in Canada. Amidst bitter heartburning, two of the CEF battalions which had depended on English-speaking Montreal for their recruits were disbanded in the field and replaced by battalions from Nova Scotia and Ontario. Later, in August 1917, two more battalions, hitherto associated with British Columbia, were transferred to the Second Central Ontario Regiment, reflecting the relative exhaustion of recruits from the west coast as well. To conserve manpower and achieve faster return of wounded soldiers, Perley adopted the British system of command depots in which medically unfit troops were subjected to a combination of military training and medically-supervised physiotherapy.[74]

Reorganization could not necessarily guarantee effective training and, in the short run, it drastically increased the number of surplus and aggrieved Canadian officers. Except for a last, hopeless effort to attract French-Canadian recruits to a 258th Battalion organized by General Lessard and the postmaster general, P.-E. Blondin, no more CEF battalions were authorized after 1916 (though two battalions of conscripts were organized as Canada's contribution to the Siberian expedition of 1918-19). However, more than 250 different units in various states of organization existed somewhere between the recruiting centres and the trenches and the melancholy process of dissolution continued throughout 1917. Despite repeated protests from Perley and warnings that officers from Canada would have to revert to the rank of lieutenant if they wished to see active service, understrength battalions continued to arrive in England, most of them with a generous complement of colonels, majors, and captains. The new regimental system for reinforcements, devised by Turner, at least gave some promise that friends and neighbours would no longer be arbitrarily scattered through the Canadian Corps as they had been in the Hughes era.[75]

In one area at least, Hughes's policy was followed. Despite continued pressure from enthusiasts in Canada and overseas, Sir Sam and his colleagues had firmly resisted pressure to create a Canadian air force. A government which had entered office in 1911 highly critical of the development of a separate Canadian navy was at least consistent in resisting pressure to launch into a third dimension although it was soon apparent that individual Canadians would become eager and adept airmen. Unfortunately one of the more ardent overseas advocates of a separate Canadian air service, Grant Morden, had been one of Sir Sam Hughes's personal staff officers. While Perley overcame that prejudice and was sufficiently impressed by Morden's arguments to pursue them with the War Office and with the prime minister, there was no hope of overcoming the prime minister's rooted objection to the idea. The idea of a Canadian air force, as S.F. Wise has indicated, eventually achieved reality by the end of the war but, despite the sympathy of Perley and the growing enthusiasm of Sir Richard Turner, air matters could never displace the grim preoccupation of providing fit, trained men for the Canadian Corps. That was the real task of the Overseas Ministry.[76]

The reorganization of the Canadian infantry reinforcement system and the adoption of a uniform fourteen-week training syllabus slowly began to make a difference. Even in late December, Lieutenant-Colonel W.E. Thompson, a former Liberal MP, reported perceptible improvement in the training camps.[77] From Ottawa Borden relayed a number of congratulatory letters from officers at the front. 'The difficulties here were appalling,' Perley modestly admitted, 'and I have no intention of ever trying to explain them to you in detail.'[78]

In fact, many of the problems had to be shared with the prime minister. Even the most minor often involved potential political landmines. Senator James Mason, given the rank of brigadier-general by Hughes though he was seventy-five years old, went to France ostensibly to inspect Red Cross hospitals and ended up as a nuisance visitor among front-line units. It was left to Perley to persuade the old veteran to return to England and to soothe indignant British pass authorities.[79] Other Hughes appointments, including Major Byron Greene and Lieutenant-Colonel Grant Morden, continued to hold vague military functions without the slightest military qualification. Each removal brought a minor political tempest.[80]

None of them compared to the hurricane in the medical services. Not even Perley can have been fully prepared for its violence or duration. On 28 December the Babtie committee submitted its report on the Bruce investigation. As Perley had expected, the report went a long way to rehabilitate Surgeon-General Jones and to denounce the proposition that Canadian and British patients could successfully be segregated. If, as Bruce had complained, there were far too many unfit soldiers at Canadian bases in England, that was the fault of medical officers in Canada who accepted over-age, under-age, and obviously disabled recruits.[81]

It was now Colonel Bruce's turn to feel aggrieved. He could claim, with some justice, that he was a political victim of Sir Sam Hughes's downfall. He could point out that the great majority of his specific recommendations had been adopted and that, apart from the segregation issue, most of what was at stake was a question of personal manner. However, as he would prove in his long career in medicine and politics, Bruce was an aggressive and effective controversialist with an eye for public prejudices and a gift for invective that Sam Hughes might have envied. Despite the presence of Ashton, expected to be his ally in the Babtie investigation, Bruce denounced the entire Babtie board and its proceedings. The three Canadian medical officers from France, he insisted, could know nothing of conditions in England. (If they had come from England, Perley noted sourly, Bruce would have accused them of prejudging the situation.) As for Babtie, his own medical arrangements for the Mesopotamia campaign had been condemned for bringing terrible suffering to British and Indian sick and wounded. Though he was promptly exonerated by the Army Council, Babtie had plainly been an unfortunate choice to pass judgment on others.[82]

Babtie's past record, probably unknown to Perley at the time, helped to confirm a theme which both Hughes and Bruce's supporters would develop against the overseas minister: subservience to incompetent British officials and to feckless aristocrats. Even before his dismissal, Hughes had shocked a Toronto audience with the charge, drawn from the Bruce report, that 'thousands of Canadians had lost months and sometimes a year, in hospitals not under Canadian control when they should have been back in the trenches.'[83] The VAD hospitals, often established in the country houses of wealthy Britons, were depicted as 'matrimonial agencies' where wounded soldiers lolled under the attentions of untrained English ladies. Denunciation of Canadian medical services touched a highly sensitive nerve among Canadians at home. Most had been raised on the legend of the Lady of the Lamp, Florence Nightingale, doing battle for suffering soldiers against venal, ignorant army surgeons. It was easy to believe that Bruce, handsome, delicate-featured, and apparently disinterested, was a latter-day Nightingale though there was a disquieting element in his crusade to speed up the return of wounded Canadians to the slaughter of the trenches.[84]

Perley was vulnerable to the charge of anglophilia. His preference for the high commissionership was evidence that both he and his wife were conscious of cutting a figure even in the austerity of wartime British society. 'Under certain circumstances,' Borden had warned him, 'a cry may be raised ... that Canadian rights will not be strongly asserted under your administration and that Canadian direction and control will not be properly maintained.'[85] It was a charge Perley had at once refuted but the choice of Babtie to reject Bruce's nationalistic arguments had been unfortunate. When Colonel Bruce resigned as director of medical services, Perley immediately reinstated General Jones. Despite Borden's strong misgivings, Perley insisted that it would be popular and sound from 'a business point of view.'[86] Certainly it was overdue justice to the veteran army surgeon and it helped win Perley the confidence of a badly shaken Canadian Army Medical Corps. However, the prime minister's warning was well founded. Doing justice to Jones gave proof to Hughes and his allies that the overseas minister would be an ally of the hated permanent force and the 'professionals.'

Both in Ottawa and in London the government did its best to protect itself from the consequences of what Perley considered 'the most serious and difficult of all the many troubles here.' If Colonel Bruce brought his grievances back to Canada, the prime minister advised, Sir William Osler must be persuaded to follow him.[87] The prestige of the Canadian-born Regius Professor of Medicine would be a powerful counterweight to Bruce's campaign. In the event, Bruce swallowed his indignation for a time and accepted a hospital appointment in France. Perley's plan for medical reform was completed when Major-General G.L. Foster, a Nova Scotian doctor serving as the Canadian director of medical services in France, crossed the Channel and took up the same appointment in England. His prestige and experience, backed by a supporting staff also drawn from the Canadian Corps, helped to launch a new spirit in the Canadian hospitals in England. General Jones was removed to the somewhat ornamental role of medical commissioner, with a small staff and the hurriedly improvised task of co-ordinating medical services between Canada and England. A year later an appointment was found for him at Militia Headquarters in Ottawa.[88]

By the beginning of 1917 Perley had established his department, chosen his key officials, and weathered his first major crisis. There would be many more.

6

Gaining Control

While Sir George Perley had busied himself with the creation of his new ministry and coping with the aftermath of the Bruce inquiry, dramatic changes had occurred in the offices and corridors of Whitehall. It was, A.J.P. Taylor has suggested, 'a revolution, British-style.'[1] To leading Canadians it could hardly have been more welcome.

The first two years of the war had been utterly disillusioning for Borden and his colleagues. Confident of the experienced competence of British leaders, presumably long accustomed to managing complex world affairs, the Canadian Conservatives had been dismayed by the Asquith government's feckless amateurism, inefficiency, and favouritism. Sir Robert Borden had been shocked when his minister of militia had accused British commanders of military ineptitude during the second battle of Ypres but his own midsummer visit to England in 1915 led him to revise some of his criticisms. Only Lloyd George, once the dangerous radical and pro-Boer of Britain's Liberal party, struck Borden as showing the requisite energy and earnestness in the struggle.[2]

The costs of incompetent British leadership had become intolerable by the end of 1916, even for Britain's own ruling class. The year had opened with the final withdrawal from Gallipoli. Good fortune in getting the British and Australian troops away without loss was no compensation for their bloody, mismanaged, and futile struggle. In April came an even worse humiliation when 10,000 British and Indian soldiers surrendered to the once-despised Turks at Kut-al-Amara. Few would survive captivity. At the end of May came Jutland, a confused encounter between the British and German battle fleets. Whatever the long-term consequences for German naval power, no one could conceal that British ships had suffered far heavier losses than their adversaries. In Ireland the long-festering issue of autonomy had burst into open rebellion on Easter Monday. It began with Irish opinion massively arrayed against the rebels; when it ended in the mass execution of Irish leaders by the British garrison, opinion dramatically and permanently shifted. Then followed the long agony of the Somme offensive. Lord Kitchener, the creator of armies of young enthusiasts, had drowned on 5 June when the cruiser *Hampshire* was sunk by a German mine. Kitchener's soldiers perished just as helplessly when on 1 July, they rose and walked forward into the German machine guns and wire: 19,000 died in a single day. The British army eventually admitted to 57,000 casualties, 710 of them from the little Newfoundland battalion at Beaumont Hamel. By the time Sir Douglas Haig was persuaded to call off the Somme offensives, British casualties totalled 420,000.[3]

There was no question of the commitment of the young men who died in these successive tragedies; the question lay with the competence and commitment of the leaders who precipitated such tragedies. What could Canada's own leaders do? The year of British disasters had been a year of growing Canadian self-confidence and competence. At home Borden could believe that he had systematically resolved failures and problems in Canada's war effort. The Imperial Munitions Board was taking aggressive steps to end the confusion and profiteering of Hughes's Shell committee. Recruiting, purchasing, finance, the export of nickel and other crucial raw materials had been brought under control. The reform of the overseas administration was only one of a host of problems that Borden and his colleagues had tackled during 1916 and the unexpected resolution he had demonstrated in handling the errant Sir Sam reflected his own change of attitude. Moreover, Borden could take pride in the performance of the expanded Canadian Corps as practical evidence of Canada's contribution. In the Somme offensive, the Canadians had taken Pozières Ridge after the Australians and New Zealanders had been slaughtered in vain for the objective. The 2d Division, led by the valour of the French-Canadian Twenty-second Battalion, had captured Flers-Courcelette. The 3d Division took the heavily-fortified Farbeck Graben. Although the Corps failed, despite heavy casualties, to capture Regina Trench, the newly fledged 4th Division managed the feat in October.[4]

Such accomplishments and sacrifices entitled Canada not only to take control of her own military organization overseas but also to have a say in the war effort. During his 1915 visit and for months afterwards, Borden tried desperately to infect British leaders with a sense of his own urgent commitment. Canada's promise to provide a quarter of a million soldiers from her population of only seven million had been such a gesture. So was the New Year's promise to double the contribution to half a million men. From Britain there was no serious response. In May 1915 Herbert Asquith had yielded reluctantly to a coalition with his Conservative and Unionist opponents but, apart from damping criticism in Parliament, the new government marked no significant change in Britain's war management. The new colonial secretary was the Canadian-born Conservative leader, Andrew Bonar Law, but Borden found little response to his demands for information and consultation. Law's polite sympathy was accompanied by a complete unwillingness to find practical ways of meeting Canadian desires. As Law pleasantly explained to Perley, 'if no scheme is practicable then it is very undesirable that the question should be raised.'[5]

Borden was furious at such a response and his indignation burst out in both his offer of half a million Canadians and in a letter he wrote to Perley four days later. Although the letter was inspired by the pain of lumbago as well as indignation at Law's response, and accordingly was quickly cancelled, it gave Borden sufficient pride that he later included it in his memoirs:

During the past four months since my return from Great Britain, the Canadian Government (except for an occasional telegram from you or Sir Max Aitken) have had just what information could be gleaned from the daily press and no more. As to consultation, plans of campaign have been made and unmade, measures adopted and apparently abandoned and generally speaking steps of the most important and even vital character have been taken, postponed or rejected without the slightest consultation with the authorities of this Dominion.

It can hardly be expected that we shall put 400,000 or 500,000 men in the field and willingly accept the position of having no more voice and receiving no more consideration than if we were toy automata. Any person cherishing such an expectation harbours an unfortunate and even dangerous delusion. Is this war being waged by the United Kingdom alone or is it a war being waged by the whole Empire? If I am correct in supposing that the second hypothesis must be accepted then why do the statesmen of the British Isles arrogate to themselves solely the methods by which it shall be carried on in the various spheres of warlike activity and the steps which shall be taken to assure victory and a lasting peace?[6]

Throughout 1916 there was really no answer to Borden's complaint – in large measure because he made no effort to provide one. Indeed, the Canadian prime minister was too preoccupied with a procession of domestic issues and crises to give relations with London much thought. The problems of the bankrupt transcontinental railways, of marketing bonds, of Sam Hughes, of recruiting, and of provincial defeats conspired to keep Borden close to Ottawa. Suddenly the situation changed.

Throughout 1916 members of Herbert Asquith's uneasy coalition had grown steadily more troubled by his leadership. A man of personal charm and eloquence, he was also painfully indecisive and, like many such leaders, utterly mistrusted by his few aggressive, clear-minded lieutenants. Of these none stood out more than David Lloyd George. As chancellor of the exchequer, he had launched war finance. Appointed minister of munitions, he galvanized Britain's obsolete industries and created a staff of sixty-five thousand and a labour force of three million, producing far more than the generals had asked for – though barely as much as was needed. Next, as secretary of state for war, he had first sought glory from expected victories and then raged when fumbling generals failed to deliver. To fellow-Liberals, looking desperately for a leader determined to win the war, only Lloyd George was available. Among the Tories, Bonar Law realized that he could only hold his leadership if he, too, contributed to a more dynamic war effort. The man who led him steadily to Lloyd George was his fellow New Brunswicker, the inveterately scheming Max Aitken. By the night of 7 December, after an infinity of going and coming, conspiracies and counter-conspiracies, bluffs, threats, and misunderstandings, Asquith was out and Lloyd George was in.[7]

Like most revolutions, Lloyd George's overthrow of Asquith led to widespread devastation of obsolete but cherished symbols, innumerable institutional alterations, and the steadfast continuity of the old problems. Instead of an overly large cabinet, Lloyd George proposed to run the war through a five-member war cabinet, only one of whose members, Bonar Law, the chancellor of the exchequer, had departmental responsibilities. For the first time a British cabinet acquired a secretary, a record of its decisions, and machinery to ensure that they were properly executed. In his 'Garden Suburb,' Lloyd George built the first genuine staff a British prime minister had had for generations. At the same time, appeasing his Tory supporters meant no move against a freshly promoted Field-Marshal Sir Douglas Haig in France or against his loyal ex-ranker supporter, General Sir William Robertson, the chief of the Imperial General Staff. Businessmen, landlords, and hereditary magnates continued to run the British economy and war effort as they had before.[8]

For contemporaries, the institutional changes mattered a great deal more than the less visible continuities. For Canada, the advent of Lloyd George meant that almost overnight the 'practicability' problem of information and consultation was solved. Within a week of taking office, Lloyd George had made his thoughts known to Walter Long, the new colonial secretary: 'The more I think about it, the more I am convinced that we should take the

Dominions into our counsel in a much larger measure than we have hitherto done in our prosecution of the War.' There was no altruism in the gesture nor was there a desire, as there would be a year later, to use the dominion leaders as a counterweight to British generals and politicians. The purpose was more straightforward: 'We want more men from them. We can hardly ask them to make another great recruiting effort unless it is accompanied by an invitation to come over to discuss the situation with us.'[9]

Lloyd George was a man of gifted inspiration, not of stolid system. Colonel Maurice Hankey, the brilliant soldier who served as secretary and an increasingly influential adviser to the war cabinet, noted that nothing had been prepared to discuss with the colonial politicians. Bonar Law, who shared all of Hankey's misgivings, observed: 'when they are here, you will wish to goodness you could get rid of them.'[10] What neither they nor probably even their prime minister realized was that Lloyd George was creating a new British Commonwealth. The dominion prime ministers were to be summoned not to a routine imperial conference but as members of an extended 'Imperial War Cabinet,' armed with at least the sense that they were sharing in major wartime decisions. For Sir Robert Borden and his most influential adviser, Loring Christie, this represented an opportunity not to be missed. The Canadian Parliament was summoned unusually early, on 18 January, and adjourned so that Borden and two of his less significant ministers, Robert Rogers and J.D. Hazen, could sail on 15 February.[11]

While Borden's two colleagues from Canada busied themselves with a simultaneous Imperial War Conference, Borden took Sir George Perley with him to the Imperial War Cabinet, pointedly identifying him as minister for overseas forces, not as acting high commissioner. However, it was more often Douglas Hazen, the minister of marine and fisheries, not Perley, who accompanied Borden to the later meetings. Australia's outspoken William Hughes did not come and South Africa's prime minister, Louis Botha, sent his remarkable minister of defence, General Jan Christian Smuts. Sir Edward Morris represented Newfoundland, New Zealand's fractured domestic politics demanded two separate voices and, as an afterthought, India was granted three assessors 'in recognition of its enormous contribution of men and money to the Imperial effort.'[12]

Beyond the adoption by the Imperial War Conference of Resolution IX, a delicately worded statement of the autonomous nature of the dominions within an 'Imperial Commonwealth,' it is not easy to see what either the 1917 conference or the war cabinet sessions achieved in influencing the direction of the war. In essence Resolution IX, drafted by Borden with contradictory pressures from Smuts and from the highly imperialist W.A. Massey of New Zealand, reflected the problem. A 'cabinet' implied a body of ministers competent to make binding and agreed decisions. That was what Lloyd George had intended as the reward for the time spent at its meetings. Instead, each dominion prime minister did his utmost to make clear that there was to be absolutely no surrender of dominion autonomy in a common cause. 'Each nation,' Borden told the Empire Parliamentary Association on 2 April, 'has its voice upon questions of common concern and highest importance as the deliberations proceed; each preserves unimpaired its perfect autonomy, its self-government, and the responsibility of its Ministers to their own electorate.'[13] If Lloyd George had imagined that he could manage the war effort of a united empire by proclaiming dominion prime ministers a 'cabinet,' he soon recognized his error. The dominions had passed from colonial status to become junior but highly autonomous allies.

For Sir Robert Borden, the chance to thresh out such concepts, together with detailed, factual briefings on the progress of the war, gave the sense of involvement and commitment he had demanded. The First Sea Lord and the chief of the Imperial General Staff both appeared before the prime ministers to give grim reports on their respective spheres. When high casualties in the Royal Flying Corps caught the attention of the overseas politicians, Lieutenant-General Sir David Henderson, its commander, was summoned to report. From 7 April, when the United States declared war on Germany, Borden could feel a special, if unauthorized, sense of importance. He had worked long and hard to bring that event about and now he could interpret for the new belligerent within the British family. Of more concern was the evidence that Imperial Russia was collapsing and that the enormous German forces deployed against her might soon be available on the western front. Lloyd George had plenty of evidence for his stern warning at the outset of the Imperial War Cabinet session that planning on victory in 1917 might well be a fatal miscalculation.[14]

The dominion prime ministers gained little share in the direction of the war and only slightly more in the ostensible purpose of their meeting: the definition of war aims and peace terms. Lloyd George's war cabinet continued to meet separately during the visit of Borden and his colleagues and it was there that the real decisions were made. The Imperial War Cabinet was allowed to decide that German towns should be bombed in retaliation for the sinking of hospital ships and that the French should be urged to press forward on the Salonika front but these were issues Lloyd George and his British colleagues had already settled. When the overseas politicians dispersed, they had had nothing to do with Lloyd George's decision to back the Nivelle offensive on the Chemin des Dames, with its disastrous consequences for

French army morale and discipline, nor would the dominion prime ministers be consulted about the British drive towards Passchendaele. Instead, Borden and the others went home, as Lloyd George had hoped they would, determined to gather still more recruits for the western front.[15]

The Canadian prime minister had come to England, of course, with more on his mind than the proposed Imperial War Cabinet and Conference. Perley's Overseas Ministry had been in operation for four months and Borden wanted first-hand evidence that his plan of reorganization was working. During the brief parliamentary session, Sir Sam Hughes had had his chance to launch his counter-attack, dragging out past scandals, grievances, and allegations to the delight of the Liberal opposition. Throughout a long and rambling speech, the ex-minister had returned to two fundamental charges: the new ministry was extravagant and bloated with staff and Canada had deliberately sacrificed her autonomy to the British.[16] George Kyte, Hughes's chief accuser in the Shell scandal, denounced Borden on the basis of Hughes's own claims while Charles Murphy poured the Bruce report into the debate, revelling in statements that 'dope fiends and alcoholics' had been numbered among the trusted officers of the Canadian Army Medical Corps.[17]

Borden and his colleagues, particularly the aggressive young Arthur Meighen, had beaten back the attacks as best they could but they were plainly hampered by a lack of precise information. A cabinet minister held more than an executive rank in government; a minister was also part of collective cabinet decision-making and an official directly answerable to Parliament. Separated by the Atlantic, Perley was barred from performing the full functions of a minister and the debate on Hughes's speech of 30 January illustrated part of the problem. It was hardly less awkward for Perley to retain the full confidence of his fellow Conservative ministers, and his difficulties may well have been aggravated by the fact that he had spent all but a couple of months since June 1914 in England. When so many of the practical issues of military administration seemed to pit Canadian against British interests, was it true, as Hughes regularly implied, that Perley and his wife were too eager for a place in London society to represent Canada adequately?

The greatest area of potential friction when a new department is split off from an old is the division of responsibilities. Although the Atlantic provided an unmistakable dividing line, it was easier to divide functional roles than to separate political responsibilities. In Ottawa Sir Edward Kemp was immediately and directly accountable to Parliament and through the press for the consequences of Militia Department policies and problems on Conservative political fortunes; in England it was possible and entirely to Perley's taste to suggest that the Overseas Ministry was above crude partisan considerations.

The outcome, for all Perley's confidence that the two ministers could cooperate, was repeated friction.[18]

Nothing had enraged Hughes more than the consistent rejection of Canadian arms and equipment by the British. From the Ross rifle to the Bain wagon, from boots to entrenching tools, the Canadian model had been scrapped for the British. The reasons might seem unanswerable to anyone but Sir Sam but the outcome was the same: British suppliers profited; the Canadian government was left with huge stockpiles of rejected purchases; Canadian manufacturers found themselves shut out from lucrative war markets. The problem did not end with Hughes's departure, and was not necessarily limited to Canadian designs. Sir Edward Kemp could not understand why the Savage Lewis gun, ordered in Canada by the Imperial authorities, manufactured according to British specifications, was not used at the front. The question was politically embarrassing since Kemp had felt obliged to assure his fellow Conservatives in the Ontario government that a stock of the weapons, purchased by Ontario for use by the CEF, had done good service against the Germans. Why, too, did the British refuse to buy 200,000 Canadian winter overcoats, now surplus to the needs of the Militia Department? It was obvious that the design of the coats was identical to the British pattern and the quality must be far higher. And why could the British not accept 100,000 more Ross rifles which, unfortunately, Ottawa was committed to purchase from the factory? Surely the British could use the rifles somewhere in the world?[19] Borden went to England in 1917 to investigate.

Unfortunately, as Borden discovered, Kemp had not always known all the facts. The Savage Lewis guns were unsuitable because subsequent modifications of the British pattern prevented most of the parts from being interchangeable. Under pressure, the British agreed that they might be useful in a minor theatre of the war. Negotiations for the purchase of the Canadian greatcoats were proceeding, Perley reported, but far from being superior, the Canadian cloth had been cheaply manufactured with a cotton, not a woollen, warp. The Ross rifles in the hands of the Canadians had been replaced at no cost by Lee-Enfields and Perley prudently wished to complete that transaction before trying to burden the British with more of them. In a report prepared for Perley by his quartermaster-general, Brigadier-General McRae, there was a tone of barely-contained indignation at Kemp's pressure:

May I be permitted to refer to the note of impatience which is discernible in the letter from the Honourable, the Minister of Militia and Defence. Appreciating that it is quite impossible for the Honourable the Minister to have a true appreciation of the results of two years of bad administration and the problems which it has left us to clear up, the desired results cannot be obtained without much patience. Matters of this kind must follow regular procedure and if in the end we are successful in disposing of these problems to the credit of the Government and without loss to the Canadians, we have reason to feel well repaid for our patience.[20]

Perley, of course, had his own disputes with Kemp. Once again efficiency and political pressure were at odds. As battalions recruited during 1916 continued to arrive in England, the problem of surplus officers grew worse, not better. Indeed, it grew much worse because politically-influential officers from the 1915 battalions had often been accommodated in the expanding training and reinforcement organization or in the offices of Carson's burgeoning headquarters staff. Now there was no more room at all. On 5 March Brigadier-General P.E. Thacker, the adjutant general, with Perley's approval, directed the Militia Department to send no more officers and warned that even lieutenants sent overseas might be compelled to revert to the ranks. Well aware that any such order would provoke an explosion in Canada, Kemp immediately pleaded with Borden to intervene: 'Whole matter should be reviewed. These officers have raised their units in good faith and when their battalions are taken away from them on the eve of sailing they become disappointed and resentful against Government. A large number of troops are about to embark and there are indications of great unrest among the officers, as well as the men, because of what appears to be a breach of faith on part of Government.'[21]

The overseas minister was obliged to concede ground because of what officers and men of the newer CEF battalions considered 'fair politics' but the only outcome was that the Overseas Ministry took the blame, not Kemp's department.[22] The bitterness was hardly diminished and the cost was significantly increased but the political resentments were grounded as far from Ottawa as possible. More than surplus officers were involved. As Perley had discovered, virtually every aspect of his new responsibility presented him with difficulties and many of them derived directly from the expansive favouritism of the Hughes and Carson era.

Next to the medical services, Perley's biggest political problem was undoubtedly with the chaplains' department. Religious questions were quite as explosive as care of the wounded and the political rivalries were complicated by denominational issues. The director of chaplains' services was Lieutenant-Colonel R.H. Steacy, an Anglican clergyman of very little administrative talent or personal authority. Like others in the CEF, Steacy had to create a new institution from unfamiliar and often conflicting elements. Denominations watched their quota of chaplain vacancies with a vigilant eye and the chaplain's appointment in many of the CEF battalions had proved to be the most bitterly contested issue in the unit's creation. Colonel Steacy, a Hughes appointment, wrestled helplessly with his problems, rejected British influence or example, promised promotions and appointments he could not deliver, and steadily lost prestige.[23]

While his relations with Protestant chaplains were unsatisfactory – both Methodists and Anglicans were furious when he had tried to help a Methodist chaplain switch faiths – it was the Roman Catholics who were most aggrieved. Much of their dissatisfaction arose not so much from Steacy as from his self-appointed assistant, Mgr Alfred E. Burke. The former editor of the Catholic *Register* and the extrovert promoter of a long succession of causes, from imperialism and scientific agriculture to a tunnel to his native Prince Edward Island, Burke had quarrelled with a number of powerful Canadian Roman Catholics during his long career. None the less, during Senator James Lougheed's brief tenure of the Militia Department in 1914, Burke prevailed on the Roman Catholic politician to appoint him chief Roman Catholic chaplain to the CEF.[24] When Hughes returned, he refused to endorse the appointment but Burke set out for Europe with no better authority than his own remarkable self-confidence. That was enough to gain him a brief visit to the western front and to Gallipoli and an audience with the pope. This, in turn, endowed him with sufficient prestige to be accepted without further ado as Steacy's deputy. In itself, that might have been a solution for the Roman Catholic chaplains, resentfully subordinate to an Anglican, but they soon blamed their overwork, lack of support, and other grievances on the ebullient monsignor.[25]

As an Anglican himself, the new overseas minister gratefully passed such ecclesiastical problems to his colleague, Charles Doherty, minister of justice and spokesman in the cabinet for English-speaking Roman Catholics. Doherty's inquiries solved nothing. As the minister of justice soon discovered, among Burke's mortal enemies were Bishop Michael Fallon, arch foe of anyone, like Burke, who had not joined in denouncing the pretensions of French-Canadians. On no account, Perley was instructed, must Burke be allowed any senior appointment.[26] The overseas minister still hesitated to enter the chaplaincy dispute until Borden's arrival at the end of February. The prime minister firmly disposed of Burke's claims and, with his lieutenant discountenanced, Colonel Steacy was retired. As usual, Perley found his successor in France. Lieutenant-Colonel J.M. Almond, principal Protestant chaplain with the Corps and a persistent critic of Steacy, was brought to London as his successor while Major W.T. Workman, the senior Roman Catholic chaplain, displaced Burke. Though both Steacy and Burke did not cease from troubling, the new team gradually brought administrative order and reasonable tranquillity. Within a month, Almond had restored relations with his British counterparts, established authorized totals of chaplains for each denomination, arranged remuneration for British clergymen visiting Canadian sick and wounded, and won approval for a system of promotions within the young Canadian service.[27]

Equipment and personnel problems caused recurrent friction between the Overseas Ministry and its counterpart in Ottawa, much to the dismay of both ministers. However, it was Perley's duty to seek out matters which the British government would cheerfully have ignored and press them to solutions more satisfactory to Canada. Whatever the high symbolism of the Imperial War Cabinet and prime ministerial consultation, the real advances for Canadian autonomy had first to be made at a far humbler level. By staffing the Overseas Ministry with officers who had earned their reputations in France, Perley had recognized that battle experience had given Canadians proficiency. With his support, Turner now began to press for more Canadian staff officers in the Corps itself, displacing the British officers who had held key appointments ever since the 1st Canadian Division had left Salisbury Plain. According to Turner, the Corps could still be efficient if only a handful of vital appointments – the brigadier-general, general staff at Corps headquarters and the general staff officers, grade I, in each division (the right-hand men of their Canadian commanders) – were British staff college graduates. To give Canadians experience for more junior staff positions, Turner pressed hard for more attachments to General Headquarters and to the headquarters of the five British armies in the field.[28] Sir George added yet another Canadian claim when he pressed the colonial secretary for a more generous share of the foreign decorations distributed to British army officers. By mid-February, he complained, Canadians had received only one of 35 French decorations and nine of 225 Russian decorations.[29]

However important these efforts were for the morale and self-esteem of CEF officers, they hardly compared with the significance of Perley's bargaining with the British government for the payment of the costs of the Canadians overseas. The negotiations, which opened formally in March 1915, had involved Perley from the outset. Like so much else, there was no precedent and no pre-arranged plan. In the mood of 1914, Canada had insisted that she would pay the full cost of 'equipment, pay and maintenance.'[30] For their part, while the British had made arrangements to keep accounts for the direct charges, nothing was collected for accommodation, furniture, hospital stores, or transportation by land or sea once Canadians had reached Britain. When negotiations opened, Canadians began with the proud boast that they would meet 'the entire cost in every particular of their own contingents.'[31]

From the outset, Perley had insisted that Canadians should not establish a separate system of supply and certainly any such arrangement in France, together with the necessary accounting, would have been unwieldy and costly.[32] The solution, advanced by the War Office and endorsed by Perley, was a per capita payment for Canadians in France of six shillings per man per day. Of this, five shillings was reckoned as the per capita cost of maintaining a British soldier in the field (apart from pay, allowances, and pension costs) including food, fuel, clothing, equipment, transportation, replacement of arms, transport and horses, and small arms ammunition. The remaining shilling represented the cost of artillery ammunition used on behalf of Canadian forces. As for the Canadians in England, Perley agreed that Canada would pay the actual cost of all supplies and stores and the transportation costs of Canadian personnel and stores on British railways. Britain would absorb the cost of all accommodation, including barrack and hospital stores.[33]

The negotiations between Perley and the War Office, with Canadian generosity quailing before the enormity of the wartime financial burden, finally ended with cabinet ratification on 24 January 1917. However, the agreement had included a clause that the rate of six shillings would continue 'unless conditions should so alter as to make it clearly unfair either to the Imperial or the Dominion Government.'[34] No sooner was a settlement arranged than the War Office concluded that the one shilling a day rate for artillery ammunition, based on conditions a year earlier, was now unrealistic. Sir Charles Harris, assistant financial secretary and the chief British negotiator with the Canadians, notified Perley on 2 March that the figures must be changed. From July to September 1916 (the height of the Somme battles) expenditure per soldier for artillery ammunition alone had averaged seven shillings and sixpence a day.[35] Nothing better illustrated the altered mood of the Canadian government in its commitment to the war than Perley's immediate riposte that any increased obligation must date only from Sir Charles's notification. The British official promptly replied (with considerable justice) that the higher rate should prevail from the time when the previous rate of six shillings was no longer equitable. A paper battle had opened which would preoccupy Perley until the end of hostilities, with about four million pounds sterling at issue.[36]

Once Perley had begun to put the Canadian administration in England on a more orderly footing, his next concern was to establish a more satisfactory relationship with the Canadians in France. Once again the advantages and the difficulties of having a Canadian cabinet minister in London soon became apparent. Sir Max Aitken, though still the recipient of the ex-minister of militia's outspoken confidences, had cheerfully switched his allegiance to the new régime. He was not about to sacrifice the Canadian rank and uniform that guaranteed him access to the gossip and secrets of General Head-quarters. However, the Canadian eye witness spent much of November and December coaxing and prodding his friend Bonar Law in the intrigues which led to the fall of Asquith. Aitken's reward for his role, accepted with unusual lack of political acumen, was a peerage.[37] As Lord Beaverbrook he was barred from both the British and the Canadian House of Commons and he no longer found time to serve as Canadian representative in France. His successor was a survivor from the Colonel Carrick period, Lieutenant-Colonel R. Manly Sims. Beaverbrook continued to sponsor the work of the Canadian War Records Office, granting it space in the offices of his news-paper and launching ambitious programmes for Canadian war art, exhibi-tions and publications.[38]

Sims was to play a discreet but increasingly important role in extending direct Canadian authority over the Corps. That was by no means apparent in the arrangements proposed to the War Office on 25 January. Sims would, Perley proposed, serve as a representative for the Overseas Ministry at General Headquarters and as a liaison officer between the minister, GHQ, Canadian headquarters in London, and the Canadian Corps. As Sir George delicately explained, he wanted Sims to provide an informal channel to the commander-in-chief on 'all matters of a semi-official or purely domestic nature' which had 'caused difficulties on various occasions.' Sims was also given a staff of three officers and a few motor cars to take care of another difficult responsibility – looking after prominent Canadian visitors to the front.[39] It was evidence of the end of Hughes's back-slapping informality that Sims's new instructions for administration and financial accounting covered eleven closely-typed pages.[40]

Although discreetly asserted, Sims's role was the first in a series of steps which would expand Canadian influence over the Corps. No one questioned that the Canadians in France were under the full tactical control of Sir Doug-las Haig. However, the administrative and personnel aspects of Canadian participation would no longer be left by default to the British. An example was the authority to promote Canadian officers. A Canadian order-in-council of 19 December 1916 gave the overseas minister full authority over the promotion of CEF officers outside Canada. To his surprise, promotions he had never seen continued to appear in the London *Gazette*. A reminder from Gow, the deputy minister, brought the unexpected news that the War Office still acted on the authority of a much earlier Canadian order-in-council of 16 September 1915. Hughes's order of 23 February 1916, giving himself the ultimate authority, had never even been noticed.[41]

Though it took a few days, Perley's authority was acknowledged by the British.[42] The main resistance came from the Canadian Corps itself, resentful of delays and suspicious of renewed political meddling. Once again the new efficiency at the Overseas Ministry made a difference. An angry charge from the Corps that promotion of certain artillery officers had been delayed as long as fourteen months, until some of them had been killed and wounded, was carefully investigated by Turner and Sims. The real responsibility, they proved, lay in the Corps headquarters itself.[43] Using Sims as a channel and by checking the information submitted, the Corps could be promised that any promotion would be confirmed and gazetted within two weeks.[44]

Promotions were not the only issue. Perley's first crisis in relations with the Canadian Corps came in early January with news that the ex-minister's brother, Brigadier-General St Pierre Hughes, had been relieved of his command of the 10th Brigade. The explanation was a dramatic falling-out between Hughes and his divisional commander, Major-General Watson. According to Hughes, Watson had fired him as soon as Sir Sam was gone as an act of retribution against the ex-minister and to conceal his own incompetence. To Watson, Hughes was simply unequal to the burdens of command, his brigade was disorganized, and his front line had been successfully raided by a German patrol.[45] There may have been arguments on both sides. If St Pierre Hughes's dismissal may have been politically motivated, so was his appointment to a 4th Division brigade in the spring of 1916, over General Turner's discreet reservations.[46] Whatever the truth, obscured in charges and counter-charges about the respective failures of Hughes and Watson, the episode inflamed survivors of the Hughes faction and added fresh venom to Sir Sam's attacks on his successor.

While St Pierre Hughes was persuaded to postpone his demand for vindication by appointment to one of the reserve brigades in England, the shadow of Sir Sam Hughes fell darkly over much more major changes in the Corps in June 1917.

As part of a British commitment to help the French offensive on the Chemin des Dames, Haig had agreed that his Third Army would assault the German line on the Scarpe while Byng's Canadian Corps would attempt to capture Vimy Ridge. After the precise, detailed rehearsals Byng introduced to Corps planning and more than two weeks of relentless bombardment, the entire Canadian Corps advanced in line on Easter Monday, 9 April. The result was one of the few dramatic victories on the western front. At a cost of 3,598 Canadian dead, an almost impregnable position was taken, and by 12 April the Germans had withdrawn to new positions across the Douai Plain.[47] Later, as the British divisions battered hopelessly against the Scarpe, the Canadians managed to capture first Arleux and then Fresnoy. Such successes, if costly and minor, raised the esteem of the Corps in its own eyes and in those of its British commanders. On 5 June, when Haig learned that

General Sir Henry Allenby would be sent to revive the disorganized British advance into Palestine, Sir Julian Byng had his reward: command of the Third Army.[48]

For both Byng and Haig, there was only one possible Canadian successor to the command of the Corps: a newly knighted Major-General Sir Arthur Currie. As W.B. Kerr, a young gunner in the Corps noted, 'even among men who could not mention his name without some coarse allusion to his personal appearance,' there was never any question about Currie's military skill.[49] In youth a venturesome scapegrace, Currie in middle age had turned to corpulence and a certain ponderousness of manner but he had addressed his military avocation with unusual seriousness of purpose. He was brave, cool, and systematic. He also took advice where he found it, whether from British staff officers or from some of the remarkable specialists who had found their way into the ranks of the Canadian Corps. General Seely of the Cavalry Brigade recalled a visit by Currie during 1916 in which Currie had condemned the mining operations on Seely's front. Their designer was, in fact, a corporal named 'Foghorn' Macdonald who boasted long experience in Canada as a mining engineer. When Currie finished his comments, Macdonald, who had been sitting on a table in the background, butted in: 'Look here, old man Currie, you don't know the first thing about mines. I have forgotten more about them than you will ever know. You may say what you like about the rest, but don't try coming over me about the mine just because you're the stud duck in this puddle.' Currie had the grace to burst out laughing.[50] In other circumstances, Currie showed that he was far less able to win the affection and respect of his men than the popular Sir Julian Byng. However, such limitations were more damaging to his postwar reputation than to his wartime performance. Byng and Haig were right. On 6 June Currie was summoned to Corps headquarters to learn of his new appointment.[51]

Perley learned of the change only on 8 June, the same day that Byng left to take over his new command. Colonel Sims was the intermediary, explaining that though the change was described as 'temporary,' Byng was unlikely to return. The Overseas Ministry faced a painful quandary. Currie was now the senior Canadian major-general in the Corps and he had a distinguished fighting record. In November Perley had concluded that Currie's abilities were greater than Turner's. At the same time, Turner was the senior major-general in the overseas forces, he had sacrificed his own ambitions in order to obey Perley's summons and, as a condition, he had reserved the right to be considered for the command of the Corps when it became vacant. On the other hand, as Perley had also learned, there were serious questions about

Turner's tactical competence and he had been away from active service for more than six months. Obviously, some sort of arrangement had to be made.[52]

When Sims arrived at Corps headquarters on 10 June, after a hurried visit to London, he had more to offer than congratulations: 'Apparently wanted to suggest a dicker,' Currie noted in his diary.[53] By 13 June, when the Canadian cabinet had met and approved what it regarded as a *fait accompli*, Perley summoned Currie to London. By the evening of the fourteenth, Currie had met with Perley and Turner. Turner, also newly knighted, surrendered his bid to command the Corps. In return, he would be promoted to lieutenant-general, retain his seniority over Currie, and extend at least his nominal authority over the Canadians in France. Currie had the real prize and both men knew it.[54] The really tough bargaining came in the choice of Currie's successor in the 1st Division. Six months earlier, the prime minister had pressed hard for a divisional command for Garnet Hughes. Instead he had been given a consolation prize, command of the 5th Canadian Division suspended in permanent home defence duties at Witley. Now, surely, Garnet would have his claims satisfied.

On the face of it, Currie should have been delighted. His own selection as a brigadier in the First Contingent was due to the urging of his good friend Garnet Hughes in 1914. As senior major in the newly created Fiftieth Regiment of Highlanders in Victoria, Hughes had urged his commanding officer's claims on his father and then persuaded Currie to accept the repeated offer.[55] However, for reasons which remain obscure, Currie had come to the conclusion that Hughes was unfit for higher command. Instead he had chosen his own successor: Brigadier-General Archibald Macdonnell, a tough, colourful officer from the permanent cavalry widely known as 'Batty Mac.' According to Currie, he was subjected to relentless pressure to change his mind. 'I was importuned, threatened and bullied. I was told that Garnett [*sic*] Hughes would have to get the 1st Division, that there was a combination in England and Canada for him, that neither I, nor any man, could beat; that his father wanted him to get the position and that God help the man who fell out with his father.'[56] On the evening of 15 June, as Currie and his wife finished dinner at a London hotel, Garnet Hughes himself arrived from his headquarters at Witley. Conversation grew heated. After three hours, Hughes burst from the room shouting: 'I will get even with you before I am finished with you.'[57]

Undoubtedly, Perley did his best to argue Garnet Hughes's claims, if only out of loyalty to his friend the prime minister. Borden, indeed, had assumed that the younger Hughes would get the appointment, softening the ex-minister's resentment and counteracting some of the consequences of removing

St Pierre Hughes. However, the impression (which Currie left with his bio-graphers) of ruthless and irresponsible pressure from the politicians fades on closer inspection. Even before the meetings on 14 and 15 June, Perley had supported the nomination of Macdonnell and Borden offered no pointed rejoinder. Both men would gladly have pacified Sir Sam but Perley in particu-lar had seen enough of the aftermath of Hughes's patronage and croneyism to recognize its price. Nothing in Perley's account of the interviews even hints at Currie's claims of heat and pressure. Like their professional counter-parts, even citizen soldiers may find it difficult to argue with the wishes of their political superiors and, on this occasion and later, Currie found the experience humiliating and infuriating. Currie may also have been justified in believing that Hughes's supporters bore him no good will. However, he was the author of much of his own personal unpopularity in the Corps and his sense of martyrdom may have concealed a justifiably bad conscience.[58]

On 15 June, the very day that Sir George Perley concluded an agreement with his two senior generals, an old and exceedingly delicate matter was laid before the Militia Council in Ottawa. It concerned the long-standing claim of the Glasgow firm of Moore Taggart against the Fiftieth Highlanders of Can-ada for uniforms delivered in the spring of 1914. The outstanding sum, £1,276.17.3, should easily have been covered by a government cheque for $10,883.73, issued to the regiment in late July 1914. However, months of desultory and embarrassed correspondence left only one unavoidable con-clusion: the public funds had been pocketed by the commanding officer, deposited in his personal account, and used to cover his private debts. The commanding officer had now become the first Canadian-born officer to com-mand the Canadian Corps.[59] As resourceful bureaucrats, the Militia Council members merely agreed to bundle up the damning evidence and deliver it to the discretion of Sir George Perley. Showing no undue haste, Sir Eugène Fiset dispatched the file to his opposite number in London on 25 June.

Currie's sympathizers, largely unaware of the real nature of Sir Arthur's offence, often implied that the Hughes faction had conspired to bring him to a sudden and acute state of financial embarrassment as vengeance for Gar-net's disappointment. The fear of exposure by Hughes, who had every opportunity to know of the scandal, may have indeed impelled Currie to clear his debt with a determination he had not shown since he had left Victo-ria almost three years previously. On 25 June Currie wrote to a friend and successor in command of the 50th, Lieutenant-Colonel Charles A. Forsythe, to inform him that he could now draw on Currie for the missing amount. In fact, it was not until 10 September, with funds borrowed from Major-

General Watson and Brigadier-General Victor Odlum of the 11th Brigade, that Currie was really in a position to pay the debt.[60]

Quite independently, the papers revealing the Currie scandal made their way to London to land on Sir George Perley's desk on 21 July. Though he was no lawyer, Perley understood at once that the only possible outcome of further investigation would be a court martial, the certain disgrace, and the possible imprisonment of Canada's most prominent fighting soldier. 'Much upset by record shown in file just received from Militia Council regarding high officer at front,' he cabled the prime minister, 'Think would be disastrous from every point of view if matter became public.' While he would summon Currie at once, he offered another expedient 'Would Kemp be willing to put up half the money personally if I do the same?'[61] As two of the wealthiest ministers in the government neither man would feel the hardship. Perley's message may, indeed, have been Borden's first real intimation of the scandal and more than a week passed before his reply: 'Kemp informs me that his department will pay account and recover same from officer after the war. Therefore no further action is necessary.'[62] A draft order-in-council was prepared in early August and then, without explanation, allowed to stand over for three months. For all the intertwining of circumstances and the coincidence of dates, it seems almost certain that Currie never actually knew that his guilty secret had been shared with his minister, the cabinet, and the Militia Council. As accomplices in a cover-up, they had exercised a beneficial discretion.[63]

The cover-up of Currie's personal scandal and the efforts on behalf of Garnet Hughes were by no means the only intrigues set afoot by the change of command in the Corps. Almost light relief was a campaign by General Steele on behalf of his fellow westerner, Brigadier-General Ketchen. The plot miscarried. A telegram to the dependable Robert Rogers was intercepted by the British censor and deposited on Perley's desk. The overseas minister was not amused. 'As you know,' he complained to Borden, 'we are trying to manage the Overseas Department as a military organization, and to make all appointments and promotions entirely on the grounds of efficiency ... I do not say that any action should be taken regarding this particular incident, but it gives me the opportunity to say to you again that I think General Steele might be most useful in Canada, particularly in connection with recruiting in the West, where he has great influence ... I do not think he has as much work to do as he is capable of performing.'[64]

In the new relationship between Currie and Turner, the latter was formally designated as holding 'the senior military appointment in the Overseas Military Forces of Canada.'[65] Both were appointed on the same day and Haig was invited to go through the pretence of choosing between officers of equal seniority. Some delay was occasioned while Sir Julian Byng's appointment to command the Third Army was confirmed but the promotions were formally gazetted on 23 June.[66] Later in the month, Perley sent his deputy minister to France to report on the new arrangements. Gow returned convinced that there could be no further question of raising Garnet Hughes's prospects: 'Speaking generally I found a very much better feeling existing on all hands as to the relations between London and the Front, than existed when I was in France last year. Everywhere the statement "Things are so much better now than they were. The drafts which came over from England are much better trained and the relations between the field and the forces in England seem to be much closer and better in every way." That I think is a fair epitome of the many statements made to me on the subject.'[67]

By no means all issues had been settled. A memorandum of agreement, drafted on 14 June explicitly withheld powers of appointment and promotion from the Corps commander but Currie insisted that he must have authority over the arrangements made in his own formation. 'I am only too anxious to do everything possible to promote and preserve harmony,' he wrote to Perley early in August, 'but I must respectfully submit that, as I am the one who must assume final responsibility for the efficiency of the Corps, there must be no interference with my prerogatives in the matter of recommendation.' Recent promotions, Currie complained, threatened to 'create a similar confusion and ill-will as was formerly created by the late Minister of Militia's practice of slapping people on the back and telling them their rank was so and so.'[68] This was neither tactful nor fair to Perley but the overseas minister avoided replying in kind. Instead, the dispute was settled late in August when he and Turner visited France and agreed that Currie would pass his advice on appointments, particularly in the supporting services, through Colonel Sims.[69]

By the summer of 1917 both the Canadian Corps and the Overseas Ministry had achieved significant success. Having presided over a substantial administrative reform, Perley had rendered himself somewhat superfluous. Increasingly, Turner, Gow, and other officers of the department settled problems that had earlier burdened Perley. At the same time, as a cabinet minister, Sir George was still compelled to answer to a distant House of Commons. To arm himself for fresh attacks, Sir Sam Hughes placed questions of ingenious length and complexity on the order paper. On 23 May 1917 the Overseas Ministry was called on to furnish a list of all officers not attached to a definite unit on 12 March 1916, the nature of their duties, the amounts paid to them, and 'all relevant correspondence.'[70] The difficulties were only slightly relieved when the date was corrected from 1916 to 1917. A reply was finally sent on 9 August. The ex-minister also adopted a popular refrain that the staff of the Overseas Ministry had grown enormously. On 30 January he had told the Commons that 'Poor old General Carson and Colonel Murphy had about thirty officers assisting them at comparatively small cost – but I am told that there are six or seven hundred around the place now, and the Lord knows how many more there will be before the war is over.'[71] In fact, Perley was informed, Carson's staff by 1 December 1916 numbered 134 officers and 566 other ranks; by August 1917 the Overseas Ministry included 139 officers and 486 other ranks. Eleven training brigades had become six; a reserve cavalry brigade had been cut to a regiment; Cleveland House and the luxurious Hotel Cecil, for which Canada had paid rent, had been exchanged for free quarters.[72] However, with Perley in London, there was no one but Kemp or Borden to present the case to Parliament.

Early in August, with the House of Commons still rancorous over the passage of the Military Service Act, Sir Robert Borden set out to clarify the legal, if not the political, position of the Overseas Ministry. Perley's status, as well as that of the parliamentary secretaries for external affairs and for militia and defence, rested only on orders-in-council. All three would be given a statutory basis by means of an omnibus bill. The financial resolution, introduced on 7 August, proposed a salary of $7,000 for the overseas minister and $5,000 for each of the parliamentary secretaries. For most members of parliament, it was an opportunity to debate the concept of a cabinet minister wholly absent from the centre of government; for Sir Sam Hughes, it was a second chance to assemble his grievances. These had become sufficiently repetitive that the government no longer showed much concern, though Hughes obviously found an echo when he sought support from the numerous MP's whom he had transformed into colonels and who had returned as surplus to the CEF's needs.[73] More to the point was Laurier's complaint that, while there were now two ministers of militia, he could get information from neither of them.[74]

On the second reading, the criticisms of Perley took shape and grew. E.M. Macdonald, a Liberal from Nova Scotia and a future minister of national defence, offered his view that Sir George, trained only in business and civil life, could not possibly direct military matters.[75] It was a contrast to a more familiar viewpoint that only a businessman could be a competent manager. Another Liberal, Rodolphe Lemieux, spoke of a 'leap in the dark,' of 'too great, too serious a departure from the spirit of the British Constitution and of British institutions.' Lemieux's concern, it emerged, was with the neglected voters of Perley's Argenteuil constituency.[76] Hughes resorted to personal abuse of Perley and of his long-suffering chief of the general staff, General Gwatkin: 'I was right in the fact that he did not know much but I was wrong in thinking he would interfere.'[77] On 18 August, after two full days of debate, the bill was carried on division.

Like most such performances, the debate did not show the House of Commons to its best advantage. Members had recognized fundamental problems when they spoke of divided jurisdiction and the problem of securing information but both Liberals and Tories felt inhibited in launching a frontal attack on the administrative situation which had led to the Overseas Ministry. The Conservatives had no desire to attack their own record while the Liberals, lacking definite information, still trusted that Hughes might prove a new-found ally in denouncing the Borden government.[78]

Politically, the Overseas Ministry would become increasingly vulnerable almost precisely because of Sir George Perley's attempts to drive out the patronage and favouritism of the Carson era. The penalty was an accumulation of charges that Perley was cold, lacking in the human touch, and too much bound up in the routine of his office. A disproportionate number of the surplus senior officers were prominent Conservatives and they had no inhibitions in bringing their grievances to Borden and his colleagues. During his spring visit to England, the prime minister urged his friend to employ not only a few diplomatic and resourceful assistants to receive and mollify disappointed favour-seekers but also a confidential secretary to keep him in touch with mood and grievances.[79] The advice was embarrassingly reminiscent of the personal spies and favourites who had been so closely associated with the Hughes régime but, soon after Borden went back to Canada, Perley asked Kemp to recommend: 'a trustworthy, tactful and reticent officer who does not talk too much and would assist me with those having troubles and grievances and generally smooth over difficulties. Hard to define his duties but they will be important. He should be man of experience not too young and Conservative but not too partisan.'[80] Kemp offered a number of names, all Toronto Tories, but when it became apparent that Premier Hearst of Ontario had decided to press the claims of Colonel William Price to the appointment, Perley lost interest. An assistant appointed by patronage would not be much of an asset in dealing with other favour-seekers.[81]

In any case, the Overseas Ministry had not been established to dispense party favours but to prove that Canada could administer her own military affairs in a systematic, responsible manner. That achievement must be its own reward.

7

Conscription

The new British government had convened the colonial ministers for one real purpose: to convince them of the need for more recruits for the struggle on the western front. The experiment was a success. Even Maurice Hankey was convinced: 'The great drain on the time and energy of the British Ministers ...' to say nothing of the risks and inconvenience for the overseas politicians 'were felt to have been well worth while.'[1]

For Borden, the stunning revelations about the dismal progress of the war, the collapse of Russia, and the effectiveness of German submarine warfare had not been the only sources of persuasion. The delay in starting the sessions gave him time to visit the major Canadian camps and hospitals in England and to spend four days with the Corps in France. As he talked to convalescing wounded and discussed the war with officers, the Canadian leader realized that there was another guiding principle to set beside the need to support a flagging Allied war effort: Canada must keep faith with her fighting men. Ever since 1915 Borden had preached the need for earnest commitment. Who were more earnestly committed than young Canadian soldiers?

That might not be the mood in which the soldiers necessarily saw themselves. The last traces of romantic optimism had perished in the disastrous offensives of 1916. No longer could men believe that a 'Big Push' would somehow shatter the German line and open the road to Berlin. Instead they talked of being 'fattened up' for offensives. Men whose courage had withstood months of horror began to fail. In 1916 eleven Canadians had been shot by firing squad, all but one of them for desertion in the face of the enemy.[2] In 1917 the toll would continue. It was the horrible by-product of a system that condemned wounded to return again and again to the front until they were either killed or so terribly hurt that no medical officer could consider them fit for active service. Of those wounded, roughly 80 per cent had to return to face battle again.[3]

How would men respond to the apparent inevitability of death or mutilation? They could accept their fate while urging brothers and friends to do everything to spare themselves, particularly since the only means of support for aged parents might well be a surviving relative, or they could turn a savage resentment on the 'slackers' who had refused to take their share of the common burden. Both reactions were apparent among Canadian soldiers, but it was the latter mood which Borden himself was predisposed to find and he would later present his apprehensions with an eloquence born of conviction: 'If what are left of 400,000 such men come back to Canada with fierce resentment in their hearts, conscious that they have been deserted and betrayed, how shall we meet them when they ask the reason?'[4]

By the time Borden left for England in February, the flow of volunteers for the CEF had slowed to a trickle. In January 1916 30,000 men had come forward. A year later, the total was less than 10,000. In April 1917, when Canadians might have been swept into patriotic euphoria by the dramatic victory at Vimy Ridge, only 5,000 recruits came forward. Of them, many would fall by the wayside as physically inadequate even by reduced medical standards or as mental or disciplinary misfits. During 1916 the government had tried a number of expedients, responding as much to complaints from employers that valuable skilled workers had enlisted as to the rising patriotic outrage at 'slackers.' An attempt to allocate manpower more efficiently had begun with a National Service Board, headed by a prominent Montrealer, Sir Thomas Tait. When Tait resigned to protest alleged political interference, he was succeeded by R.B. Bennett, an aggressive Calgary lawyer, Tory MP, and foe of Sir Sam Hughes. Bennett was responsible for an ambitious, highly publicized but ultimately unsuccessful plan of national registration, designed to identify men who should be available to enlist. Only about 60 per cent of Canadian men actually submitted completed cards and of these 286,976 were judged by the board to be in non-essential occupations. Their names were ponderously distributed to recruiting officers but to negligible effect. Of 4,497 names canvassed in the Quebec City area, only four volunteers were obtained; in Military District 10, covering Manitoba and north-western Ontario, 1,767 contacts produced not a single recruit.[5]

In Quebec, increasingly denounced by English-speaking patriots for its undoubted reluctance to share in the national war effort, a special attempt was made by authorizing yet another CEF battalion, the 258th, to be commanded by the postmaster general, P.E. Blondin, aided by the fading prestige of General Lessard. The recruiting parties met jeers, stony rejection, and occasional violence and the entire effort netted perhaps ninety genuine recruits. The battalion left for England with fifteen officers and 221 men, most of them rejects from previous Quebec battalions.[6]

In another expedient the government insisted, despite the reservations of Gwatkin and most members of the Militia Council, that some men might volunteer for home defence to replace troops still guarding canals, internment camps, and coastal fortifications. A 50,000-man Canadian Defence Force of forty-seven battalions would be commanded by a Hamilton militia officer and prominent Liberal, Major-General S.C. Mewburn. Although the government promised recruits full equality with the CEF, the results were pitiful. By the end of April only 1,858 recruits were found for the new force and two-thirds of them promptly switched to the CEF. Super-patriots and Liberals alike, fully armed with hindsight, had a host of explanations of why recruiting had failed, most of them based on real or alleged government blunders. The scapegoating was largely irrelevant. By early 1917 with close to half a million past and current members of the CEF, Canada had effectively reached the limit of the young men who would volunteer for military service. That was the counterpoint, beating in on Borden in successive telegrams from Kemp and other colleagues, during the prime minister's two months in England.[7]

Borden returned to Canada with a very clear sense of what he must do. 'Slow to move or to decide on his course,' as Granatstein and Hitsman have observed, 'Borden normally worked his way through the facts of a situation, chewing over the details until he had mastered them. And then, once his mind was clear, he held to his direction with great tenacity and bulldog determination.'[8] The process by which he transformed the Canadian political landscape by his decision and the incredible, wholly unexpected process by which a government headed toward certain and dismal defeat was able to claim smashing victory six months later has been recorded elsewhere from both friendly and hostile perspectives.[9] However, the outcome of the conscription crisis was as vital to the Canadian Expeditionary Force and to Canada's changing status in the war effort as it was to the fortunes of Borden, Laurier, or to the politicians and parties caught by the issue. That fact has been much more cursorily considered.[10]

One consequence of Borden's visit was his realization that the problem of reinforcements could not be resolved by any further reform of the Canadian overseas administration. Thanks to Hughes, charges would continue to be made that the Overseas Ministry was grossly overstaffed by 'slackers in uniform' and by 1918 it would become a positive refrain, often fed by surplus officers who had failed to find a billet on the staff. Borden could be satisfied that this was largely nonsense and that Sir George Perley had achieved a dramatic transformation in both the efficiency and the prestige of his organization. No one suggested, as they would in the Second World War, that conscription might somehow have been unnecessary if the military had only managed a rigorous comb-out of their own organization.[11]

Borden also returned to Canada with the clear understanding that he could no longer postpone a general election. It was a grim prospect. If there was any certainty in politics, it was that his Conservative party would lose. Since 1915 Conservatives had lost seven out of seven provincial elections, often in humiliating routs. Only Ontario had a friendly government. Liberals were united, fully armed with evidence of government corruption, bungling, and uncertainty.[12] The British had offered Borden assurances that they would endorse an amendment of the British North America Act further postponing an election, even if it were passed only by the Conservative majority in the House of Commons but Borden knew that the outcry would be too great. Moreover, he had no confidence at all that conscription would do more than add to his enemies. In Australia, far more homogeneous and committed to the war, compulsory service had been rejected by a 1916 referendum and it would fail again in 1917.[13] In Canada it would meet solid opposition from Quebec, from the non-Anglo-Saxon voters of western Canada, already showing their political strength in provincial contests, and from farmers determined to hang on to their sons at a time when labour was scarce and prices were soaring. Later, Liberal apologists would accuse Borden of introducing conscription as a brilliant stroke of opportunism, designed to rob Laurier of his legitimate political comeback and to divide Canada on racial lines. That was not the prospect facing Borden when he prepared to meet his cabinet colleagues on 17 May. If the outcome was almost wholly unexpected, it was a triumph of political leadership, patience, courage, ingenuity, and ruthlessness in a cause which many Canadians might later come to doubt.

To many ardent Tory partisans, Borden had missed his chance when he failed to call a patriotic, national unity election in 1914 or early 1915. Though the Liberals would also have been confident of victory, some of their most obvious targets would have been missing. After 4 August Sam Hughes looked more prescient than foolish. The Liberal-inspired blockade of Conservative aid to the Royal Navy would have become difficult to justify to war-fevered electors. While Borden weighed his options, Perley raised an important point: 'Am informed large proportion Canadian troops are Conservative. Doubtless you have considered this as affecting election.'[14] Almost certainly Borden had not, Canadian election law presumed a stable, largely rural electorate, uninterested in absentee ballots or proxy voting. No one had thought of enfranchising Canadian soldiers in South Africa during the 1900 general election. This time, with Conservatives in office and vastly more Canadians in uniform, the concern was real. In early 1915, as election talk revived, Borden was again pestered to allow soldiers to vote: 'from ninety to ninety-five per cent of the men that have gone or are going to the front, west of Lake Superior, are Conservatives,' warned a Manitoba MP, 'and some plan, if possible, should be adopted to give these men a vote.'[15] It was not easy. British and Canadian military regulations formally discouraged political activity by men in uniform. On the other hand, both Australia and New Zealand had provided voting rights for their soldiers. In their December 1914 national election, New Zealand troops simply marked their ballots for the government or the opposition.[16]

The upshot of Conservative concerns, doubtless urged on by Borden's coarse-grained 'Minister of Elections' Robert Rogers, was a Soldier's Voting Bill, studied during March 1915 by a small parliamentary committee and introduced on 8 April by Charles Doherty, the minister of justice. The legislation excluded women and minors in the CEF from the franchise, allowed soldiers to choose any constituency in which they had spent at least thirty days prior to enlistment or, if that failed, any other. Soldiers would fill out an affidavit, put their ballot in a sealed envelope under an officer's supervision, and mail it to the clerk of the crown in chancery in Ottawa. The envelopes would be sorted by constituency, mailed to returning officers, and counted in the presence of candidates or their agents.[17]

Despite Borden's professed eagerness to accept Liberal improvements, nothing could make the opposition like the idea of soldiers voting. Marking ballots simply for the government or the opposition would undermine the constitution. What was good enough for New Zealand, 'the hotbed of socialism' as Michael Clark described it, was unacceptable in Canada.[18] When Laurier finally entered the debate, the argument became explicit. 'We have laws and regulations, the result of the wisdom and experience of the ages, which have determined that we may expect the blood and sacrifice of the soldier,' the former prime minister explained, 'and yet the soldier is not entitled to cast a vote in the administration of the country.' Soldiers, he insisted, were entitled to no more special consideration than any other labourer. Moreover, Laurier maintained, Canada had no legal authority over her troops: 'Every one of the 50,000 men who have left the country, or will leave the country, is no longer under the jurisdiction of this Parliament, he is a part of the British Army and he is under the jurisdiction of the War Office, and the War Office alone has the right to pass legislation for him or against him.'[19]

The Conservatives were unmoved by the Liberal protests and doubtless treasured the more extreme expressions as election ammunition. The Liberal-dominated Senate hesitated to kill the bill but it did force Borden to go through the indignity of obtaining British permission. On 5 May the British cabled their approval but two days later the soldiers' vote was, quite literally, sunk. Armed with a militia commission and a large supply of ballots, Harold Daly, a former Vancouver lawyer and now a Hughes aide and all-purpose fixer, had embarked on the *Lusitania*. On 7 May his voyage ended in the frigid waters of the Irish Sea. Unlike most of his fellow passengers, Daly survived to cable Rogers from London: 'I am still quite willing to die for the Conservative Party but am glad I didn't drown for it.'[20]

Daly's survival proved an acute embarrassment. His mission and his vestigial rank might have given colour to German claims that the huge ship was packed with British soldiers and munitions. Daly's presence in England became a deep, if temporary, military secret. However, there were better reasons for postponing an election. Borden himself proved increasingly unenthusiastic. Patriotic feeling, far from swinging to the Tories, now began condemning the government's confused and sometimes corrupt war preparations. Other elections did occur, however, and Canadian politicians got some evidence of how soldiers might behave politically. In the autumn of 1916 British Columbia soldiers participated in a provincial election on terms closely resembling those of the Soldiers' Voting Act. On 13 September, W.J. Bowser's Conservative régime was annihilated in one of the most decisive shifts in the province's electoral history. Soldier voters still in Canada followed the provincial trend; those in England and France had remained staunchly Tory. In referenda, the British Columbia soldiers ran counter to strong civilian support for prohibition and favoured votes for women far less strongly than electors at home.[21]

Alberta and Saskatchewan also gave votes to their soldiers but, with strongly entrenched Liberal régimes, took precautions. Instead of allowing military voters to influence their home constituencies, they hived them into special 'soldier' constituencies. On the basis of numbers, each province should have given the soldiers eight to ten seats; each government conceded only three. Alberta voters showed a lively interest, with 25,601 ballots cast for twenty-one candidates. The winners included Roberta McAdams, a nurse and the second Canadian woman to be elected to a legislature. The Saskatchewan election took place under the shadow of the 1917 federal election. Only eight thousand voters bothered to participate: they chose two officers and a blinded private.[22] The provincial experience was proof to both Liberal and Conservative politicians of the potential of managing the military vote. 'I think if properly organized in plenty of time,' Senator Rufus Pope was advised by his soldier-son, 'the thing could be done and a plum picked.'[23] 'The men were marched to a hall and voted,' Lieutenant-Colonel George McLeod reported to Laurier, 'there were plenty of cigars around but no scrutineers, and the vote went the way the returning officer wanted it to go.'[24]

Borden was reasonably aware of the potential of the overseas vote. In a contest which would obviously become a referendum on conscription, he needed no persuasion to involve the men of the CEF. Equally, the Liberals could be depended upon to oppose and condemn any military franchise. On 5 July eighteen Liberals joined the Borden government to defeat Laurier's proposal that conscription be put to a national referendum; eleven French-speaking Conservatives joined Laurier on the question. It was the key division on the issue of the Military Service Bill. Twelve days later, the Liberals refused Borden a one-year extension in the life of the twelfth Parliament; an election was inevitable.

The machinery of the Soldiers' Voting Act was now obsolete. The CEF was eight times larger than in 1915 and the overseas component had grown tenfold. Three western provinces had extended the franchise to women and nurses and other female members of the forces surely deserved the same right. So did Indians and minors who wore the King's uniform. The earlier act had required all ballots to be sent to Ottawa. That would now impose an unacceptable delay and, with the resumption of German submarine warfare, inadmissable risk of loss.[25] While Arthur Meighen took charge of the Wartime Elections Act, drastically reshaping the civilian franchise, Charles Doherty as minister of justice assumed responsibility for a new law. The detailed work was done by W.F. O'Connor, architect of Canada's unique War Measures Act. To ensure that service and civilian voting would end on the same day, nominations in all but remote constituencies like the Yukon had to be complete four weeks before election day. While military voters in Canada would deposit their ballots on the same day as civilian electors, the overseas vote would be collected over several weeks. Teams of 'presiding officers' would oversee the collection of ballots, forwarding them to the Canadian high commissioner in London or the commissaire du Canada in Paris. 'Special returning officers' and clerks nominated equally by the government and the opposition would sort, authenticate, and count the votes.[26]

Probably nothing could have reconciled the Liberals to extending the soldier vote; the advent of conscription guaranteed that they would be enfranchising their enemies. Liberal MP's poured fire on virtually every clause of Doherty's bill but section 3 drew their hottest indignation. If all British subjects in the CEF were to have the vote, the franchise would be open to a number of British soldiers in the contingent and a much larger group of Britons who had come directly from the United States to enlist. Since voters would influence specific constituencies, those without Canadian domicile had to have some place to cast their ballot. In his *Memoirs*, Sir Robert Borden summarized the rules: 'If a voter could specifically designate the electoral district wherein he last continually resided for four months immediately preceding his enlistment, his vote should be applied in that district. If he could not so state or specify the electoral district but could state an electoral district wherein he had at any time resided, his vote should apply to that district. Otherwise, he should be deemed an elector in such electoral district as he might indicate.'[27]

If there is one topic on which MP's are not novices, it is election law. The Liberals did not need a guidebook to know that Doherty's bill fulfilled a campaign organizer's dream – the right to deploy a clutch of reliable voters wherever the struggle was closest. Liberals became almost apoplectic. Frank Oliver called it 'a deliberate outrage'; William Pugsley raged that it was all being done to benefit mere Americans who had enlisted for high pay and a free transatlantic passage.[28] Such abuse was welcomed by the government and Doherty responded sweetly that the game, after all, could be played on both sides: 'Why is it presumed that there will be a greater power on the part of one party than on the part of another to indicate places which they would desire these men to select as their place of voting? The field is open.'[29] Doherty was being disingenuous. The bill strictly limited the parties to a total of six scrutineers, selected equally from each party and paid by the government. Perley had warned that General Headquarters had no intention of allowing squads of political agents to patrol the battlefield. Beyond extending the official ballot to allow Labour supporters to indicate their choice, the government made no concessions. By 31 August, as debate concluded, E.W. Nesbitt, an Ontario Liberal, could only plead that honesty might prevail over temptation: 'My experience has been that while men may be absolutely honest in business transactions, they sometimes look on things as, what they call smart in political transactions ... I hope that those charged with the administration of this Bill will not take advantage of their opportunities to commit irregularities.'[30]

Among those charged with administration was W.F. O'Connor, appointed general returning officer and left to wrestle with such complexities as whether the submarine blockade had left enough paper in England to print the ballots. To run the election overseas Borden appointed a fellow Haligonian, Willard P. Purney, president of the newly formed Great War Veterans' Association. It was a convenient gesture to an unfamiliar new constituency: war veterans. However, the key role in organizing the overseas vote would have to be played by Sir George Perley. As overseas minister he would be in a position to manage the complicated machinations made possible by the new legislation.[31]

To his dismay Borden discovered that his old friend seemed a reluctant warrior in the developing political struggle. Utterly preoccupied with the task of dissolving Liberal party unity, the prime minister did not need apparent faint-heartedness from an old friend. The truth was that Perley, like his British hosts, did not want a wartime election. 'It seems to me unthinkable,' Perley had proclaimed to Borden in November 1916, 'as the energies of everyone are needed to assist in winning it [the war], and spending a lot of time on party strife would be most unfortunate.'[32] It would also be unfortunate for Perley's own career. His constituency of Argenteuil had been utterly neglected since 1914 and the conscription issue, bursting among his French-speaking supporters, now guaranteed that it would be unwinnable. Even his own patronage interests had been overlooked when Perley's nominee for a cherished senate vacancy had been bypassed in favour of Smeaton White, president of the Montreal *Gazette*.[33]

Because Perley was despondent about his own political prospects, his advice on the overseas vote tended to sound half-hearted and untrustworthy. It was, however, much sounder than the pressure from Canadian-based ministers to mobilize every resource to organize the soldier vote. While Canadian-based politicians thought in conventional terms of organizers, lists, patronage favours, and a ruthless struggle to deliver every possible supporter to the polls, Perley recognized that his own greatest achievement had been to adapt his new ministry to the apolitical mood of the Canadian Corps. He resented the association of the Hughes era of favouritism with 'politics' but, in fact, by eliminating one he had for a time eliminated the other. To bring that era back, releasing officers with political experience to work their partisan wiles, manipulating discipline and arousing partisanship, would be counter-productive. 'I believe that any attempt to "use" the military organization would do more harm than good,' he warned Borden.[34] Even before talk of a wartime Union government had turned into serious action, Perley had grasped the essential political tactics:

A great many who are ordinarily Liberals will support you on the win-the-war issue and nothing should be done to offend them. I think the best way to reach the individual must be through the good offices and unsolicited efforts of these men, scattered through the various units, who will naturally support the Government strongly on this issue at this critical time. There are a great many of them over here and if each of them talks with those whom he happens to meet and impresses on them that the coming election is to decide whether we are to continue to strongly prosecute the war and do everything necessary to keep up reinforcements or whether the action of Canada in the future is to be governed by Laurier and the opinions of the French Canadians, the effect should be satisfactory and the result over here hardly doubtful.[35]

Anyone who understood the political attitudes of soldiers would have recognized the soundness of the advice. Borden's colleagues had no such sensitivity. Determined to mine every last overseas vote, Conservative politicians demanded that Perley release trusted henchmen from military service to help in the campaign. Borden directed that fifteen or twenty officers and men be shipped back to Canada to make the case for conscription.[36] Earlier he had insisted that Sir Arthur Currie embellish his acceptance of the Corps command with a firm proclamation of the need for extra men.[37] In return the prime minister offered to send over spokesmen from the new returned soldiers' organizations to preach to their former comrades. Perley firmly quashed the proposal with a warning that General Headquarters would never allow it.[38] Other ministers demanded to know what English newspapers were read by the troops. F.B. McCurdy, facing a powerful Liberal machine in Nova Scotia, was almost beside himself at the apparent negligence of the overseas minister. The men, he warned Borden, would vote as they did in civilian life if firm action were not taken. 'If it is desired to secure a very large favourable vote overseas, it is most important ... that every province should send over a skilled campaigner. At least there should be a strong committee of hard and skilful workers there whether they are gathered there or sent from Ottawa.'[39]

Perley promptly solved the problem. In a mood of deep depression and frustration he had proposed to Borden in June that he would carry on through the election campaign as overseas minister but without standing as a candidate. Once the election was over, he could then revert to the appointment he had always cherished, the high commissionership. Someone else could take over Perley's ministry.[40] Borden never acknowledged the letter but reports from Perley's supporters in Argenteuil were consistently gloomy. Bitter and resentful that his plea for sympathy had never been answered, Perley again cabled Borden on 14 September. Regretting that he had never had a reply to his earlier message, he concluded: 'In my opinion best solution make me High Commissioner, appoint another Overseas Minister. Am finding this additional work too heavy carry on permanently ...'[41] Again there was no reply from a prime minister totally immersed in negotiations which were shattering the English-speaking wing of Laurier's party.

Those negotiations, launched furtively and with many setbacks during the summer, were suddenly sent hurtling when Meighen's War-Time Elections Bill was rammed through the House of Commons. With the help of closure, the Conservatives literally rearranged the franchise to suit themselves in a conscription referendum. The wives, mothers, daughters, and sisters of soldiers won the vote; aliens from enemy countries, naturalized since 1902, lost it. In a few days, the electoral prospects of the Liberal party were utterly reversed. On 6 October Parliament was dissolved and a week later the arrangements for a wartime coalition finally jelled.

The political transformation, combined with a four-day holiday, had transformed Perley's mood and his prospects. His constituency agent was now jubilant. Perley cabled at once to Borden to withhold action. 'Am now prepared continue my present work here,' he assured the prime minister, 'It has been represented to me that my leaving Cabinet now might be misconstrued and that change in Overseas Minister just now might prejudicially affect soldiers' vote.'[42] It was far too late. Faced with squeezing ten Liberals into his cabinet, Borden had held Perley's proffered resignation as a valued bargaining chip. Even the high commissionership had been offered at one stage to the venerable and unlikeable Sir George Foster. In a hurried message on 13 October Borden gave Perley the news; 'Have arranged your appointment as High Commissioner in view of your strongly expressed desire but it may be necessary within six months or year to make different disposition ...'[43] When the new Union cabinet was announced, Sir Edward Kemp was transferred from the Militia Department to the Overseas Ministry and his place was taken by one of the earlier Liberal recruits to the coalition, Major-General S.C. Mewburn of the ill-fated Canadian Defence Force.

Perley was bitterly hurt. Characteristically, Sir Robert Borden had never realized that his friend had really wanted praise and reassurance, not a tentative and brusque appointment as high commissioner. The prime minister had never understood why Perley could prefer the appointed office to the ministry and he was doubtless astonished when Perley poured out his injured feelings in a long letter of acceptance. Obviously, Perley implied, Borden had made the appointment reluctantly and against his own best judgment. That, he complained, was unfair: 'Any time that your opinion and mine have varied, I have usually found you were right.' At long last, he could complain about his lengthy ordeal:

I have been under a very heavy strain for a year. I have said little about it but the military organization here was in very bad shape and I really did not know myself what a mess it was in. I imagine that no one can ever realize what I have gone through in putting it right except those immediately around me. No money could have tempted me to do it in peacetime and I only tackled it out of loyalty to you and desire to do my utmost in this war. At the same time the work was most interesting and from now on it will not be nearly so difficult. I think Kemp will find things in good shape & I will do anything I can to assist him.[44]

An abashed Borden found a few moments to dictate a cable of reassurance and gratitude before returning to the endless electoral crises of his new Union organization. Perley was also instructed to continue to deal with 'all matters large and small' until Kemp would arrive at the end of November.[45] That, of course, would include electoral duties. Once again, Perley balked. The precedent of highly partisan high commissioners had, of course, been well established by Sir Charles Tupper, who had alternated his London duties with regular salvage operations for the Tories during the Macdonald era. Perley felt differently. 'If the High Commissioner is to fight in elections,' he told Borden, 'the only argument in favour of his present legal status falls to the ground and he should be a member of the Government.'[46] However ingenious, this attempt to revive Perley's old dream of cabinet status for Canada's London representative was no more acceptable to the prime minister than before. Instead, if the government wanted an overseas campaign manager, it would find someone else.

The choice fell on Hector McInnes, a Halifax corporation lawyer and active Conservative who happened to be in London on behalf of his client, the British Empire Steel Corporation. At Perley's request, McInnes threw himself into the struggle.[47] The large pool of surplus Canadian officers may not have represented much military expertise but it included a galaxy of political talents. The quartermaster-general at Overseas Headquarters, Briga-dier-General A.D. McRae, took charge of British Columbia voters in a pro-vince where Conservatives had been shattered and Unionism was never strong. His assistant, Colonel Donald M. Hogarth, a Conservative member of the Ontario legislature for Port Arthur (and one of Carrick's dependents) looked after his own province's soldiers. At McCurdy's insistence, Lieute-nant-Colonel Joseph Hayes, medical officer of the Eighty-fifth Battalion, was given leave to look after Nova Scotia voters and later was assigned to manage voting by Corps headquarters units.[48] Sir Edward Peacock, a brilliantly suc-cessful Canadian-born London financier, became chief fundraiser for the overseas campaign. Lord Beaverbrook, who had long since forgotten his pro-mise to run for Borden in the Ontario riding of Northumberland, automati-cally became chief publicist for the campaign. He supplemented a flood of pamphlets, posters, and handbills by launching the *Canadian Daily Record*, a tabloid newspaper that conveyed the government's viewpoint with a wholly deceptive air of objectivity.[49]

The formal campaign organization for the overseas election, with its culling of lists and its production of what politicians insist on calling 'literature,' was supplemented by the usual combination of promises and good works. A knighthood was expedited for the distinguished literary doctor, Andrew Macphail, ostensibly because he was that year's Cavendish Lecturer at Oxford, more substantively because he forsook his accustomed Liberalism, defended the government from the allegations of Colonel Bruce, and even volunteered to stand as a candidate in his native Prince Edward Island.[50] Men of the 5th Division, their formation as superfluous as ever, were assured that conscription and a Union victory would guarantee a transfer to France. Otherwise, the division would be broken up and its officers and men would become scattered reinforcements.[51] When a Conservative organizer, busy censoring letters from the troops, discovered an unexpected opposition to conscription, action was taken. 'In searching for a reason,' Lieutenant Earle Logan reported to Perley, 'I find that the men are "fed up" and do not want their relatives to come out. Again, I find that in a great many cases the brothers of those here are the sole support of the family in Canada.'[52] The result was a promise, backed by extensive publicity throughout the CEF, that the next-of-kin of men already in the army would not be conscripted.

The Conservative-Unionist campaign was spurred by dramatic warnings from McCurdy and Dr J.D. Reid, the minister of customs, of frantic Liberal efforts. A cable drafted on Borden's instructions warned Perley that the prime minister had 'reliable information that trenches are being flooded with Laurier campaign literature.'[53] A few weeks later, on 12 November, Reid warned: 'No doubt whatever Liberals have money and organization ... they are enthusiastic over organization in England and France for soldiers' vote.'[54] This would have been news to Laurier. Having fought the Military Voters' Act, the Liberal leader seems to have given little further thought to its implications. The English-speaking Liberals who might have been concerned were often in the throes of defecting to Borden. Even the task of finding three Liberal scrutineers to supervise the overseas vote showed a party in disarray. Senator Raoul Dandurand declined the honour on the grounds of his wife's health. Charles Hyman, a former cabinet minister, was not only ailing but pro-conscription. A former lieutenant-governor from Saskatchewan first accepted and then declined. As the deadline approached, Laurier reluctantly settled on W.R. Hearn, a Glace Bay lawyer, Godefroy Langlois, Quebec's agent-general in Paris, and the notorious W.T.R. Preston.[55]

A former newspaperman, company promoter, and immigration agent, Preston had first been hired by the Liberals in the 1880s to perform some of Oliver Mowat's less elegant election chores. His rewards were a succession of patronage jobs, including legislative librarian, an evil reputation among Tory partisans and Liberal purists, and the nickname of 'Hug the Machine' Preston. He brought to his task, which he had actively sought, a thorough knowledge of electoral skulduggery, a voluble righteousness which had doubtless commended him in his day to Mowat, and a total commitment to Laurier. As for the major issue of the day, 'I would join the rioters,' he assured Laurier, 'before I would allow any conscription Act to be administered by that gang of political pirates in Ottawa.' It was, perhaps, significant that Laurier had ignored Preston's repeated offers of help until the last possible moment.[56]

Formation of a Union government abruptly ended negotiations for $25,000 from P.C. Larkin, the Toronto tea magnate, to fund the Liberal campaign in England and France. Alexander Smith, another veteran Ontario Liberal organizer offered sound advice on the way to approach soldier voters: 'in my opinion the work should be handled by persons who have been in (or are in) and understand the soldiers' game. Returned soldiers could take this work on and permit me to suggest that those at the front not be bothered with campaign literature.'[57] However, not even 'Silent' Smith could find such workers. In desperation, Laurier turned to an old supporter, Alexandre Clément, a pharmaceutical agent in London. Would Clément be willing to mail literature sent to him from Canada? Clément would be delighted – if $600 were deposited in his Paris bank account.[58]

There was no such pricetag for Preston's services. Even in early September, he began to feed his leader with allegations of electoral manipulation and chicanery and if the details were vague they also fed Laurier's growing sense of betrayal and conspiracy. By the end of October Preston had established his headquarters in the premises of the National Liberal Club, down the street from the Canadian High Commission. He was busy devising leaflets, pursuing possible supporters, and cultivating sources within the notoriously leaky Canadian headquarters. As an official scrutineer, Preston received twenty-five dollars a day and expenses but there was no official help for his campaigning. 'With regard to your request as to the carrying out of propaganda and organization,' Sir Richard Turner stiffly informed him, 'I can only say that the activities of all political parties in this respect must be subject to the provisions of King's Regulations and Standing Orders.'[59]

The campaigning styles of the two overseas Liberal scrutineers were in marked contrast. Like Laurier, Langlois made no pretensions to military knowledge. After decorous consultations with Perley and Preston, the veteran Quebec politician was assigned a staff car and an escorting officer and spent the campaign in leisurely tours through the war zone.[60] For his part, Preston was indefatigable. He also opened total war on the Canadian military authorities. 'I beg to inform you,' he warned Turner, 'that the office of the High Commissioner for Canada is instructing officers of the Canadian Expeditionary Force to canvass and organize the Soldiers Vote for Government candidates, and also that a list of Constituencies has been given to officers with instructions that they are to do the utmost to secure the election of the Government candidate in those seats.'[61] Military ambulances, he claimed, were shuttling loads of campaign literature through the streets of London. Medical officers were canvassing the sick and wounded. Chaplains at Witley had delivered pro-government sermons to men of the 5th Division.[62] 'Under instructions from Sir Robert Borden's Cabinet, Army Officers who are filling "safety" jobs are mobilized to organize and secure your vote in support of the Government,' proclaimed one of Preston's newspaper advertisements, 'It is no secret that this horde of "cushey" officers is to organize and distribute the "floating vote" to constituencies in which, but for this nefarious work, the Government Candidate will be defeated.'[63]

There was substantial truth to many of Preston's charges. The military organization, over Perley's misgivings, was undoubtedly doing its best for the Borden government, particularly in England. Answering one of Preston's tirades, Turner made it clear that he did not view political neutrality as an officer's obligation: 'It is my view that an Officer has the right to allow his views on political questions to become known to the men of his Command provided that in giving expression to these views he does not violate the provisions of the "King's Regulations" referred to. When an Election is being held, as in the present case, it is not only desirable but necessary that the soldiers should be permitted to discuss the National issue with those to whom they look for information and guidance in all their affairs.'[64]

In retrospect, one might wonder why the Unionists tried so hard with their soldier voters. Surely soldiers were sufficiently favourable to conscription and to a more vigorous prosecution of the war not to need harangues from chaplains? Surely there was no point in stretching military discipline by a reversion to politics? Even if opinion polls had been available to spread their dubious assurances, the campaign might still have been strident and unethical. In England particularly it was the work of the surplus or soon-to-be surplus officers. Robbed of a chance to do much in the war, humiliated by the charge that they had grabbed safe jobs, they turned to the campaign as a way of making themselves useful using skills which, in many cases, had earned them their commissions. Lieutenant-Colonel W.E. Thompson, the former Liberal MP and eventually appointed as one of the three Unionist scrutineers, was a case in point. An able but elderly militia officer, he had spent his time since his battalion had been broken up inspecting camps and performing various odd jobs. Meanwhile, one of his sons was wounded in France and another was crippled for life.[65]

The McInnes organization had two basic tasks: to secure the support of the great majority of soldiers and to ensure that their votes were applied, when possible, to the constituencies where the contests were closest. To the first task, it brought government promises – preservation of the 5th Division, a furlough to Canada for the 'Old Originals' of the First Contingent, exemption from conscription for brothers or sons still in Canada. Sir Douglas Haig was annoyed by a Canadian request to move the Corps – exhausted and decimated by its costly symbolic victory at Passchendaele – into a quiet sector so politics could proceed.[66] Distributing votes was more complicated. Paradoxically, it was made easier by the Liberal insistence that section 3 of the new act was wider than it was. Read scrupulously, the right to choose a constituency was limited to at most a few thousand soldiers. Read under the impression that a 'forgetful' voter could apply his ballot wherever he chose, it was an open invitation. In the election forms, nothing in block capitals, bold type, or plain English instructed the troops to vote where they claimed to live.[67]

The mechanism for directing votes was simple. Party managers in Canada – usually cabinet ministers or their nominees – forwarded their assessment of needs to A.E. Blount, Borden's private secretary.[68] Few extra votes were needed for the west, more for Ontario, and a good many for Nova Scotia, where the provincial Liberals played double games with the Unionist cause and old party loyalties ran deep. As usual in electioneering, perfection fell victim to human nature. The McInnes organization could not possibly identify all the voters eligible to use section 3 nor could it forestall attempts by candidates or their friends to do a little private organizing. Speaker E.N. Rhodes profited from his brother-in-law's command of the big Canadian ordnance depot at Ashford. Brigadier-General W.A. Griesbach, the popular commander of the 1st Brigade, could count on a special effort to beat his veteran Liberal opponent in Edmonton West, Frank Oliver. An Ontario colonel in the Canadian Forestry Corps confessed that he simply could not keep his men from voting for him. 'Hepburn is here,' McInnes reported to Blount, 'and I am writing for the purpose of saying that so far as he is concerned he is playing the game fairly and does not want to gather a great many votes to the disadvantage of others. It is not easy to control the men who are voting in the constituencies named by others; there are not very many, but they insist on voting as I have said.'[69]

As the polling period approached, propaganda rained on the troops. Eight Liberal members of the new government explained their differences with Laurier. Eighteen Liberal editors, headed by Stewart Lyon of the *Globe*, J.W. Dafoe of the Manitoba *Free Press*, and Joseph Atkinson of the Toronto *Daily Star*, assured soldiers that the new régime in Ottawa would 'deal with conditions in Canada and abroad, which have been subject to criticism in the past.'[70] More than paper was used, if Dr Hayes was typical of the overseas organizers. Having done his duty by the Eighty-fifth Battalion and the Second (Coloured) Construction Company, both of them Nova Scotia units, Hayes took charge in the Corps rear area: 'Many O.C.'s lined their men up and told them plainly what they wanted them to do as a matter of duty ... Also many of the Chaplains took the stump and gave 10 minute addresses before the curtain at the shows each night.' In this atmosphere it was not hard for Hayes to collect a couple of hundred votes for each of the nine Ontario and seven Nova Scotia constituencies in need of help.[71] The Liberal counter-barrage was barely discernible. One surviving brochure, addressed to the 'Soldier-Boys of South Huron,' would have bewildered any recipient. Preston's final broadside from London was longer on vitriol than argument:

While you, with true British courage and amazing fortitude, have faced and are preparing to face, appalling conditions and stupendous sacrifices, political vultures at home have been fattening and are prepared to fatten still more, upon public expenditures and public necessities. Colossal fortunes have been amassed by Government pets through exorbitant profits, who have made no personal sacrifices nor suffered any personal inconvenience. The political hangers-on in Ottawa have been raking in the gold, while you and your comrades were being raked by German shells.[72]

The overseas polls opened for voting on 1 December. In Britain, senior officers like General Garnet Hughes and Frank Meighen served as presiding officers for their camps while colonels and majors supervised polling in their own units. In France, a special organization under Colonel Frank Reid gathered junior officers and clerks at Boulogne and then dispatched them across the war zone to find the scattered members of the CEF. Eventually teams travelled as far as Italy and an officer dispatched to Gibraltar and Salonika drowned when his ship was torpedoed.[73] According to Reid, the prospect of voting aroused great enthusiasm. In military hospitals he claimed,

'Certain instances exist in which the patient was sufficiently interested in the election to cast his ballot even although his condition was so serious that his decease followed within two or three days immediately succeeding.'[74]

No other accounts reflect such a mood. In the Fifteenth Highlanders, there were no speeches; only an implied threat that anyone who voted for Laurier would be ducked in a nearby horse pond. In an Alberta battalion, the orderly sergeant was allegedly posted by the ballot bag to instruct soldiers to place their 'X' next to the Union government. Other officers regarded the election as an annoyance or a colossal irrelevancy. During some of the campaign period, Seely's Canadian Cavalry Brigade was involved in the battle of Cambrai. During the last desperate phase of the battle, surrounded by Germans, with dead and dying all around, Seely's sole surviving signaller decoded an urgent message: 'Reference Canadian General Election now proceeding, please note your signal troop will vote as a unit and not with the Royal Canadian Dragoons.'[75]

One officer who resolutely and angrily stayed out of the campaign was Sir Arthur Currie himself. He had no doubts at all about conscription, and he had been delighted when Newton Rowell, the Ontario Liberal leader, had put that cause above party. By autumn his mood had changed. Though he had obediently included an appeal for men in his message accepting the Corps command, he angrily refused to be used in the Unionist campaign in the autumn. What had seemed a necessity had now become a political game, particularly as Borden and his colleagues successively watered down the Military Service Act with exemptions. By November there were no men to replace the 15,654 casualties suffered at Passchendaele. Promising to keep the 5th Division became mere politics in Currie's eyes. Not only did it deny him men for his depleted ranks; it preserved a venomous enemy in a position of influence.[76] Increasingly Currie blamed high-ranking intriguers around the Overseas Ministry for the vague and hostile rumours circulating about his management of the Corps, particularly at Passchendaele. When Perley, on a flying visit to the Corps on 4-5 December, pleaded with Currie to send a pro-government message to Canada, the Corps commander refused. Was it vengeance or a deliberate insult that the message from the Liberal newspaper editors had been addressed to Currie 'or to the Acting Commander of the Canadian Corps'?[77] At once he complained to Perley and was indignant when Sir George refused to take his grievance seriously. To his friend Harold Daly Currie poured out his anger: 'The truth of the matter is this, Harold, that the Government supporters are quite anxious to see that one is protected ... There are some things occurring which make me suspicious that there are in England now some, whom one might expect to play the game but are not doing so.'[78] Fortunately for Currie, cooler advice from McInnes, conveyed through his London bank manager, reassured the Corps commander that the Unionists' victory was assured and that he did not need to relinquish his political neutrality.[79]

In England, the atmosphere during the weeks of voting was much more fervid. The war was remote, the military politicians in command of training battalions could treat the election as a campaign, and Preston was available as an enemy. Sir Richard Turner had none of Currie's inhibitions about using his influence. 'If the people of Canada would only realize that in order to maintain our Divisions at full strength men who have been wounded have to be rushed back as soon as they are fit without the leave or rest to which they are entitled,' he wrote in an election message, 'I believe there is not a patriotic civilian in Canada who will not stand heart and soul behind you in your endeavours.'[80] In France, Langlois motored complacently from polling station to polling station, reporting that all was above-board: in England, Preston was busy collecting evidence which, he believed, could annul the election. Not only were officers like Turner openly partisan; Laurier supporters had been deliberately transferred to the front; 'Twelve such men were sent out to "No Man's Land." Not one of them ever returned.'[81] Even such charges paled beside his own unceremonious treatment by military authorities. On 4 December, a day after voting began at Witley, Preston invaded the polling station of the 208th 'Irish Canadians,' announcing: 'I am Mr. Preston and I protest that vote in the name of Sir Wilfrid Laurier.' Lieutenant-Colonel W.P. Malone, the commanding officer, promptly shut the poll for lunch. When Preston returned in the afternoon with undiminished zeal, Malone demanded his credentials. Preston had none. A guard was summoned and Preston spent the rest of the afternoon in the battalion guardroom before an officer from 5th Division headquarters arrived to offer a half-hearted apology.[82]

A week before voting ended Sir George Perley could report that most of the ballots had been collected and that everything had gone as the government could have wished. The credit belonged to McInnes and to two politically ambitious soldiers, Hogarth and Brigadier-General Manly Sims, who had abandoned his role at Haig's headquarters to throw himself into the campaign in France. Understandably, Perley appropriated some of the honours for himself: 'The foundation had been laid during the past twelve months as I have endeavoured to make the force feel that everyone gets fair play irrespective of politics or favouritism ... A year ago there was a general feeling of dissatisfaction but I shall be very much surprised if the vote now over here is not very strongly in your favour.'[83]

The outcome of voting in Canada made the overseas campaign almost irrelevant. Except in a few close contests, the soldiers could not settle the election. With only civilian voters, Borden could command a majority of 45 in a House of Commons of 235 members. In view of the storm of suspicion raised by the Military Voters' Act and its operation, it was just as well.

Throughout the campaign, Laurier had pleaded in vain for Preston to furnish evidence for his violent charges.[84] In fact, Preston's proof could only be found in the mounds of ballot bags now growing in Paris, London, and Ottawa. Much turned on procedural technicalities. Before completing his ballot a soldier filled out a questionnaire on the back of a covering envelope. In addition to the familiar questions about name, rank, number, and branch of service, a soldier stated whether or not he was a British subject, had voted previously, and had enlisted in Canada. Question 6 asked for an address at which the soldier had lived for at least four months before enlisting while question 7 asked him to specify the appropriate electoral district. For those who professed themselves unable to answer either question 6 or 7, question 8 asked a soldier to state an address, however transitory, at which he had lived. Finally, for the benefit of those who had never resided in Canada at all, question 9 invited a would-be voter to choose a constituency. Once an officer had certified the answers, a soldier received a ballot and could mark it for the Government, the Opposition, Labour, or an Independent or, if he ignored strong warnings, he might even write in a candidate's name. The ballot was sealed in the envelope and stuffed through an aperture in specially made ballot bags.[85]

Even in defeat, Preston and the Liberals could win themselves consolation by proving that the election had been stolen. In London the counting process became a running battle. Preston lost the first round when Colonel Purney, not W.J. Griffiths of the High Commission, presided. He won a second round when he insisted that Liberal observers must be present when the ballot bags were opened. At once they found suspicious evidence: tightly rolled bundles of envelopes, too thick by far to have passed through the aperture. Any experienced postal clerk would have explained that letters frequently wadded during the handling of mailbags. Instead the Liberals, specially sent over from Ottawa, demanded that the bags be set aside. Purney pleaded, argued, and finally threatened to fire the Liberals on the spot, leaving them to pay their own way back to Canada. With Laurier's approval, they capitulated. The next battle was more serious. Thousands of soldiers, admitting Canadian addresses, had ignored questions 6, 7, and 8 and claimed a constituency under question 9. A bag from the ordnance depot at Ashford was almost wholly directed to the Cumberland riding where civilian voters had narrowly rejected Speaker Rhodes. Another bag gave 132 of 231 votes to an Ontario constituency in which only one voter, the Unionist candidate's son, professed to reside. In Paris and Ottawa, Liberal scrutineers found identical evidence. In Paris, Langlois derived a certain gaiety from the combinations: 'Des quatres coins de la planete une pensée aimantée a dirigé le cœur de ces hommes vers le Témiscamingue, terre de prédilection et d'espérance.'[87] Even more flattering was a fondness for a region of his native province: 'Je dois insister sur le fait que tous ces electeurs qu'un sympathie aussi vive que particulière a orienté vers le Gaspé, sont tous des soldats de langue anglaise.'[88]

Perhaps if the election had been closer the Unionists might have fought harder for the questionable ballots, bolstering their argument with the widespread sympathy for the rights of the soldier. Instead the new government conceded that the Act had miscarried. Rowell, the intensely moral Methodist who had precipitated the Liberal Unionist movement, expressed horror when a former clerk reported to him that he had been asked to switch his vote from West Lambton to Hamilton West. 'Surely such ballots should be disallowed,' he expostulated to the prime minister.[89] They were. O'Connor and J.G. Foley, the clerk of the crown in chancery, agreed without apparent cabinet interference that ballots from soldiers who had enlisted in Canada but who had not answered questions 6, 7, or 8 would be set aside. The results were drastic. In Paris, Langlois reported that 8,200 out of almost 130,000 ballots had been ignored – and there might have been more if his British Columbia scrutineer had not been in collusion with his Unionist partner. In London, Preston estimated that 13,000 out of almost 100,000 ballots were rejected while Hearn in Ottawa claimed 15,000 out of only 52,000.[90]

By late February the military results began to filter into the press. Borden had hoped that the soldiers might add as many as five seats to his margin. He underestimated. The Canadian portion of the military vote, released a week before the overseas results, altered two critical seats. In Cumberland, Rhodes was saved; in Edmonton West, Oliver was ousted by General Griesbach. On 1 March, as the overseas totals were added, Liberal margins began to crumble. In fourteen ridings, five in Nova Scotia and two in Prince Edward Island, the soldiers altered the outcome. McCurdy, McInnes, and Hayes had not laboured in vain.[91]

Thanks to Preston, the echoes of the attempt to manipulate the soldiers' votes would resound for years while few noted that the suspect ballots had never been counted. In a clumsy subterfuge, suspected by British police as a sudden outbreak of German espionage, Preston tried to collect details about

Canadian military voters at Witley.[92] Then, abandoning his lawsuit against Colonel Malone, he hurried home to Canada to arm a shrunken Liberal caucus with his shocking evidence. A nervous government gradually relaxed and the House emptied as a burly A.B. Copp droned on through the myriad of details and allegations. The government easily defeated Copp's motion for an investigation by 92 to 61 and even the Liberals had grown tired of their champion before long.[93]

In time Preston's version of the villainy in the overseas election would become a familiar fragment of Canadian history. The fact of massive, organized vote-switching would survive; the accompanying fact that the votes were ignored would be forgotten. 'Is there not something very sad about the demoralization of the youth of our country,' wrote a beaten William Lyon Mackenzie King in 1918, 'when their first experience of the franchise resolves itself into base deception of the high purpose they have at heart in their exercise of it?'[94] Neither the soldiers nor the future prime minister would ever understand each other. In a life stripped to the basics, the overseas soldiers wanted a government which would take them and the war seriously. They voted with a grim cynicism and without much thought of the consequences for Canadian unity or French-Canadian disaffection. Major C.G. Power, who had returned to his native Quebec to run as a Laurier candidate, had at least an understanding of the soldiers' reasoning: 'I do not think any impartial student of history would give any verdict other than that very extensive frauds were practised. However, he would also come to the conclusion that these frauds were neither systematic nor effectively organized, and that, as far as the military voters were concerned, the tide of sentiment was running so strongly for what they really believed to be the patriotic cause that it is difficult to attach much condemnation to the acts of fraud that were undoubtedly committed.'[95]

8

Kemp's Ministry

If there was one Unionist minister who could be confident of re-election, it was Sir Edward Kemp in his old constituency of Toronto East. Born in a modest farming family south-east of Montreal in 1858, Albert Edward Kemp was almost an archetype of the self-made man, starting as a bookkeeper and ending as the millionaire president of Sheet Metal Products, director of the National Trust and Imperial Life Insurance, and past-president of the Canadian Manufacturers Association. A devout Tory partisan, bustling, aggressive, and sometimes pompous, Kemp was a contrast to the man he succeeded. Perley had been punctilious, patient, and diplomatic and very much in love with the British society in which the war had found him; Kemp was blunt, decisive, and, from the first, found London a bleak, frustrating, and largely uncongenial environment.[1]

Kemp's introduction to his new department was certainly ill-starred. Leaving his supporters to demolish his opponent, Kemp sailed for England a fortnight before the general election. An Atlantic crossing in winter is often an ordeal and, during wartime passages, Kemp discovered that cabin doors were kept open to prevent jamming in the event of being torpedoed. As a result, the new minister spent his first two weeks in London recovering from pneumonia. When he was able to take up his responsibilities, he found little to restore his spirits. British morale sagged disastrously in the wake of the Passchendaele tragedy. Lord Lansdowne, a former governor general of Canada and Conservative foreign secretary had publicly asserted the need for a negotiated settlement and the answering indignation only partially concealed a fear that the elderly aristocrat might be right. The bright hopes which had launched the Lloyd George government a year before were now badly tarnished. In official circles savage gossip undermined the reputations of politicians and generals alike.[2] A growing food shortage, the outcome of submarine warfare, added to demoralization. 'I met many people,' Kemp reported, 'who are well able to pay for all the food they can obtain, who admit to me that they are not getting sufficient nourishment.'[3]

In such a frame of mind Kemp easily found fault with the department he had inherited: 'I find the organization here somewhat peculiar in many ways, as it does not follow along the lines altogether, of any organization of similar character either here, or in Canada. It seems to have evolved out of a situation which developed in the early stages of the war. I intend to make some changes which I think will be of advantage and cause things to run more smoothly.'[4] To his surprise Kemp found that his predecessor had never really established either a proper office or a personal staff in the ministry. In large measure Sir George Perley had appointed officers and officials like Turner and Gow and left them to carry on with a minimum of interference. It was an arrangement which had given a very large measure of satisfaction to the senior soldiers and it had spared Perley the unwelcome burdens of routine administration. The new minister had different ideas. He would run the ministry on his own business-like terms and he would run it personally.[5]

Kemp was also clear that he was now the ranking Canadian official in England. So was the prime minister. When Perley reported that the British government would now welcome a Canadian minister at renewed sessions of the Imperial War Cabinet 'for purposes of information and counsel,' it was Kemp who attended. Perley's renewed claim that his office of high commissioner should be a cabinet portfolio was dismissed even more brusquely than usual.[6] In the power game Perley had clearly lost. Kemp's burden of representing Canada appears to have been limited to sessions on 2 and 5 January 1918, at which he basked in general rejoicing over the Unionist electoral triumph and delivered a sharp warning that Canada's manpower had been stretched to the limit and that Canadians felt like waiting until the Americans had contributed a proportional share.[7]

However, the new overseas minister was more concerned with correcting the problems of his own department than with war cabinet diplomacy. Some of his new problems, like the surplus officers, had been aggravated by his own policies as minister of militia. Earlier he had insisted that the government must keep faith with the men who had raised dozens of understrength CEF battalions; once in England he had to deal with the consequences. In his first report to Sir Robert Borden, Kemp announced that he had launched a further comb-out.[8] The consequences were predictable and bitter. Summoned to Argyll House to discuss the alternatives of reversion to the rank of lieutenant or prompt return to Canada, the surplus officers turned their rage against the ministry and its officials. Now it was Kemp's successor, Major-

General Sidney Mewburn, who had to listen to their complaints. The outrage of Major A.T. Hunter, a Toronto lawyer and Liberal-Unionist, was typical though his language was more picturesque than most:

Those of us who are returned superfluous in France to be disposed of at the English Base found an atmosphere more fetid than ever. We found that Argyll House reeked with the smell of the Winnipeg Tory kennel. It is true that there were ornamental officers who were supposed to deal with personnel. But these know no more about the personnel than you know of political 'discretion'. I took the trouble to find out who were running the machine. General Turner is not; he is a lock-up fetish.

This Argyll House cabal is too thick for either a decent Liberal or a decent Conservative. I travelled back on the Missanabie with 150 surplus officers fresh from their experience in callous insult. To say that they were peeved would not express it. If the steamer had lost her coal, she could have put a few of these gentlemen below the boilers and come home on her own steam. Their experiences will not be forgotten or forgiven even when senile decay sets in.[9]

The direct targets for much of the abuse were Turner's aide-de-camp, a son of Robert Rogers, the former minister of public works, who acted as gatekeeper against disgruntled officers, and Major F.F. Montague, another Winnipeg Conservative, who had been summoned from France in March 1917 to take on the delicate and thankless task of dealing with the extra officers. By January 1918 he had persuaded 476 officers to revert to lower rank, at considerable loss of pay as well as status, but not all could qualify even for lower rank and very few, like Hunter himself, would admit that adverse reports were justified.[10] 'Very few of these surplus officers were willing to return to Canada,' Sir Richard Turner explained, 'and practically all of them had grievances of one kind or another.' Turner could speak from experience: he had seen most of the senior ones himself, sometimes on three or four occasions.[11] For Kemp it was an exasperating and politically costly legacy of the Hughes recruiting system, but he was soon persuaded that his officers had handled the problem with fairness and patience: 'Some of these men carry back to Canada weird tales and grievances, some of which have to be taken with a grain of salt. The greatest amount of patience has been exercised by everyone here who has had to deal with these officers and statements to the contrary are unjustifiable. I cannot refuse to see these officers personally, and I have given all those who desired to see me a hearing, although it has been done at a great sacrifice of valuable time.'[12]

The problem of the surplus officers which had plagued the CEF since 1915 suddenly found a possible answer within a month of Kemp's assumption of responsibility. As a result of the losses in the Passchendaele offensive and the government's refusal to trust Haig with Britain's last, failing reserves of military manpower, the British Expeditionary Force had to be reduced. An ingenious solution was adopted: the number of infantry battalions in each brigade would be reduced from four to three. The total number of divisions would remain the same but the infantry, which suffered the greatest casualties, would be cut by a quarter. It could also be argued that the Americans at some time in the future might provide enough infantry battalions to rebuild the British infantry divisions to their old strength.[13] Since the Canadian Corps generally abided by the establishments set for the British army, the War Office assumed that the Canadians would follow suit. However, with conscription guaranteeing an additional 100,000 men in uniform, Canada had no need to reduce her manpower at the front. Instead, with the addition of a mere six battalions from England, she could have six of the smaller divisions at the front instead of four. These, in turn, could be organized into two corps under a small army headquarters. By adding only a few thousand men, Canada could help the Allies to boast that they had actually increased the number of divisions braced for the inevitable German spring offensive.[14]

The idea appealed to a good many powerful interests. It was forcefully promoted by Field-Marshal Sir William Robertson, the chief of the Imperial General Staff, who conceived of his responsibility, in Lord Beaverbrook's dismissive phrase, as 'sending every possible man and boy to fight the Germans in France.'[15] It would appeal to Canadian pride that the dominion finally had a full army in the field and one more division than the Australians. Sir Sam Hughes's boast of a fifth and sixth division would finally be fulfilled. To no group was the prospect more welcome than to the Canadian officers, particularly those in England, who would almost certainly share in the rain of promotions and staff appointments necessary in creating headquarters for an army, another corps, two divisions, and six new brigades in France. Alive to the rumours, Major-General Garnet Hughes had offered to bet his former friend, Arthur Currie, any amount he wanted that the 5th Division would be in France in 1918.[16]

The 5th Division was a growing embarrassment. Although the British kept home a surprisingly large force against the remote risk of a German invasion, it was increasingly far-fetched to suggest that Hughes's division at Witley was making any contribution to victory. In Canada Borden had discovered that, whatever its other merits, conscription was no quick solution to the problem of manpower. Political promises and widespread exemptions had allowed most apparently eligible young men to avoid service. It would take months to transform the remaining conscripts into soldiers, transfer them across the submarine-infested Atlantic, and funnel them through the reserve battalions in England. Meanwhile, reports that barely convalescent soldiers were returning to the front while healthy, well-trained men of the 5th Division rested in England had troubled the election campaign. On 7 November 1917 Borden had warned Perley that the new cabinet's war committee wanted the division broken up for reinforcements.[17] Determined to harvest votes at Witley, Perley ignored the directive. On 4 January, when the prime minister demanded a progress report, Perley replied evasively that Kemp 'has it in hand.'[18] Borden was not pleased.

It never seems to have occurred either to the War Office or to the Overseas Ministry that the Canadians might not imitate the British reorganization. On the very day that Robertson's formal proposal arrived at Argyll House, General Turner was in France to consult Currie about possible senior commanders and staff officers for the new organization.[19] Sir Edward Kemp was easily convinced of the undoubted efficiency of the 5th Division and of the folly of leaving it in England. The arguments were persuasive. The war effort was approaching a crisis. Canada would certainly have to commit more manpower to the western front but, since the equivalent of the artillery for five divisions was already in France, only eight thousand more infantry and five thousand men for other arms and services would be needed. Surely Canada could sustain such a modest addition. Finally, and unsaid, was the prompt and pleasant solution of the problem of surplus officers, to say nothing of satisfaction for the impatient General Garnet Hughes and his officers.[20] In Ottawa Borden felt that he could only concur in Kemp's recommendation but his reply was unexpectedly unenthusiastic:

Having regard to present conditions we feel that the increase proposed by the War Office involves a supply of reinforcements during the next twelve months which it will be extremely difficult, if not impossible, to provide. On the other hand we thoroughly realize that in the presence of a tremendous enemy offensive such as seems imminent it is our duty to put forth an effort even beyond that which it may eventually be possible to sustain.

You are therefore authorized to carry out the proposals of the War Office if you are convinced that the necessities of the situation imperatively demand it. We shall do our utmost to provide reinforcements which will keep the six divisions up to strength but the War Office must distinctly and positively be informed that we do not and cannot give any absolute undertaking that this will be possible. In that case it may be necessary to reduce to five divisions of ten battalions each, which is practically the strength which has been maintained since the Canadian Army Corps was officially constituted.[21]

Kemp was chastened by the prime minister's distinct warning note. It had already become apparent that any such reorganization would have the rooted and forceful opposition of the Corps commander. No sooner had Sir Richard delivered his message on 11 January than Currie dispatched an urgent invitation to the overseas minister to join him in France: 'This question involves so much and influences so greatly the fighting efficiency of our Expeditionary Force that I feel that I should explain to you personally my views in all their detail.'[22] Having maintained it as a unit during the summer and winter battles of 1917, and having devoted considerable thought to the strengthening and better use of its supporting arms, particularly the engineers, Currie was indignant at any suggestion that the vaunted Corps should be split into two smaller and weaker forces. He knew very well that the small Canadian army headquarters would be a feeble symbol, not a forceful expression of Canada's military maturity. Worse yet, Currie suspected that the entire scheme was being promoted by incompetent, politically influential officers with Garnet Hughes at their head. Finally, Currie was indignant that such a fundamental reorganization had apparently been hatched without his prior knowledge.[23]

Burying his personal pique and jealousies, Currie mustered an impressive case against the proposed changes. The Canadian Corps, he insisted, had developed a strong team spirit and there would be more than disorganization if that *esprit de corps* were shattered. What seemed like an advantage to Kemp – and even to Borden in Ottawa – was wasteful overhead to Currie. The additional artillery units, ancillary services, and no less than ten additional staffs would add very little to fighting efficiency, while they would drain the pool of trained talent in an organization in which competent staff officers were already at a premium. Still, for all his arguments, Currie felt that he had not persuaded his new minister when he received a personal summons to London on 2 February.[24]

Kemp had, in fact, been badly shaken by Currie's opposition and by Borden's warnings. In London Sir William Robertson pleaded with the colonial secretary, Walter Long, to wire the governor general in Ottawa, expressing the British government's strong wishes in the matter. Long referred him politely to Kemp. Instead Robertson went to Perley to seek his support. Lord Beaverbrook, urged on by Garnet Hughes, asked Lloyd George to intervene. He was politely rebuffed: 'Our cock won't fight,' he told his friends.[25] When Currie reached London on 5 February, he was armed with the views of his own senior officers and a strong statement from Sir Douglas Haig. Whatever Sir William Robertson might feel, the British commander-in-chief claimed that reorganization of the Canadian Corps was neither necessary nor desirable for the time. If it were pressed, then Currie must be promoted to general and given command of the new Canadian army headquarters. On 6 February Currie met with Kemp, Turner (who had been converted to his views),[26] and Walter Gow. At the end of the session, Currie's objections were embodied in a lengthy and persuasive memorandum, reciting arguments about wasteful overheads and the potential damage to the cohesion and morale of the existing Corps. As a counter-offer, Currie proposed to add a hundred men to each of the existing infantry battalions, a proposal which would actually put twelve hundred more men in the line than the proposed increase to six smaller divisions. It would also be easier, if reinforcements failed to materialize, to withdraw this increment than to disband a whole division.[27]

Kemp was persuaded although he waited until 8 February to announce his decision. Haig's support was important but Kemp had also been impressed by Currie's blunt, factual arguments and perhaps also by the fact that the Corps commander was also arguing against his own promotion. Currie's memorandum formed the basis for Kemp's memoranda to both Borden and Lord Derby, the British secretary of state for war, explaining why the Canadians would not be moving to the new organization. After a few weeks, while the War Office sought confirmation of Haig's views, the matter dropped.[28]

That decision settled the fate of the 5th Division. It also aggravated the problem of the surplus officers. On the very day that Currie had argued persuasively against the new organization, a telegram had arrived from Borden urging that at least a third of the positions in the new divisions be reserved for officers in England while those who had reverted to get to France should have a chance to regain their old ranks.[29] Now there would be 460 additional officers to place and, apart from subalterns, captains willing to revert, and a few highly technical officers, the rest must shift for themselves. Indeed, the problem was aggravated because the British, by disbanding 145 of their own battalions, now faced a surplus of forty-five hundred officers of their own. Currie offered the best terms he could, taking former Corps officers back at their old ranks, accepting captains as supernumeraries in his own battalions, and absorbing any of the divisional staff for whom vacancies existed.[30] By the end of the month, the adjutant general of the Overseas Ministry could report that 3,050 of the men of the division were on their way to France as reinforcements while the remainder were being dispersed to the reserve battalions.[31] Despite the bitterness and frustration, there were no overt demonstrations of protest.

Disposing of Major-General Hughes proved more difficult. Turner offered him the command of the largest Canadian training camp in England. Instead

Hughes insisted that he was entitled to return to France. He demanded that Kemp recall Major-General L.J. Lipsett, a British officer who had served on the militia staff before the war, come out with the First Contingent, and who now commanded the 3d Division. Dismayed at the prospect of presenting either Currie or the War Office with such an ultimatum, Kemp checked with the prime minister. To his relief, he discovered that the Hughes clan had finally exhausted its political credit. General Hughes was obliged to settle for unpaid employment with the War Office.[32]

Though he had succeeded completely in persuading his new minister, Currie was by no means satisfied by his success. As in earlier arguments over his appointment to the Corps command or his role in the 1917 election, Sir Arthur seems to have believed that his authority, at least within the Corps, should be not only pre-eminent but also unchallenged. It had become too easy for him to see legitimate arguments as manifestations of conspiracies, a paranoia which in some cases though by no means in all, might be justified. As the senior Canadian officer in the field, Currie had willy-nilly to accept that he was now subject to the buffeting of public opinion, whether from the followers of the ex-minister of militia or from his own irreverent and increasingly disparaging soldiers. Much later, Currie would profess to Canadian audiences that 'My fight was not with regular officers at all. It was with Canadian authorities in London.'[33] In fact, the extension of effective Canadian control over the CEF by Perley and Kemp meant that the Corps commander, too, would be accountable to his own government.

That kind of accountability was Kemp's explicit goal. If Perley had been satisfied that Canadians gained control over their own military administration, his successor took the next step by subordinating that growing authority to civilian, political control. As a critic of the Carson organization, Sir George Perley had insisted that what was needed in England was a unified authority: by appointing Turner to be general officer commanding, Perley had implemented his own idea. Kemp, for his part, was determined to transform the Perley system into the structure he had come to know as minister of militia. He was also determined to extend the effective influence of the Overseas Ministry over Canadian forces at the front, particularly to the thousands of railway and forestry troops spread across much of France. Both goals demanded an extensive reorganization.

Perley's Overseas Ministry was closely analogous to the Canadian Department of Militia and Defence before 1904. Under a minister of militia, authority had been divided between a general officer commanding and a deputy minister. This arrangement, associated with increasingly public quarrels between the ministers and their generals, had been transformed in 1904 when Laurier and Sir Frederick Borden had remodelled the departmental hierarchy to follow the British example. The new Militia Council allowed the minister to meet with a number of senior staff officers and civilian officials and the senior military adviser, the chief of the general staff, was more the first among equals than a commander.[34] Though there was no evidence in the Overseas Ministry of the civil-military friction that had led to the 1904 change, Kemp plainly preferred a system with which he was familiar and which allowed him to be a fuller participant in decision-making.

The obvious loser was Sir Richard Turner. The vague additional powers he had gained in June 1917 as compensation for Currie's command of the Corps had never really materialized. His right to 'consult with the British GHQ on matters of policy and administration connected with the Canadian Forces in the Field' had remained wholly symbolic.[35] Perley's attempt to find an amicable and clear basis of co-operation between his two senior generals had not really succeeded. Simply because he held the more important appointment, Currie could deal directly with the overseas minister when he chose, and he had done so.[36] Perley had attempted to reassert Turner's authority in a long memorandum addressed to the War Office on 27 November 1917, underlining that his GOC held the senior appointment, but such demands made little difference in the internal dynamics of the Canadian administration.[37] Now, after three months of consultation with Turner, other senior Canadians, and Sir Arthur Currie (who frankly regarded the changes as irrelevant), Kemp was prepared to move. The long-suffering Borden, who must have presumed that he had heard the last of overseas reorganizations, was subjected to a long explanatory cable:

Organization which existed after the Overseas Minister was appointed and up to the present time must be considered as tentative although a step in advance. I discovered soon after arriving that there was friction between Corps Commander and our Liaison Officer who represented Minister in France [Sims] also between former and G.O.C. London. Besides this there was absolute lack of co-ordination between different important branches which led to inefficiency and perhaps what was of more importance there was lack of appreciation of what was understood by constitutional methods as against Military control.

In addition to strengthening his political authority over his senior officers, Kemp was concerned about the growing army of Canadians outside the Corps. By the beginning of 1918 more than 50,000 men were working in forestry units or in railway construction and operation, playing a vital role in solving Allied logistical problems but largely beyond Canadian control. They could hardly come under Currie while Turner was uncertain of his authority over them. However, the central problem was the relationship between Currie and Turner. The former wanted Kemp to have proper military guidance on policy decisions but he was not confident that Turner gave good advice. The answer, worked out despite threats of resignation, was a replica of the Militia Council, advisory in role, co-ordinating in function. 'It relieves the Minister practically of no responsibility,' Kemp explained to Borden, 'but it will be of much assistance to him and his Deputy Minister and all concerned in forming substantial organization to deal with important problems which otherwise are dealt with unfortunately by individual judgement and assist in bringing about co-ordination of work of different administrative branches in London which are unavoidably in six different localities separated from one another in some instances by two or three miles.'[38]

Kemp had, in fact, felt acute frustration in coming to grips with the Overseas Ministry. In an early letter to the prime minister, he had complained of the lack of political awareness of his senior officers: 'The men holding the more responsible positions have in the past for the most part taken very little interest in public affairs in Canada. The most of these men have been over here three years or more and the more of military life they have seen, the less likely they are to appreciate such a thing as Public Opinion in Canada.' If Perley had prided himself on eliminating political considerations from the overseas administration, Kemp found himself trying to restore at least a sense of political realities: 'One of my greatest difficulties is to endeavour to instil into their minds that all we have done has been done by the grace of public opinion.'[39] The effort was not welcome. In a pale reflection of the simultaneous struggle between British politicians and generals for control of the war effort, Kemp faced senior Canadian officers who insisted that the overseas forces must be under strictly military management. It was, after all, the system adopted by both the Australians and the New Zealanders and though there might be real friction between the generals in the field and the respective defence ministers, it was not widely known.[40] Pressure against Kemp's proposed overseas council took the form of an anonymous memorandum proposing that Sir Arthur Currie should become general officer commanding Canadian overseas, reporting directly to Ottawa, eliminating all the intrigue and petty scheming which allegedly prevailed.

Unlike the British controversy, which ended with the forced resignation of Sir William Robertson, the humiliation of Lord Derby, and the removal of several of Haig's senior staff officers, the Canadian dispute ended quickly and peacefully, with both Turner and Currie backing the minister. When a copy of the anonymous memorandum reached Currie, he dispatched it immediately to Kemp, offering to comment only if invited.[41] Turner backed his political superior with a strong memorandum, noting the advantages of having a cabinet minister on the spot, able to gain direct access to the British secretary of state for war and arguing that Canadian and Australian circumstances were quite different. While the latter had few units in England and conducted their training under British auspices, half the overseas forces of Canada were located in Britain and a third of the Canadians in France were outside the Corps. A consultation with the high commissioners of Australia and New Zealand, Turner suggested, might reveal that their arrangements had not proved an unqualified success.[42]

Once the principle of an overseas council had been imposed, it remained to choose the members. Kemp's original nominees included Turner as general officer commanding, Thacker, the adjutant general, Brigadier-General D.M. Hogarth, who had replaced McRae on 19 February, as quartermaster-general, the accountant-general, Colonel Ward, and the director-general of medical services, General Foster. Borden, concerned perhaps because Kemp's system resembled the ill-starred Sub-Militia Council and certainly because the London version might force changes on the Militia Council in Ottawa, asked that any appointments be held over until his forthcoming visit to England. In any case, he wanted the director-general of medical services to be no more than an associate member while there should also be an associate member to represent the Canadian forces in France.[43] Kemp refused to wait. He gave way on Foster's status, promised future consideration on a representative from France, and insisted on an order-in-council signed by the prime minister himself. By 11 April he had his wish.[44]

Having won, in effect, a vote of confidence from his Ottawa colleagues, Kemp showed no precipitate haste in organizing his new council. Since one of its advantages was a proper recording and implementation of decisions, a secretary had to be chosen with considerable care. The choice fell on Major Gordon Harrington, a young lawyer who had already served for two years as mayor of the turbulent coal mining town of Glace Bay and who was destined later to lead his fellow Conservatives as premier of Nova Scotia from 1930 to 1933. On 1 May Kemp could inform Lord Milner, the new secretary of state for war, that Turner's designation would henceforth be Chief of Staff, Overseas Military Forces of Canada, with duties as 'First Military Member of the Overseas Militia Council, and Chief Military Adviser to the Minister, Overseas Military Forces of Canada.'[45]

Between them, Kemp and Harrington set out to prove that the new council would be a healthy contrast to Carson's version. Procedures resembled those of the Militia Council in Ottawa, with memoranda submitted in advance, a set agenda, and a formal report on decisions reached. At the first meeting, on 14 May, all members were present except the ailing Walter Gow. Committees were appointed to investigate a number of departments. A report was demanded on the cost to Canada of loans of personnel between the British and Canadian forces.[46] Though a month and a half separated the first and second meeting of the council – doubtless due to the arrival of Sir Robert Borden, meetings resumed on 27 June and continued at regular intervals, with three in July, three in August, and twenty-seven in all by the time the Overseas Ministry closed its operations in London in September 1919. During the council's lifetime, it recorded 434 formal decisions. The extent of its concerns is reflected in its own final report:

The subjects considered from time to time have been so varied in character as not readily to admit of classification. Generally speaking the decisions which Council has been called upon to give have related to organization and policies, financial and other relations with the British Government, expenditures of an extraordinary nature, the write-off or charge to individuals of losses of public property, pay and allowances, establishments of all units and formations, and confirmation of all promotions and appointments within the O.M.F. of C.[47]

If Kemp was slow to assemble his new council, it was because even more of his energies had been directed to strengthening his authority over the Canadians in France. It was obviously a more difficult and a more important initiative. Apart from a few initial excursions, more to resolve problems than to assert a principle, the War Office had never questioned Canadian authority over the CEF in Britain; in France, interference with the doctrine of a unified command of all imperial forces was obviously more disquieting, even for Canadians like Currie. It had not been apparent to the Corps commander, for example, that his interests in the reorganization controversy had been better served by Kemp than by Sir Douglas Haig.

Kemp made no claim to interference in the tactical employment of the Canadian Corps but he was increasingly concerned at the growing number of Canadians, for whom his government would be expected to pay, who served beyond Currie's authority. During his visits to France, Kemp had been delighted by the reputation of the Canadian railway troops, and their commander Brigadier-General J.W. Stewart had been acknowledged, he told Borden, as 'the ablest railway construction administrator there is in France.'[48] The companies of the Canadian Forestry Corps, scattered from the Scottish Highlands to the Jura Mountains and the border with Spain, beat the German blockade by their timber production for the British army. More thousands of Canadians, some of them surplus junior officers, had joined the Royal Flying Corps – officially, 13,345 had transferred to the Royal Naval Air Service, the RFC, and their successor, the Royal Air Force by 1 April 1918.[49] These units and individuals and even small fighting formations like the Canadian Cavalry Brigade might easily be forgotten when Canada's war effort was compared with the Australian or New Zealand contribution but they would not be overlooked by the financial officials at the War Office.

In September 1917 Brigadier-General Thacker, as adjutant general, had proposed that he should become officer in charge of administration for the Canadians outside the Corps.[50] The suggestion was not accepted and, during his months as acting minister, Perley had neither the incentive nor the power to pursue the matter. Indeed he was quite satisfied with the services of Colonel Manly Sims at General Headquarters and he was more than grateful for his vigorous electoral services as the Union government's chief scrutineer in France. Unfortunately, Sir Arthur Currie had grown to detest the Canadian representative as an ill-intentioned meddler.[51] It had been apparent to Perley that the right way to assert Canadian authority in France was through a Canadian officer at General Headquarters; it was soon apparent to Kemp that the officer could no longer be Sims.[52]

After extensive talks with officers in France and England, Kemp had evolved a plan. Slightly reformulated by the deputy minister, Kemp's proposal called for the creation of a Canadian section at the Second Echelon of General Headquarters, commanded by a brigadier-general who would both represent Canadian interests and assume responsibility for Canadian units outside the Corps. The proposed section would include representatives of the adjutant general, quartermaster-general, director-general of medical services and of the chaplains' and dental services. Except for military operations, it would be a direct channel between the Canadian Corps and London. 'It is believed,' Gow wrote, 'that this would have the full sanction of the War Office as it had been repeatedly intimated that it is only in matters affecting military operations that it is felt G.H.Q. must be consulted.' Obviously too, Gow argued, the officer selected to command the Canadian section must be acceptable to Currie: 'One clear-cut point emerges from consideration of the present conditions and that is that the sooner the situation is recognized and the remedy applied, the better; otherwise matters will grow steadily worse and chaos ultimately result.'[53]

The War Office showed no particular opposition to the expanded organization and enhanced responsibilities of the proposed Canadian section once the Canadian representatives had reiterated that they had absolutely no intention of interfering with the operational authority of the British command. Indeed, it might well be preferable to have a single channel through which the Canadian minister could exercise his authority. At a meeting at the War Office on 19 March such full agreement was achieved that Currie was summoned from France to add his own views.[54] The Corps commander was of decidedly mixed feelings even when he learned that Sims would not be part of the new organization. More clearly than Kemp or Turner, he perceived that the head of the Canadian section would rapidly become more powerful than a mere intermediary particularly if, as the British proposed, he would have discretion in deciding what to refer to the British commander-in-chief.[55]

Unfortunately, Currie did not have much leisure to express his views. Summoned to London on the nineteenth, he arrived on the twenty-first, the day the great German offensive was finally unleashed. That night he was ordered back to France and, although he had time for a brief meeting next day, he was back at his headquarters on the night of the twenty-second.[56] It was just as well. The German assault had turned into the greatest British military disaster of the war. The weakened divisions of the Fifth Army, still recovering from their experience at Passchendaele, dissolved under German artillery and gas bombardment and disintegrated in the face of the new German infiltration tactics. Currie's 2d Division had been pulled into GHQ reserve, the 1st Division was held in army reserve, and the 1st Canadian Machine Gun Brigade, the pride and joy of the innovative Colonel Raymond Brutinel, was ordered south to shore up the crumbling British defences.[57]

For the first time since the early autumn of 1914 the Allies faced the real prospect of total defeat. Virtually throughout the war and with terrible losses, troops in trenches with even limited artillery support had been able to throw back attackers. Now British troops, who had always prided themselves on bulldog defence, had apparently simply given up.[58] Currie, for one, was appalled. Was this the outcome of the vicious, demoralizing slander campaigns in the London clubs and the lobbies of Westminster? After Passchendaele, he had warned that Canadians would never again serve under General Sir Hubert Gough; it was now Gough's army that had collapsed.[59] Within a week, to meet the desperate pressures on his front, Haig had taken all four of Currie's divisions, scattering them among two armies under three corps headquarters. Currie's headquarters went into reserve.

As the Canadian commander knew, this was inevitable. An army corps was merely a grouping of two or more divisions and the Canadian Corps had been unusual in retaining its cohesion for so long. However, Currie was also convinced that his four-division corps was a brilliantly effective tactical instrument as well as a national symbol and he wanted it restored. To Haig's chief of staff, Lieutenant-General Sir Herbert Lawrence, Currie made his point as trenchantly as he could: 'From the very nature and constitution of the organization it is impossible for the same liaison to exist in a British Corps as exists in the Canadian Corps. My staff and myself cannot do as well with a British Division in this battle as we can with the Canadian Divisions, nor can any other Corps staff do as well with the Canadian Divisions as my own.'[60] To Kemp he wrote on 27 March explaining what had happened to his organization: 'For a time it may be that the Corps will be divided. I have urged verbally and in writing that to get the best out of the Corps it must be kept together and I have intimated that I am sure this is what the people of Canada desire most. I know that the Commander-in-Chief is most sympathetic with this point of view, but when a terrible battle like the one raging now is going on it is not an easy matter to withdraw at once a whole corps from the line ...'[61]

When the overseas minister got Currie's letter on 29 March, he was shocked. No one had told him that an army corps was normally a flexible organization nor, beyond frightening rumours could he be aware of the desperate state of the British Expeditionary Force. At once, assuming that Currie's letter was a veiled appeal for backing, Kemp went into action. In a letter to Lord Derby, he urged the reunification of the Corps: 'Without in any way presuming to interfere with the conduct of operations in France, permit me to point out that the Canadian Corps has become most efficient under its present leadership and it is believed that the high morale which exists in the Corps is due to the fact that it has been kept together.'[62] The request was equally promptly forwarded to Haig and the harried British commander-in-chief, bitterly resentful at the interference, managed to restore three of Currie's four divisions by 8 April. Currie, who had by no means expected to alter his chief's dispositions, was marked down in Haig's diary as suffering from a swollen head.[63] Almost unintentionally, Currie and Kemp had interfered with operational decisions. As a result, most of the Corps had been reunited and left to guard a long and vital stretch of the line from Vimy Ridge to Arras, almost twenty-five miles. Fortunately, the Germans chose other objectives for their subsequent assaults.[64]

Faced with defeat and the likelihood of a growing gap between his armies and the French forces, Sir Douglas Haig had finally abandoned his opposition to the appointment of a supreme commander for the western front. On 26 March at Doullens, French and British representatives met and accepted General Ferdinand Foch as over-all commander of the Allied armies. Even as the British generals painfully accepted their subordination, Sir Edward Kemp pursued his own efforts to clarify and extend Canadian authority over the Canadians in France. On 29 March the Overseas Ministry formally sub-

mitted its organizational proposals to the War Office and asked for a conference to work out the details. A chart accompanied the proposals, indicating
that the Canadian section would be the intermediary not only for the Canadian Corps and Canadian troops outside the Corps but for the Canadian
reinforcement and records organizations at the BEF's Third Echelon as well.[65]

Despite other preoccupations, the War Office organized a meeting with
Kemp, Turner, General Thacker, and Harrington on 2 April. British representatives led by the director of staff duties all offered their own reservations.
The director of personnel services reminded Kemp that the Canadians were
subject to the Army Act for discipline and that its administration rested with
the commander-in-chief. The deputy director of operations insisted, perhaps
in light of the controversy over the Corps, that Haig must be able to send
reinforcements where he chose and that he must also be consulted on senior
appointments. Kemp cheerfully conceded both points. The assistant military
secretary wondered whether British officers serving with the Canadians
would be replaced without reference to GHQ. The deputy director of staff
duties insisted that details of establishments must be passed through General
Headquarters. In both cases Kemp satisfied the War Office misgivings.[66]

The potential for misunderstanding survived, however, as Kemp discovered from the War Office letter recording the results of the conference.
'The Canadian authorities do not wish to interfere at all with military operations or discipline,' the War Office draft recorded, 'the changes which they
wish to introduce being unimportant matters. On all important matters, e.g.
discipline, allotment of reinforcements, appointment of senior officers, etc.,
the Canadian authorities welcome the check afforded by recommendations
being sent through G.H.Q.' Such an interpretation might have reassured
Haig but to the Canadians it was almost deliberately insulting.[67] The letter
was returned to the War Office with significant amendments. For 'unimportant matters' was substituted 'in matters affecting only the organization and
administration of the Canadian troops.' The ensuing passage was altered in
tone and substance: 'On important matters such as allotment of reinforcements in emergencies, establishments, appointments of General Officers
and those which from their relation to military operations should properly
receive consideration from G.H.Q. France, the Canadian authorities will welcome the assistance offered by recommendations sent through G.H.Q.
France.'[68]

The War Office swallowed the amendments and dutifully forwarded the
letter to Haig. It was just as well. When Walter Gow returned at the end of
April he complained that Harrington should have made it clear that even in
emergencies GHQ could act only in an advisory capacity. However, Gow was

eventually persuaded that his point was superfluous.[69] A more substantive question was how the machinery of consultation with General Headquarters would actually work. As at least Harrington now understood, considerable discretion would remain with the head of the Canadian section, particularly in deciding when matters of administration and organization might have a bearing on operations. On the promotion of general officers, the head of the Canadian section would first obtain an informal approval from GHQ, followed by the unofficial approval of the minister. Only then would formal recommendations pass through the successive levels of Corps, Army General Headquarters, and Army Council to be published in the *Gazette*. The section would exercise full administrative control over Canadian units outside the Corps.[70]

Because of the successive German offensives, it was not until 6 May that Kemp paid a visit to General Headquarters at Montreuil, spent a few not altogether friendly minutes with Haig, and left a copy of Harrington's memorandum. At the end of May, Harrington visited France to win approval from the senior officers of the Corps. After preparing the ground with Brigadier-General N.W. Webber, Currie's trusted senior staff officer, Harrington saw the Corps commander. Once he realized that the head of the Canadian section would be no more than a brigadier-general and that his own access to Haig would remain, Currie warmed to the idea. He approved Harrington's memorandum and concluded that, if the arrangement did not work out well, it would be a matter for Canadians to settle among themselves.[71] Much relieved, Harrington could now present the British commander-in-chief with both a united front and the most explicit statement to date of how autonomous the Canadian overseas forces had become:

For matters of military operations the Canadian Forces in the Field have been placed by the Canadian Government under the Commander-in-Chief British Armies in France. For matters of organization and administration, the Canadian Government still retains its full responsibility regarding its Forces. Matters of organization and administration frequently have a direct bearing on military operations and discipline and vice-versa and it is therefore considered that where they have such bearing these matters should be made the subject of conference between the Canadian authorities and the G.H.Q. To meet this situation in the most effective manner a Canadian Section has been formed at G.H.Q.[72]

Unfortunately, the controversy was by no means at an end. British politicians and the War Office might be willing to concede something to Canadian autonomy; GHQ had more old-fashioned views. On 23 June Sir Herbert

Lawrence returned with a comprehensive list of amendments, all of them restoring the Canadians to a state of dutiful subordination. Instead of the complicated consultative process for promotions, appointments of brigadier-generals and above must be submitted as formal recommendations to the commander-in-chief. No transfers or changes of skilled officers in the Canadian administrative troops could be made without the approval of General Headquarters. No change in scales of equipments or supplies or the methods of issue and return would be made without the approval of the quarter-master-general.[73] However, Kemp and his officials had learned a few lessons of Whitehall bureaucracy. The Overseas Ministry acknowledged Lawrence's letter, expressed polite thanks for the assistance of GHQ in allowing recommendations of general officers to pass through its channels, and ignored the rest.[74] Lawrence evidently decided not to pursue the matter.

Among the minor casualties of the German offensives was the career of Brigadier-General Manly Sims. Lord Beaverbrook, his former chief, had held open a position in his newly created ministry of information as long as he could but, by the time Kemp and Currie had agreed on a successor, the offer had long since expired. The unhappy Sims found, like others before him, that political services had not guaranteed him employment.[75] Kemp would have been delighted to get Brigadier-General James MacBrien, a highly respected young permanent force officer with lengthy staff experience, but Currie would not part with an officer who might soon be needed to command a division.[76] Instead, the choice fell on Brigadier-General J.F.L. Embury, the former commanding officer of the Twenty-eighth Battalion, a brigade commander in the 5th Division, and, briefly, of the 2d Brigade. Currie had concluded that Embury was really too old for active service but he had every other qualification. Politically, he was a dependable Tory, a perennial candidate for his party in the pre-war years, and a Unionist scrutineer in the overseas election. In explaining the appointment to Lord Milner, the new secretary of state for war, Perley also explained that, in addition to recommendations from Turner and Currie, Embury had just been appointed to the Saskatchewan bench. He could thus bring judicial as well as military qualities to the appointment.[77] Embury, on leave in Canada, returned promptly and submitted dutifully to the principles Kemp had worked out for his new creation:

(1) That the will of the Canadian Government through its responsible Minister, is supreme in all matters relating to Canadian Forces and Canadian Personnel.

(2) That in matters relating to Military operations, there has been delegated to the Commander-in-Chief of the British Forces control of all Canadian Troops under his command with respect to Military operations.

(3) That the Officer Commanding the Canadian Corps shall not have the Corps' personnel or policy interfered with without his consent. In cases where differences arise which cannot otherwise be disposed of, the matter shall be referred to the Minister for decision.

Embury's instructions then dealt systematically with the possible conflicts between the various principles, indicating the officer who, in each case, would have the authority to make a final decision. Throughout the document it was apparent that Kemp wished nothing to interfere with the development of the Canadian Corps as a homogeneous organization nor did he wish the Canadian section to develop into an independent authority. Having dealt at such length with potential disputes, Kemp belatedly added a more positive-sounding fourth principle: 'it is essential that all questions be approached in a spirit of mutual trust and good will, and that a sincere desire shall prevail to work in common accord for the efficiency of the whole.'[78]

In mid-July, General Embury took up his new appointment. Although Currie had protested the possibility that he might lose control of senior service and departmental appointments in the Corps, both Kemp and Embury had set his mind at rest.[79] Like Sims, Embury took over the costly responsibility of entertaining Canadian official visitors and, somewhat to the alarm of Overseas Ministry officials, the Canadian section began to grow at a healthy rate. 'It is urged with great respect,' Embury reported on 22 September, 'that this Section should be given more scope than that suggested in the initial stages of its career, and the time for putting forward proposals for a Permanent Establishment shall have arrived.'[80] To meet his needs, Embury demanded sixteen officers, seventy-three other ranks, eleven cars, three motorcycles, and seven horses.[81] In London Turner protested feebly against such an expansion from Sims' modest entourage but conceded to Kemp's priorities: 'As this Section was practically organized under the Minister's instructions, I presume he accepts the responsibility for the necessity.'[82] Embury stuck to his guns and the establishment was approved. At Kemp's insistence, the Canadian section was also formally approved by a Canadian order-in-council on 22 September. In that way, Kemp hoped, 'such an important matter as our relationship with the British Army may be thoroughly understood by the Government generally.'[83]

Embury's Canadian section continued to function and to grow until the war's end, when it assumed even greater responsibilities for the demobilization of the Canadian Corps and for the adjustment and settlement of Canadian affairs in France. Kemp looked with pride and joy on his creation, commenting after the war that: 'After the Canadian Section at G.H.Q. had been working for a short time, it became apparent to the Imperial authorities that the new department was a great success and they expressed their entire satisfaction with the arrangements. It was of great use to General Currie and the Corps. There was splendid co-operation in every way and it resulted in more efficiency, less delay, and greater satisfaction generally.'[84]

In six months, Kemp had wrought significant changes in the overseas organization. If Perley had done much to eliminate the confusion and political manoeuvring of the Hughes-Carson era, his tool had been the new generation of Canadian soldiers tested by experience in France and endowed with a prestige that Carson and other militia politicians had utterly lacked. Kemp had restored political control without restoring more than a slight infusion of the old political favours. As a self-made businessman he had sufficient respect for the self-made generals of the CEF to consider their opinions. An even greater contrast between Kemp and Perley was in their respective attitudes to Britain and the empire. If Sir George was more protective of Canadian interests than his critics alleged, he remained at heart an imperialist, at home in English society, eager to see Canada flourish within the glory and the constraints of the British Empire. Kemp could certainly give a strong imperialist speech; he could hardly have survived otherwise in Toronto Tory politics. At the same time he arrived in England with a confidence in Canadian ways and a contempt for those of England which grew steadily in the ensuing months. If Canadians had to leave Canada to get a good opinion of themselves, Sir Edward Kemp was living proof. So were most members of the CEF.

9

Final Stages

By creating the Overseas Ministry and the Canadian Section at GHQ, the Canadian government had established means to control all but the tactical disposition of its expeditionary force. A force which had entered the war as virtually an integral part of the British army had developed in three years virtually to the status of an allied army. It was both a paradigm and a precedent for Canada's own transformation from self-governing colony to sovereign nation.

However, control by Canada did not necessarily mean control by the Canadian people. To the undoubted dismay of officers accustomed to the complacent Sir George Perley, Kemp had forcefully reminded his staff that 'all we have done has been done by the grace of public opinion.'[1] By 1918 that public opinion had turned querulous from exhaustion. For most of the remaining belligerent powers the war was now little more than a desperate endurance contest. The French army, driven to mutiny in 1917 by its pointless sacrifices, could hardly be depended upon. The British, bled white by Passchendaele and the March losses, faced drastic cuts in fighting strength. Having twice rejected conscription, Australia could no longer fill the ranks of her AIF. Thanks to conscription, Canada would have men but they would be no substitute for the eager volunteers of 1915 and 1916.[2]

Borden's electoral triumph on 17 December only appeared to unite Canada for the last phase of the struggle. Backed by eight provincial governments, all Conservatives of note, many Liberals and almost every English-speaking newspaper in the country, the new Union government seemed to have no critics left outside French Canada. That was an illusion. Large numbers of Canadians had ignored patriotic appeals and voted for Laurier. Thousands, disfranchised by the War-Time Elections Act, masked their feelings but felt no allegiance. Unleashed and vociferous were those who had denounced the Tories for a half-hearted, mismanaged, or corruption-smeared war effort and who now demanded a drastic reform. Why else had Liberals like Newton Wesley Rowell or Frank Carvell entered the government? Why else had Liberal organs like the Manitoba *Free Press* or the Toronto *Globe* or *Daily Star* supported them?[3]

Almost inevitably, the demand for changes focussed on the Overseas Ministry. Liberals had not forgotten their opposition criticisms of the experiment merely by crossing the floor, and Sir Sam Hughes continued to feed the hostility. So did returning Canadians. The Ottawa *Citizen* published a long letter from Lieutenant John Quinney describing an imaginary tour of Argyll House to visit officers promoted from political favouritism, a former amateur golf champion earning promotion by teaching senior officers how to play, and the sons of Tory politicians sheltering safely from war in a paradise of 'slackers in khaki.' In a later issue, Corporal H.L. White, formerly of the Pay Department, claimed that few of the non-commissioned officers in his department had ever seen active service. The Quinney and White claims were widely reprinted, often to be bolstered by charges from returned officers.[4]

Quinney and White may well have been false witnesses. Colonel Ward reported that White's father had first asked for his son to have a safe job in the Pay Office and then confessed that the young man 'had a screw loose.' Quinney had been returned to Canada after a court martial and a claim by his former commanding officer that he was 'below average in courage.'[5] However, the image of an oversized, arrogant military bureaucracy nestling safely in its red tape coincided with a public prejudice. Toronto's *Saturday Night* blithely denounced an institution that 'does what it pleases, spends what it likes and is under no sort of control whatever.' Its editor, Hector Charlesworth, left an impression of inside sources when he wrote: 'So many returned officers have brought nothing but complaints about Argyll House – its favouritism, its extravagance, its tragedy, its tuft-hunting, its colossal dunderheadedness – that the Union Government may presently take it in hand and give it a turn over.'[6] The Toronto *Daily Star* had earlier notified its Liberal readers that two of their stalwarts in the new government, General Mewburn and the Hon Newton Rowell, president of the council, would be going to England to 'look into certain desired reforms in the overseas military establishment.' In its best populist style, the *Star* argued that 'Canadian ideals have begun to droop in Argyle (sic) House':

Some of our Canadian officers, or officials, seem to have been away from their native heath too long. They need to be sent back for a while at least to have their batteries stored again with the Canadian point of view. They need to be sent home to have their mental chronometers adjusted.

Some of these men have been exercising so much official authority abroad that it would do them no end of good to come home for a month and on the plank walks of their home towns to be accosted by everybody as plain old "Bill".[7]

Kemp was infuriated by any suggestion that Rowell could conceivably be sent to inspect the Overseas Ministry. The corollary to any belief that the new Liberal Unionists would bring drastic reform to the management of Canada's war effort was that Tories like Kemp would be expected to do penance for past mistakes. Sir Edward would not play. Patriotism might persuade him to accept a wartime coalition but he owed nothing to Newton Wesley Rowell after his tiresome and wholly unreasonable demands for an excessive share of Ontario seats in the 1917 election. In his only fight as Ontario Liberal leader, Rowell had crashed heavily in the 1914 provincial election. If Kemp had to accept the sanctimonious Epworth Leaguer as a colleague, it was just as well that the Atlantic was between them. To Borden he had protested earlier rumours of a Rowell-Mewburn visit as placing him in 'a most embarrassing position.'[8] The *Star* report, which Kemp attributed to Rowell's personal inspiration, he described as 'the cheapest and lowest down thing' in all his eighteen years in politics. To Mewburn, with whom he maintained good relations, he explained that his sensitivity extended to the officers of his staff:

I would like to have you bear one thing in mind – that the officers over here are not quite the same as they are in Canada. They are not men of the Permanent Forces, with very few exceptions, but men who have occupied high and responsible positions in the business and professional life in Canada. They are, for the most part, men of strong character and are carrying on the same as the rest of us have with the object in view of doing their best and winning the War. If you do not succeed in leading them, you need not expect to get the best results by driving them ...[9]

The attacks continued. The Manitoba *Free Press* announced that officers at Argyll House had been seen wearing the red chevrons reserved for the heroes of Mons. Mewburn's secretary warned that *Saturday Night* had dispatched H.F. Gadsby, an erstwhile Liberal pamphleteer, to pursue the attack on Argyll House.[10] In Tom Blacklock of the Montreal *Gazette*, normally one of Sir Robert Borden's closest personal allies in the press gallery, the Overseas Ministry had found a vigorous, well-informed critic. Sir Edward Kemp prepared his defences. Turner summoned statistics to prove that the department had cut its staff from 134 officers and 566 other ranks and civilians at the end of the Carson period to 109 officers and 436 other ranks and civilians by 1 August 1917. By 1 April 1918, under Kemp, totals had fallen to only 70 officers and 346 soldiers and civilians. Far from being 'slackers in khaki,' 50 of the 70 officers had served at the front, 11 were unfit or overage, and only 9 had not gone.[11] In addition to figures, the prime minister gave an aggressive defence of the Overseas Ministry staff when he rose in the House of Commons on 20 March 1918:

May I direct attention to the fact that the officers in charge of this responsible work at Argyll House are men of high reputation. They are Canadian citizens whose names, for the most part, are household words in Canada. Generally they have abandoned occupations at great sacrifice to perform a service for their country. Heads of Branches have seen service at the front and they are continually pressing claims to be freed from onerous, difficult and exacting tasks with which they have to deal at Headquarters in order that they may return to the Front. I do not hesitate to characterize this propaganda, having in view the difficulty of these officers at this distance in protesting themselves, as being not only cowardly but unjust. I would thank you to call public attention to the matter.[12]

Kemp's words, repeated by the prime minister, drew applause from government supporters but they did nothing to convert enemies. Though Sir Sam Hughes's mental powers were now obviously failing, his prestige and his seat on the government side gave his denunciations added weight. On 6 May the ex-minister dismissed Kemp's ministry as a waste of money on a par with the War Lecture Bureau or the Dominion Police. Turner, he claimed, had been warned that he was committing military suicide. Sir Arthur Currie, he claimed, had 'no more conception of a democratic army than a hen of logic.'[13] Yet it was members of the official opposition who raised the key problem of the Overseas Ministry: it could not be held accountable to Parliament or, for that matter, to the cabinet. The prime minister or General Mewburn might answer for Kemp as best they could but rarely could they do so quickly or from direct knowledge. The result was that allegations and exaggerations could pass uncorrected into the public understanding while Kemp, in London, might well wonder whether his political reputation was being cheerfully sacrificed by the likes of Rowell for the sake of future political advantage.[14]

Typical of the political issues which confronted Kemp was the promise of furloughs to Canada for men of the First Contingent. The question had arisen in the summer of 1917 as a result of pressure from relatives of the

'Old Originals' as well as from the men themselves. It had become one of the benefits, argued both in Canada and overseas, of introducing conscription. Only if more men were found would it be possible to spare the hardened but weary veterans of 1914. As minister of militia, Kemp had argued hard for the proposal; more concerned by the overseas manpower shortage and by British resistance, Perley had been more cautious. Thanks to exemptions, conscription failed to produce a flood of military manpower and War Office objections persuaded both Australia and New Zealand to shelve furlough plans for their men.[15] Caught between a highly popular election promise and practical objections, the government compromised. Eventually about a thousand married soldiers and others with strong compassionate justification were permitted to take leave in Canada. More leaves were halted by the German offensives in March and the understandable reluctance of many of the First Contingent men to go back to France when they discovered that married men had been exempted from compulsory service. When Sir Robert Borden visited troops in France at the end of June, he was met by shouts of 'Leave, leave.' Soldiers and their political representatives were easily persuaded that a promise had been broken and the Overseas Ministry was the obvious scapegoat.[16]

Borden, for one, ignored most of the criticism, supported Kemp against criticism in Parliament and the cabinet, and pointedly reminded his colleagues, after he reached England in June, of the great difficulties the overseas minister had faced and the 'really fine results which he had achieved.'[17] Borden had good reason to be pleased that his friend had achieved more than structural changes. In addition to cutting the ministry and headquarters staff almost in half, Kemp and his officers reduced the fifty-seven infantry reserve battalions to only fifteen, at the cost of sending even more disgruntled senior officers home. The end of Hughes's recruiting method of creating CEF battalions meant that drafted Canadians were now sent to England soon after enlistment. For the sake of quarantine as well as basic training, the new arrivals were dispatched to segregation camps at Frensham Pond or Bourley Wood. In the autumn of 1918 the British made available a big hutted camp at Kinmel Park near Rhyl in north Wales. Partially trained men were then funnelled to reserve battalions or to a growing array of training schools and depots at one of four major Canadian training centres in England: Witley, Bramshott, Bordon, and Seaford. For the sake of economy in money and manpower, smaller Canadian camps and training centres had been closed or concentrated.[18]

Borden's greater concern, after his arrival on 7 June, was directed more at the conduct of the war than with the efficiency of Kemp's operation. For the first time a Canadian prime minister could turn to a senior Canadian officer for professional technical advice. Sir Arthur Currie, summoned to London for a meeting with Borden, spared neither the details nor his British superiors. The painful Canadian gains at Passchendaele, won at a cost of 16,000 casualties, had vanished in a single German thrust. An angry Currie claimed that his corps had put out 375,000 yards of barbed wire defences while other British corps commanders boasted that their men had put out a mere 30,000 yards or had been kept busy laying out lawn tennis courts. The Portuguese corps commander had put out none at all: his formation collapsed under the second German thrust. British intelligence Currie dismissed as useless and misleading. The Canadian general's judgments may have been harsh and unfair; they were also frank, blunt, and not unwelcome to David Lloyd George, the British prime minister, when Borden repeated them before the whole Imperial War Cabinet on 13 June. The result, as Borden later recorded in his memoirs, was a subcommittee of the war cabinet, composed of Lloyd George, the dominion prime ministers, and General Jan Smuts representing South Africa, 'to ascertain, by enquiry on all sides, from every possible source of information, what further effort would be necessary to win the war – in what sphere, in what field could the decisive blow be most effectively struck, and at what time.'[19]

The committee, on the best advice it could summon, military and civilian, set about planning a war effort which would certainly extend into 1919 and conceivably beyond. Within two months of its creation, it was wholly bypassed by events but Currie's independent information had helped make the Canadian prime minister a member of what could have been the key strategic planning agency for a prolonged war.[20]

Currie's grievances were by no means limited to his British colleagues. Though Kemp assured the prime minister that the old friction between Turner and the Corps commander had been alleviated, Currie continued to insist that enemies in England plotted against his reputation and sought persistently to undermine his prestige. Enemies Currie undoubtedly had. Senior officers found wanting in action or perhaps overstrained by the burdens of command, were unlikely to appreciate relegation to a training command in England any more than the officers they displaced, like Brigadier-General Charles Smart, welcomed an equally precipitate return to Canada.[21] Some of Currie's problems were of his own making. He won no affection from men in the ranks though he was admired by his immediate staff and by most senior officers because of his open-minded acceptance of ideas, his preference for spending material rather than lives, and his moral courage in standing up to his British superiors.

On the very rare occasions when Canadian soldiers met their commander, they saw a stout, pompous figure, all too commonly finding fault for trivial reasons. Currie's one attempt at grandiloquence, an order of the day during the German offensive, had sounded false and insulting to men who believed they needed no reminder from a mere general to do their duty. It was the widespread dislike of Currie among junior ranks of the Corps far more than the intrigues of the Hughes faction that threatened to undermine his reputation but it was a situation which he could neither understand nor could anyone, least of all Kemp or Turner, explain it to him.[22] In Newton Rowell, who had joined Borden's party for the first half of his summer visit, Currie sought a confidant for his discontent with Canadians in London:

We have still there, and have always had certain officers of high rank, who, despite that rank and despite the honours which they have been accorded, have been a positive harmful influence to our overseas organization. There are officers now there of very high rank, who, if they performed the proper functions of their office, would have more than enough to do to keep them busy, yet, it seems to me they spend most of their time visiting hospitals and convalescent depots, where they pat the wounded on the back and commiserate with them generally.[23]

Some part of Currie's problem, undiagnosed at the time or later, was that he was as tired and overstrained as some of the more junior generals he had sent back to England. Currie had, after all, been serving continuously at the front since February 1915 with only limited interludes of leave in England. Political leaders were tired too and often ill. Sir Thomas White, the minister of finance, spent the first quarter of 1918 convalescing and other ministers were run down and edgy. An ailing Walter Gow went back to Canada in the spring of 1918 to recover his health. He returned to find Kemp exasperated by Borden's entourage of cabinet ministers. First Rowell and James A. Calder, then General Mewburn and C.C. Ballantyne, the new minister of marine and fisheries, had chosen to join Borden in England. Mewburn was kept occupied by the series of minor personal complaints which various military petitioners sought to press on the Canadian prime minister. Ballantyne took it on himself to meet with the Admiralty and the new British Ministry of Shipping about arrangements for moving Canadian troops. An indignant Kemp intervened to claim that responsibility for his quartermaster-general. An appeal to the prime minister sustained the Overseas Ministry. It was no small relief when Kemp could see off his leader and entourage on 17 August.[24]

Then it was Kemp's turn to go back to Canada in his own search for rest and renewed strength, leaving his deputy minister, Colonel Gow, in charge. The arrangement should have been perfectly satisfactory. It was not. On the eve of Kemp's sailing, the deputy minister demanded a formal declaration that Kemp had delegated to him 'all and singular, the powers and authorities possessed by me.' An astonished Kemp refused. Gow protested, producing a similar statement which Perley had apparently executed during one of his absences. Kemp was unimpressed. No civil servant could be granted a minister's powers and Kemp knew it.[25] Once in Ottawa, a fortnight later, Kemp dutifully consulted the prime minister and promptly advised his deputy that Borden had ruled any such delegation to be both unconstitutional and inoperative. Surely, he argued, frequent cable communication would resolve any problem.[26]

Much more a lawyer than a civil servant, Gow insisted on pursuing the matter. By return telegram he argued that the same ordinance that authorized a deputy minister also allowed a full delegation of powers. As it was, he insisted, he needed the minister's approval for even the smallest decision. 'Without delegation,' he emphasized, 'I have no more power than man on street ... Am daily holding myself out as having authority which apparently I do not possess.'[27] Kemp, increasingly exasperated by the long-distance argument, attempted once again to be reasonable:

Cable was not intended to convey strained interpretation as you take therefrom or to alter in slightest degree situation as it has existed. Only intended that you should refer to me important matters which in your judgement might be necessary requiring prompt action. Premier on holiday will consult him when he returns. Am confident your functions or action with approval Minister are generally similar in character to other Deputy Ministers. Whatever formalities have not been complied with or may be necessary will have attention. Ministry having been carried on for nearly two years existing conditions think can be safely continued for short time without prejudice to any interest particularly as Government is agreeable.[28]

Gow was not placated. Clearly his position in London was different from that of other deputy ministers, if only because another cabinet minister was invariably persuaded to take charge of a department when the regular minister was away. Once again Kemp was obliged to pester Borden: 'I explained to him before leaving that all he had to do was to carry on the way he was doing. He appears, however, to take a very peculiar view of the situation.' The trouble, as Kemp saw it, lay with his deputy minister. Gow had spent seven of the previous twelve months on sick leave and he had returned from Canada in 'a somewhat petulant, if not unsympathetic frame of mind.'[29] The same might well have been said of Kemp when he returned to England in mid-October. He was in no mood to receive a long, ill-tempered complaint from his deputy against General Turner. It was apparent, from Gow's account, that the chief of staff had been no more prepared to regard the civil servant as a surrogate minister than had Kemp himself. In Kemp's absence, Turner had approved promotions, authorized the transfer of two officers to Canada, and redistributed motor cars, claiming that his arrangements would stand only until Kemp's return. The crowning insult, to the deputy minister, was that Turner had personally arranged a memorial service at St Margaret's, Westminster, and had presided over a dinner in commemoration of the arrival of the First Contingent without so much as an invitation to the deputy minister. Gow's indignation had been barely contained:

It was only the strongest sense of my duty to you which made it possible for me to continue until your return. Some of the incidents are trifling enough of themselves but in the bulk indicate an attitude of mind on the part of General Turner towards the position which I have had the honour to occupy which created an impossible and intolerable situation and by reason of which I have asked you to relieve me from my duties.

My relations heretofore with General Turner have been the pleasantest possible, and I can only regard his action as a straight challenge of the right of civil control over the military. It is a case of the King and the Army against Parliament over again. The Civil Power over the Army must be supreme; if General Turner's attitude arises by reason of any animosity towards myself, that is easily cured by my withdrawal, but if he is resentful of the exercise of civilian control by the Parliament of Canada over the Forces of which he is a member, the situation takes on a different aspect and is one with which you will doubtless deal.[30]

Gow's allegations that Turner was an incipient Oliver Cromwell were swiftly dispelled. Turner had approved promotions urgently sought by Currie and well in line with precedents. The redistribution of cars consisted of sending an additional car to each of three training areas. The commemorative banquet was merely a monthly dinner organized by officers of the Pay Department, presided over by Brigadier-General Ross. The truth was that Gow and Turner had come to dislike each other and there was also more than a little truth in Turner's closing comment: 'The last paragraph of this memorandum from Gow illustrated graphically Colonel Gow's intent for mischief and endeavour, during your absence, to arrogate to himself supreme authority.'[31] Kemp's solution was obvious. Gow had resigned; he could easily be replaced by the congenial and experienced Colonel Harrington. On 31 October the change was made. Only eleven days later the war was over.

The end came far sooner than anyone had predicted even five months before. Assaults spearheaded by fresh American troops had sent German armies reeling back from the limits of their March advance. On 8 August,

Australians and Canadians, backed by heavy concentrations of tanks, had mounted a surprise offensive near Amiens. When Currie ordered a halt three days later, the Canadians had advanced eight miles at a cost of 4,000 men. Six German divisions had melted away before the assault. Before the Canadians could be blunted by hardening German resistance, Currie had insisted on shifting ground. On 27 August the Corps smashed through the Frèsnes-Rouvroy line. Within a week the Corps had done the seemingly impossible, penetrating the well-fortified Drocourt-Quéant line with a loss of 5,500 men. A year before it had cost three times as many merely to creep into the muddy, worthless ruins of Passchendaele. On 27 September the Canadians stormed the Canal du Nord. By 9 October they had liberated Cambrai. Valenciennes fell on 1 November after the Germans' Hermann line was demolished by 2,149 tons of shells delivered by Brigadier-General Andrew McNaughton's massed heavy artillery. By dawn on 11 November men of the 7th Brigade had infiltrated past a rearguard of German machine gunners to occupy the ancient frontier town of Mons. It was there that the war had begun for men of the British Expeditionary Force in August 1914. It was there that the armistice found the Canadians at 11 AM on 11 November 1918.[32]

For tired, homesick Canadian soldiers the war could hardly have ended in a more inconvenient way. The eleventh of November marked only an armistice, not a final peace. The generals insisted that fighting could resume at any moment and it was all the more likely to do so if the Allied armies melted away. By the time arrangements had been made for an occupation army (including two Canadian divisions) to cross the Rhine, winter had descended on both sides of the Atlantic. For months the only direct access to Canada would be through the ice-free ports of Halifax and Saint John. The real limiting factor in bringing Canadians home was not so much a merchant fleet decimated by U-boats as Canada's inadequate rail connections with her Atlantic ports. The British Ministry of Shipping had claimed that it could ship 50,000 Canadians a month; the two Canadian railways, the Intercolonial and the Canadian Pacific, insisted that they would be able to move no more than 20,000 troops and 10,000 dependents out of the Atlantic region.[33]

Such facts had preoccupied some Overseas Ministry staff for more than six months. Demobilization planning had been launched even earlier. In April 1917 Sir George Perley had invited Sir Hugh Allan to head a planning committee of staff officers and civilians. Kemp discovered that it had barely functioned and launched a more energetic committee under the adjutant general, Major-General Percy Thacker. The result bore strong evidence of British influence. The comparable British plan had shown a sensible concern for postwar economic dislocation. If millions of soldiers were not to be released to mass unemployment, 'pivotal men' and 'demobilizers' must go first to help retool industry for peacetime production.[34] Unfortunately, common sense flew in the face of fair play. Whatever their value to the civil economy, 'demobilizers' were almost certain to be soldiers who had spent the least time in uniform and who may never have left the safety of England. The survivors of Ypres and the Somme were probably least likely to have the skills and connections that made 'pivotal men.' In the scramble to get home, Canadians conscripted under the Military Service Act might well win first place; 'Old Originals' might come last. Like its British counterpart, Thacker's committee anticipated the argument and dismissed it. 'There is only one Canadian army overseas'; there would be no special favour for those who had been called on to serve at the front.[35] 'It has been stated that there might be an uninformed public opinion in Canada with respect to such a matter as this,' Kemp acknowledged. 'This may be so. It has been found to apply to many other things as well as this particular question.'[36]

Working closely with a demobilization committee in Canada, planners at the Overseas Ministry struggled to produce arrangements which would be cheap, efficient, and proof against fraudulent postwar claims for benefits and pensions. To cut travel costs and time, all CEF units would be dissolved and their men sorted into twenty-two 'dispersal areas' across Canada, based largely on sub-divisions of the new system of military districts. Elaborate documentation was part of the plan. British and Australian soldiers completed only three forms on their way to civilian life; men of the CEF would fill out thirteen essential documents, answer 363 questions, and collect eighteen different signatures before being allowed to embark.[37]

Much of the planning underscored the charge that Argyll House was remote from its soldiers. Sir Arthur Currie, for example, had strongly divergent views on mobilization. Proud of the 'most wonderful fighting machine in the world's history,' his private dream was to bring it home intact to show to the Canadian people, perhaps in a monster re-enactment of the 1908 Tercentenary review on the Plains of Abraham. At the very least, he wanted major units to return complete to the cities and towns that had waved them farewell years earlier.[38] Currie's men had still other views. By common consent, the Canadians in France and England had only one wish: to come home at once. Since they could not do so, there was only one fair system of priorities: first over, first back. Their views did not matter to Currie and even less to government and officials in Canada. In Ottawa the finance minister and acting prime minister, Sir Thomas White, insisted on a plan based on Canada's economic and employment priorities. So did his cabinet colleagues, employers, the railways, organized labour, and even the Great War Veteran's Association, the biggest ex-servicemen's organization. Speaking for its 16,000 members, the GWVA executive insisted on 'the vital necessity of most careful and unhurried demobilization ...' Its president, Willard Purney, claimed that 'a further enforced absence of a few months would be fully compensated for in returning to Canada when conditions would be more favourable.'[39]

Of all the influences on demobilization policy, the Corps commander carried the most weight. Both Kemp and the prime minister, who had hurried over to England as the war ended, understood that a time of acute crisis was approaching. Never far below the surface among civilians and even among officers was a nagging fear of the impact of so much killing and death on the character of fighting soldiers. How far would the crude indoctrination in hate, symbolized in bayonet-fighting drills and actualized in combat, leave permanent scars? Would Canada's fighting men return as an armed, bloodthirsty, and potentially uncontrollable mob? No risk could be allowed. Currie had practical reasons for returning at least major units intact. A 'first over, first back' policy would rob the CEF of badly-needed cooks, clerks, and other tradesmen whose seniority might be due mainly to the relative safety of their jobs. Short of polling the men, Currie had to be the authoritative interpreter of their opinions and his views, echoed by his generals, were explicit: 'I have yet to hear of a single instance in which the men do not express not only a preference but an intense desire to return to Canada by units.'[40] However, Currie's clinching argument to Kemp and Borden spoke to their hidden fears: 'I feel I cannot dwell too strongly on this matter of discipline. I know its value. It has been the foundation of our strength and the source of our power. It has been the principal factor in the winning of our battles and is worth preserving for the national life of Canada. For God's sake do not play with it, for you are playing with fire.'[41]

With the further assurance that the Australians were following an identical policy, Sir Thomas White and the cabinet grudgingly surrendered. The demobilization policy was altered. The men of the CEF would return in two separate streams. Infantry battalions, cavalry regiments, and artillery batteries in France – 100,000 men in all – would return as units under their own officers. The rest of the CEF would come home in drafts based on locality and length of service. Married men would have priority over single soldiers if only for the frugal reason that their higher pay made them more costly to the taxpayer.[42] Staff officers at the Overseas Ministry and at Canadian camps across England hurried to adapt to the new arrangements. The big camps at Witley and Bramshott in Surrey would receive units from the Corps. Soldiers with dependents would go to the former convalescent depot at Buxton. Engineers and machine gunners would go to Seaford. A British camp at Ripon in Yorkshire was made available for the 26,000 men of the Canadian Railway Troops and the Forestry Corps. Kinmel Park, the big camp taken over in the autumn of 1918 as a basic training centre, was designated as a final staging area for drafts waiting to sail from nearby Liverpool. Meanwhile, to occupy the time and energy of restless soldiers, chaplains, physical training and drill instructors, the YMCA, and the Salvation Army were mobilized to provide films, stage shows, guided tours, and the inevitable route marches and drill. The Khaki University, an elaborate adult education programme launched in 1917, recruited additional staff and planned new courses. Officials from the Soldier Settlement Board and the new Department of Soldiers' Civil Re-Establishment arrived from Canada to explain government programmes for returning men.[43]

Demobilization took place in a world turned upside down by four years of war and by the revolutions that followed in its wake. Civilians no less than soldiers trusted that the world would right itself. They were disappointed. In Britain the supplementary misery of the 1918 influenza epidemic reached a climax in November with 7,560 dead in London alone. In January the epidemic returned and by March half the British population had been affected. The virus coincided with the coldest winter most Britons could remember. Sickness and cold combined to produce a critical coal shortage in February. Miners, dockers, seamen, and even the police struck for higher wages. Disaffection spread to the British army. Mutinies by thousands of soldiers at Folkestone, Dover, and Calais in the first days of 1919 convinced Winston Churchill, the new secretary of state for war, that the British demobilization plan was unworkable. In a few days, Churchill had issued his own 'first in, first out' plan. It was almost too late. At Kempton Park British soldiers formed a 'council' and invaded Whitehall to face a bloody clash with the Brigade of Guards. At other camps British troops refused to embark for India or for expeditions suspected to be in aid of the anti-Bolshevik White Russians.[44]

Canadians were not immune from the postwar mood. At Witley and Bramshott armistice celebrations boiled into minor riots when Canadians wrecked shops in their local 'Tin Towns,' ramshackle encroachments on War Department land where merchants had gone into business to fleece soldiers. At Kinmel Park a week later, members of the Canadian young soldiers' battalion responded with rocks and jeers when they were turned away from a dance unexpectedly reserved for British officer cadets. The British cadets turned out with fixed bayonets and machine guns.[45] There was more serious trouble in the Canadian Corps itself. On 17 December men of the 7th Brigade met in the central square of the little Belgian town of Nivelles to protest against having to wear full packs and steel helmets on the march. Next day protest meetings resumed. Two companies of Princess Patricia's Canadian Light Infantry were dispersed when they tried to march through the square. Roving bands of soldiers raided unit guardrooms and rescued comrades from custody. The Nivelles protest ended that night. The commander of the 3d Division, Major-General F.O.W. Loomis, hurried back from leave. The 7th Brigade resumed its march and the 9th Brigade marched into Nivelles and seized stragglers. An official report played down the episode, blaming a few agitators 'who apparently had strong socialistic tendencies.'[46] In fact, the Nivelles mutiny was serious. More than sixty Canadian soldiers were charged for their share in the protest and the leaders, including a former assistant librarian for McGill University, were sentenced to five years penal servitude. The affair had also involved some of the best known battalions of the Canadian Corps.[47]

Sagging discipline and negligent officers lay at the root of the Nivelles affair. They were also apparent some thousands of miles away when the ss *Northland* berthed at Halifax on Christmas night. The former German immigrant ship had survived a rough passage. Conditions on the crowded, unventilated troop decks had been grim. Food for the two official meals each day had been cold and unappetizing and the ship's stewards had played the old game of selling food to hungry passengers. During much of the voyage the open decks had been reserved for officers and civilian passengers. Supervising officers had neglected their duties, sanitary gangs failed to do their work, and no one had taken charge. Finally, as a climax to a miserable voyage, the ship sat in quarantine through a miserable, hungry Christmas day. By the time they came ashore, the furious returned men had plenty to tell waiting reporters. The *Northland* scandal was designed to arouse the wrath of a public eager to welcome home its returning heroes.[48]

In Ottawa the government swiftly met public protest by appointing an Ontario judge to investigate. His report, delivered within a month, pruned away the wilder charges but confirmed the deplorable conditions on the ship. His recommendations, promptly endorsed by the cabinet, guaranteed that Canada's soldiers would come home in much greater comfort than they had gone overseas. However, the inquiry also represented an explicit, unjustified, and bitterly resented rebuke for Kemp and the Overseas Ministry. Prodded by men overseas to find any vessel fit to carry them home, Kemp was pilloried in Canada because ships acceptable even to the Americans were simply not good enough for Canadians. Nor did the public understand that negligent conducting staffs were appointed by Mewburn's department, not Kemp's. A humane response to scandalous conditions, the *Northland* inquiry made repatriation more difficult. Canada was already in competition with Australia, New Zealand, and the United States for scarce ocean shipping. Waiting for overworked, strike-prone British dockyards to complete the kind of refitting demanded by Ottawa added delays.[49]

Complaints from Canada continued to prevent any compromise with the comfort of returning soldiers or their dependents. Wives and children packed in the SS *Scandinavian* arrived in Saint John with reports of fierce Atlantic storms, an influenza outbreak, bad food, and a drunken, lecherous medical officer. The *Lapland* docked with 2,320 overcrowded Canadians while the *Scotian* crossed with 300 civilian and 1,944 military passengers packed below decks. In both cases, Kemp insisted, the officially rated passenger capacity was much higher. In one case, he suggested, the real grievance was that white soldiers had objected to sharing their accommodation with their black comrades. Canadians were unimpressed by arguments that the Americans had squeezed 2,724 soldiers into the *Scotian*.[50]

Whether ships were overcrowded or not, Canadians overseas could count on a long wait. Lord Shaughnessy of the CPR confessed that it would be a marvel if repatriation of the quarter-million Canadians and their families could be completed in a year. How long would the men's patience last? In the Corps, Kemp could at least count on Currie and his officers to maintain discipline. There was no such commanding authority over Canadians outside the Corps. Discipline had never been strict among the thousands of railway and forestry troops and many of the men were veterans of the railway brotherhoods or the radical industrial unions of western Canada and the United States. Just as volatile were the thousands of CEF members scattered in reserve battalions, convalescent depots, and the administrative and training organizations of the Overseas Military Forces of Canada. 'Where you mix up all kinds of combatant and non-combatant troops into drafts to fit into the demobilization necessities in Canada and these men are held pending shipping arrangements,' Kemp explained to the prime minister, 'they become most difficult to control.'[51] Sir Richard Turner added his own warning: 'I do not think it is fully realized the situation that may be created amongst Canadian troops during the next two months; due to the growing unrest.'[52]

Turner was right. In December Kemp had been furious when the War Office solemnly forwarded a collection of harsh charges by a Hampshire magistrate against Canadians at Bordon but later reports were all too true. In January Winston Churchill complained of a shooting affray at Ripon. Canadian engineers and railway troops had raided stores and a canteen and loosed off 150 rounds at each other, fortunately without injury.[53] On 9 January 1919 Canadians from Witley invaded Godalming and stormed the local police station in search of the hated military police. Two nights of rioting in the camp went unchecked. A court of inquiry reported that the troops had been outraged by police mistreatment of a popular black boxer and a decorated war hero, by unheated barracks, and by rumours that the Americans were monopolizing ocean shipping. In a display of toughness, Turner fired the commander of the reserve artillery, reprimanded two other officers, and warned the general commanding Witley that he would be replaced if another disturbance occurred.[54] On 15 February, when men of a reserve battalion tried another canteen raid, armed sentries raced to the scene and shot down one of the soldiers.[55]

Threats and shooting could not work forever. Kemp and his officials found themselves in a tightening bind. Discipline in the cold, cheerless camps sagged. Extended leave was useless for men who had long since spent their pay. The Military Service Act conscripts, employed for every possible camp duty, had no incentive to be efficient. Officers were as casual about their responsibilities as their men. The only real solution was to get the men home but transportation problems were constantly aggravated by slowdowns, strikes, mechanical breakdowns, and imperious directives from Ottawa.[56] Repatriation might have been much faster if Canadians could have used the 'monster ships,' the *Olympic*, *Aquitania*, and *Mauretania*, the only big liners to survive the war. However, Canadian railway officials had insisted that their huge passenger capacity would clog facilities at Halifax and cause political embarrassment. When the Canadians relented, the ships' owners said that Halifax harbour was too dangerous and that Anglo-American good will demanded that they be used only on the New York run. The British authorities also resented what they judged as needlessly high Canadian standards for troopships. 'With the fullest sympathy with the difficulties you have and anticipate,' the British shipping controller warned Kemp, '... you will appreciate the fact that you are slowing down the repatriation of your troops by declining the use of ships which, from our point of view, are perfectly suitable.'[57]

In theory, the Overseas Ministry's demobilization system was an administrative marvel. Men from the Corps, once relieved by GHQ, moved from France, went through a three-day process of documentation, left for two weeks of leave in England, and then concentrated at Witley to await shipping. Other Canadians, about 150,000 in all, passed through nine different concentration camps, went on leave, and then assembled at Kinmel Park to wait the week or ten days before a ship was available at Liverpool.[58] That was not happening. In February a succession of crises affected shipping schedules. The SS *Cassandra* was caught at Glasgow by a dock strike. The SS *Vedic* must be fitted with berths and her sanitary arrangements improved but the carpenters were on strike. Kemp, ailing and afflicted by a tragic series of deaths in his own family, struggled to make his Ottawa colleagues understand the problem: 'The men all want to get home – not next month or the month following, but this week, or tomorrow if you like to put it this way.' Goodness knows, he shared their feeling. By now, everything in Britain conspired to infuriate him, from evasive officials at the Ministry of Shipping to his own living conditions. 'The fact of the matter is the whole country is in turmoil. I am not able to get a meal in the hotel in which I live. The electricians are threatening to go on strike and the city to be thrown in darkness tonight. You have no idea of the conditions which exist here. You are living in paradise in Canada as compared with this place.'[59]

Kemp's circumstances were luxurious compared to those at Kinmel Park. A swarm of damp frame huts sprawled on the side of a long Flintshire hill, not far from the seaside resort of Rhyl, the camp had nothing to command it to the growing host of bored, homesick Canadians who gathered there. The camp commander, Colonel Malcolm Colquhoun, was a pre-war militia officer and Hughes nominee who had commanded the camp at Frensham Pond after age and poor health ended his career at the front.[60] He organized his camp in eleven highly autonomous wings, one for each of the military districts in Canada, and left matters to run their course. The result was almost precisely the kind of organization Currie had warned against. It was a random mixture of combatants and non-combatants, 'Old Originals' and recent conscripts, wounded veterans and the professional troublemakers and misfits who float to the rear of any army. The camp staff, resentful at the delay in their own repatriation, took little interest in the men passing through their hands. Neither did the officers assigned to drafts. Only a bully or a fool would have been eager to assert his authority with demobilization only weeks away. Instead, many officers fled the dreary camp for Rhyl or the bright lights of London.[61]

The boiling point at Kinmel was low. On 7 January a virtual race riot erupted when a black sergeant-major tried to arrest an insolent white soldier. Three days later soldiers from the Nova Scotia camp raided a guard room to rescue a comrade. In the scuffle a corporal clubbed the camp commander with the butt of a rifle.[62] Colquhoun's military police, mostly dispersed in neighbouring towns, were abused by officers and soldiers alike. The salvation of any staging camp is that troublemakers keep moving but during February cancellations and disruptions of shipping slowed the flow to a trickle. Bitter cold, steady rain, and a severe fuel shortage made life miserable. A few soldiers had money to spend on food, beer, and illicit games of crown and anchor; most were stony broke.[63] Meanwhile, numbers grew. By the end of February Colquhoun reported more than 17,000 men under his command; some of them had waited as long as six weeks.[64]

Strikes and shipping delays were not the only reason that men began to accumulate at Kinmel Park. It was finally the turn of units in the Canadian Corps to begin their homeward journey. Because the 1st and 2d Divisions had been assigned to the army of occupation in Germany, Currie selected the 3d Division in Belgium as the first Canadian formation to be repatriated. All at once the soldiers understood the exasperating flaw in Currie's demobilization plan. By sending home complete units, the Corps commander may have preserved discipline and *esprit de corps*; he also guaranteed an early homecoming for thousands of conscripts who had filled the ranks of the Corps during the last months of the war. Canada had imitated Australian policy while ignoring a significant difference. Instead of returning complete battalions, the Australians split their units, grouping low-priority men in the second half. At Kinmel, Canadians who had come over in 1915 and 1916 waited in dank huts while conscripts in the 3d Division received a hero's welcome at Liverpool and tramped up the gangplanks for their homeward journey.[65]

That was not all. The SS *Haverford* had been scheduled to load troops from Kinmel on 5 March. A cattle boat on the North Atlantic trade, the *Haverford*'s troop accommodation was on low-slung concrete decks built for cows. A Canadian inspection team condemned the vessel out of hand. The troop space was unacceptable; latrines were rusted and unventilated; the galleys were cramped and remote. On two days' notice the sailing was cancelled. At once there was trouble. At Kinmel, Draft 21 destined for the *Haverford* demonstrated, protested, and vented its wrath on officers.[66] An anxious Colquhoun stopped mailing reports and warnings to London and dispatched his chief staff officer, Lieutenant-Colonel R.G. Thackeray, to London with orders not to return without word of additional sailings. Argyll House lived up to its forbidding reputation. On Monday, 3 March, Thackeray learned that there would be no more sailings for Kinmel until after the middle of March. Instead, units of the 3d Division might well be funnelled through the camp because of accommodation shortages elsewhere. Fortunately, staff officers had begun to digest Thackeray's warnings by Tuesday morning. At lunch in the Piccadilly Grill, Thackeray ran into Brigadier-General Hogarth, the quartermaster-general. Perhaps something could be arranged. Units of the

1st Division would be held in Europe for two extra weeks. Two additional ships would be assigned to Kinmel. Thackeray had succeeded. Pausing at a telegraph office to wire the good news, he set out for an evening on the town.[67]

By the time Thackeray's telegram reached Kinmel Park it was too late. At 7:30 that evening rioting broke out in one of the camps. Within minutes it had spread into the neighbouring Tin Town. When nothing happened to stop the fun, excited soldiers surged back into the camp, spreading out to raid canteens and messes. By 10 PM rioters had ransacked virtually every source of food, drink, and cigarettes in the east end of the camp and more than a thousand of them returned to smash into the main canteen warehouse and tobacco depot. There was almost no resistance. To prevent complaints about extra duties, Colquhoun had refused to organize the normal guards and picquets a large camp should have had. In the dark the few officers and military police who tried to interfere found themselves alost helpless. When Colquhoun came back to camp after an evening in Rhyl, he mobilized a few officers to protect the central quartermaster stores from looters but after midnight the defenders withdrew and pillaging continued through the night.[68]

Next morning Colquhoun summoned his senior officers and issued his orders. There must be no bloodshed. Ammunition in camp must be collected and placed under guard. All stocks of liquor and beer in camp would be drained. Officers must remain in camp and spread the good news from Thackeray. On his own authority Colquhoun summoned the paymasters and ordered them to issue two pounds a man, beginning in the biggest camps. Such a humanitarian strategy would have worked better if Colquhoun could have controlled the liquor supply. While several carloads of whisky and beer were shunted out of camp, two full wagon-loads of beer were discovered near camp headquarters. In minutes soldiers had broached the barrels and collected the contents in buckets and saucepans. The beer was fuel for small parties of rioters who spread out to raid canteens and guardrooms untouched the night before. By 11 AM a rowdy crowd gathered in front of camp headquarters to jeer and throw stones at a small troop of cavalry the camp commander had summoned.

After a few feeble attempts to disperse the crowd, the cavalry withdrew, pursued by a growing and increasingly excited throng of soldiers. Still there was no effective resistance. In a few camps officers persuaded a few men to stand with them on the claim that rioters were destroying records and disrupting repatriation. In one camp, officers simply locked themselves in a hut and trembled for their lives. There was no real danger. Colquhoun later boasted that rioters had lowered their loot to salute him. While rioters concentrated on the canteens and YMCA huts, the Salvation Army hut was conspicuously spared as the only place where a penniless soldier could find free coffee and a snack. By early afternoon, rioters were headed west across the camp, meeting occasional resistance from small parties of officers and sergeants. At the Nova Scotia camp, where soldiers had rallied to defend themselves, resistance crumbled when the mob appeared. That was not the case at the far end of the big camp. Inspired by a single junior officer, soldiers from camp 20, most of them from western Ontario, seized the leading rioters as soon as they appeared. As the main crowd of rioters hesitated, the young officer and a few others dashed out to arrest more leaders. Suddenly, there was a flurry of shots. One of the defenders fell dead. Men from camp 20, armed with the few bullets they had intended to take home as souvenirs, opened fire. In a minute, the riot was over.[69]

As dusk fell, the suddenly sobered Canadians began counting the cost. Five soldiers had been killed during the afternoon rampage across the camp; twenty-five more were wounded. That night Canadian military police herded thirteen prisoners into a special train that would take them to the Tower of London. Eventually fifty-one Canadians would face courts martial for their parts in the riot. Others benefited: 'the idea of the leaders,' claimed one knowledgeable officer, 'was "the more demonstrations we make, the quicker we get sailings." '[70] Early on Thursday morning Sir Richard Turner arrived at Kinmel, toured the camp in an open car, and announced that four additional ships would be provided for the Kinmel men. Within a few days, the first drafts had left for Liverpool.

Other consequences of the riot for both the Overseas Ministry and for Canada's reputation were less easily resolved. With help from local British authorities, Colquhoun had tried to suppress news of the outbreak. He failed utterly. Local reporters at Rhyl, Pensarn, and Abergele fed wild rumours to the London and Liverpool dailies. The British public, kept in ignorance of mutinies and riots in its own forces, was spared no sensation. On 7 March London papers informed horrified readers that twelve had died and twenty-one had been hurt in two days of rioting. A Victoria-Cross-winning major had been trampled to death by crazed Canadians; another officer had been fatally beaten. Drunken soldiers had stripped the clothes from terrified canteen girls and only prompt arrival of British troops from Chester had saved the peaceful village of Abergele. Such reports, in *The Times* and the *Morning Post* were only reluctantly corrected. The superintendent of the canteen board stoutly insisted that none of her employees had been molested. The War Office denied that any British troops had been involved. The battered officer and the trampled major survived only as persistent rumour.[71]

Dramatic events deserve dramatic causes. There had to be a better reason for the Canadian riots than cancelled sailings, discomfort, and deferred pay. Why had the rioters carried red flags? Had the first assault on a canteen begun with the cry 'Come on Bolsheviks'? The answer, insisted the *Morning Post*, was that Bolshevism had made its first descent on the British Isles. If so, boasted General Turner, it had been nipped in the bud. Colonel Colquhoun, belatedly concocting an official release, claimed: 'One man raised the Red Flag in an attempt to introduce Bolshevism. He was shot.'[72] This was nonsense. There was no bud to nip. There was no conspiracy. Like other riots, the Kinmel affair had no plan and many leaders. Bored, exasperated soldiers had vented their frustration on canteens whose stock they could not afford, YMCA huts where they were treated with disdain, and civilian shops which charged inflated prices. Once the rioters found that they could act with impunity, they fortified themselves with the available whisky and beer and carried on. A few hundred active spirits had been followed by many times their number of spectators, eager to share in the only excitement in camp. 'Being of an inquisitive nature,' recalled one participant, 'I wandered pretty well all over and wherever there was a chance of scrounging a bit extra to eat, I took it.'[73]

Strangely enough, the Canadian prime minister must have been among the last to hear of the riot. The London papers reached him in Paris only on Saturday, 8 March. 'This news is very distressing and sad,' he recorded in his diary. It was also obvious that 'firmness and strength were not shown at the outset.' Why, Borden wondered, had machine guns not been deployed to stop the trouble?[74] The answer was simple. Colquhoun could either have subjected his miscellaneous drafts to the harshest test of discipline – firing on comrades – or he could have called on British troops to do it for him. Fortunately, he did neither.

In the wake of the Kinmel tragedy, as sensation flooded into the British press, Sir Edward Kemp struggled to stem the flow with promises of a thorough investigation and full co-operation with a civil inquest. In fact, such promises could not be kept. The rush of repatriation after 5 March removed shiploads of witnesses, eager to forget any potential testimony as the price of an early homecoming.[75] A military court of inquiry, presided over by the crisply professional Brigadier-General James MacBrien, wasted little time on Bolshevik conspiracies and rather more on tracking down rumours of bribery in assigning soldiers to drafts. A wealth of evidence demolished the allegation. Colquhoun's administration could be accused of many failings but corruption was not among them. By the time MacBrien's investigation was complete, few could have questioned his explanation of the outbreak: 'it is clear that the chief and outstanding cause of the discontent in the camp among the soldiers which suddenly culminated in the riots of March 4th and 5th was the delays, postponements and cancellations of sailings of ships allotted to transport troops from Kinmel Park to Canada.'[76]

It was, of course, a finding that left blame for the outbreak essentially on the British Ministry of Shipping and, by implication, on Kemp's colleagues in Ottawa. For all its devastating impact on Canadian prestige in England, the Kinmel riot did make a difference. In addition to the ships Turner could announce on the morrow of the outbreak, the British made the *Olympic* available for a single crossing. Somehow, anxiety about the safety of the 'monster ship' in Halifax harbour was outweighed by awareness of the dangerous impatience among the homesick Canadians. In February sailings had repatriated only 15,243 Canadians, the lowest figure since November. In March the total soared to 41,822. The work of the Overseas Ministry might soon be done.[77]

10

Winding Up

For members of the CEF, the main result of the Kinmel riot was a marked acceleration of repatriation. By 1 April the Overseas Ministry could boast that 110,384 soldiers and nurses and about 17,000 dependents had returned to Canada.[1] The episode also demonstrated a sharp deterioration in relations between Canadians and their British hosts. 'Every officer here wants to shake the dust off his feet as soon as it is possible to, and get back to Canada,' Kemp reported to Borden, 'and I must say my sympathies are entirely with the view they take. This condition has not come about suddenly.'[2] The sensational coverage of the Canadian riot was only an outgrowth, in Kemp's view, of the frigid hostility to the Canadians that had developed since the armistice. It was also a marked contrast to press reporting on a violent riot in London's Strand on the Sunday after the Kinmel affair. For most of the afternoon American soldiers and sailors had battled police to the very doors of the Bow Street station but Monday's reports were short and discreet.[3]

In Paris the Canadian prime minister had taken his concern to Sir George Riddell, vice-chairman of the Newspaper Proprietors' Association. He got little satisfaction. The lurid coverage of the Canadian troubles, Riddell assured him, was the inevitable consequence of the abolition of censorship. Borden's own conclusions were harsher: it was yet another example of the 'thoughtless stupidity which one so often encounters on this side of the Atlantic.'[4] Kemp was unappeased: 'Nothing since the war occurred has upset me to the same extent,' he confessed, 'it was this sort of thing that lost the thirteen colonies to Great Britain.'[5]

The immediate victims of British public opinion were the fifty-one Canadians awaiting courts martial at Liverpool. Among the potential scapegoats for the tragedy, ranging from the Ministry of Shipping, striking dockers, officials at the Overseas Ministry, politicians in Canada, and the British climate, the accused soldiers ranked very low. No one could pretend that they represented all or even most of the active rioters. Many had been rounded up on the basis of questionable identification or circumstantial evidence. Their trials, presided over by Major-General Sir Harry Burstall and before officers who included a future minister of national defence, Lieutenant-Colonel J.L. Ralston, were a political demonstration that the Canadian authorities were both innocent and stern. Convictions and penalties were intended both to placate British public opinion and to confirm a subsidiary claim that the chief role in the riot had been played by 'foreigners.' Even on that basis, seventeen of the accused were acquitted and three more were immediately reprieved on review. Sentences for those convicted ranged from ten years for a Czech-born soldier who had jeered at officers and seven years for a Rumanian-born private who spoke no English but who had struck an officer, down to a few weeks of detention for minor offenders.[6]

The judicial process did not escape criticism. Twenty-five of the soldiers had been convicted of mutiny, five more were guilty of not doing their utmost to suppress it. Was rioting really mutiny? Had anyone, apart from the junior officer at camp 20, really done his utmost to suppress it? During the courts martial, defence counsel had tried in vain to raise such questions. One of them continued the battle. Captain George Black, a future Conservative MP for the Yukon and Speaker of the House of Commons, dismissed the entire procedure as a travesty. Private soldiers, he bluntly informed the prime minister, simply could not expect justice from a court composed entirely of officers.[7] Although Black's denunciations were answered by his colleague and senior defence counsel, Major Edward C. Weyman, virtually all of those sentenced at Liverpool were reprieved and released before the end of 1919. The exceptions were the 'foreigners,' singled out for deportation.[8]

The Kinmel tragedy and its aftermath was also a signal for the many critics of the Overseas Ministry to resume their assault. More than ever Kemp felt himself isolated and deserted by his colleagues in the Union government. In Quebec's upper chamber, the Legislative Council, Brigadier-General Charles Smart rose to pour out a stream of denunciations of the Canadian overseas administration, ranging from Kinmel back as far as the Bruce inquiry. Not even the invective in Smart's charges was new, but it was shocking enough from a general, a Conservative, and a prominent Montreal businessman. Through medical incompetence, Smart claimed, an unnamed soldier had been blinded; millions had been squandered because of 'petticoat influence' around Sir George Perley; competent medical officers had been persecuted for supporting Bruce; General Steele had 'died of a broken heart' after his removal from Shorncliffe, Turner was a 'weakling,' surrounded by incompetents of his own choice.[9] It was all lively stuff, eagerly reprinted and amplified by *Saturday Night*, the Toronto *Daily Star*, the Regina *Leader* and other once-Liberal organs struggling back to their old partisanship. Smart was promptly joined by Lieutenant-Colonel A.C. Pratt, another Conservative and a member of the Ontario legislature, who specifically denounced the Overseas Ministry for causing the Kinmel riot, for allowing the 'monster ships' to be allocated to the Americans, and for countenancing a system of bribes and corruption.[10]

The Pratt and Smart charges were all the more resented by the senior officials of the Overseas Ministry because, as they knew very well, both officers had been specially favoured because of their political influence. Pratt had been returned from France with a harshly adverse report; Smart's only service in France had been brief and inglorious; it ended when he insisted on being transferred to a VAD hospital in the south of France, one of the institutions he had now condemned.[11] Smart's victims, officers like Turner and Major General Foster, could do little to protect themselves, beyond splenetic private letters of outrage and appeal. 'The malicious lying statements regarding intrigue against General Currie and lack of co-ordination between Canada, England and France,' Turner wrote, 'are without doubt bred and fostered by such disgruntled and discredited officers.'[12] Senior medical officers, aware that their professional reputations could be destroyed by Smart's allegations, were even more indignant. Foster poured out his resentment in a detailed rebuttal of Smart's charges, dipping into his own vitriol to observe: 'This Officer would now like to pose as the friend of the returned soldier ... Did he share their discomforts and face the enemy with them? No, he remained less than three months in France and as much of that time as he could was spent under the sheltering care of the Medical Service.'[13]

In Ottawa General Fotheringham suggested that word might quietly be spread that Smart had been under treatment in Ste-Anne de Bellevue and that his words should not, perhaps, be taken seriously.[14] However, both the Smart and the Pratt charges had to be aired and at length in the House of Commons. With neither Kemp nor Perley able to defend themselves and Borden still in Paris, the defence was left to Sir Thomas White (armed with a powerful brief from Sir Andrew Macphail)[15] and to General Mewburn. In any event, the parliamentary offensive proved far weaker than the government might have expected. Oddly enough, the Kinmel tragedy produced very few echoes in Canada. Pratt's charges of massive bribery aroused little interest and no confirming murmers. Smart's charges were stronger in invective than substance. Rodolphe Lemieux, leading the attack, could only repeat what the distinguished general had claimed while both White and Mewburn had damning facts to meet each allegation. The Bruce supporter banished to a remote forestry camp had been tested and found wanting as a battlefield surgeon, not as a politician. The tubercular soldier abandoned in a lean-to had in fact been treated by the contemporary faith in fresh air and had recovered. The Liberals' star war hero, Major C.G. Power, confessed that the CAMC personnel had been excellent – he had been one of them. Even the dispersal policy condemned by Bruce had been correct as an administrative measure though Power stoutly disapproved of any imperial sentimental argument: 'I do not believe in carrying on Imperial propaganda at the expense of casualties inflicted in the war.'[16]

Sir Edward Kemp would doubtless have preferred to present his own case to Parliament rather than depend on two ex-Liberals for his reputation but his problems in Britain were far from through. By the end of March he may have believed that his winter of discontent was over; instead, April proved to be one of the most worrying months he had experienced. To his dismay, the British stopped work for almost a week to observe their first peacetime Easter in five years and, when the country resumed business, the dockers went out on strike.[17] April sailings fell to only 28,884. Despite Currie's insistence that the Corps units would cause no trouble, men of the 2d Division caused at least three minor riots when they passed through the camp at Witley. Those at least could be concealed from the British press; two days of rioting at Seaford on 3 and 4 May brought sensational coverage a week later in the *News Chronicle* and *The Times*. Although Canadian officials insisted that the trouble had been the work of British radicals in the Sailors, Soldiers and Airmen's League, press reports insisted that it was the Canadians who had terrorized the little town.[18]

Seaford's own officials proved far less indignant than the London press. The Overseas Ministry was acutely embarrassed when the local Urban District Council endorsed the soldiers' grievances over low pay, slow demobilization, and alleged interference with men taking Khaki University courses, and intervened with the local Canadian commander.[19] Such sympathy had become exceptional. Canadian soldiers reaped the resentment of British civilians and ex-soldiers for their higher rates of pay and for the publicity given to Australian and Canadian exploits in the final months of the war. At Guildford, the town closest to the big Canadian camps at Witley and Bramshott, feeling was intense. On 10 May fights broke out at a local dance hall. As civil police stood by, refusing to help, Canadian military police managed to extract most of their compatriots and shepherd them to the railway station. On the following evening, gangs of demobilized British soldiers attacked individual Canadians in the streets of Guildford. One Canadian was badly hurt.[20]

If anything was needed to persuade the Overseas Ministry of a British press conspiracy, coverage of the Guildford riots was enough. Leading papers claimed that the Canadians had conducted a reign of terror in the town. When both the mayor and the chief constable deplored the outbreaks and praised the Canadians, their remarks were ignored. The *Daily Sketch* published photographs of two British corporals allegedly stabbed by Canadians. When the two soldiers signed retractions, the newspaper took no notice. The *Daily Mail* announced that Guildford had been placed out of bounds to Canadians and that the authors of the disturbances were being shipped away 'as fast as trains can carry them.' 'It was really remarkable,' noted Colonel Thomas Gibson, Kemp's assistant deputy minister, 'how small a paragraph could be so inaccurate and convey such a wrong impression.'[21]

Though Kemp immediately issued a statement to the British press, explaining that Guildford had never been closed to Canadians and that recreation in the town was necessary for men 'going through the trying experience of demobilization,'[22] the only real solution was faster repatriation. For their own reasons, the British agreed. Over protests from ship owners, the *Mauretania* was made available to the Overseas Ministry and Kemp himself was one of the passengers. Unfortunately, it was not one of the better performances by Colonel Duffin and the embarkation staff. A ferocious cable from the minister described chaos on the dockside, confusion on board, and bitter resentment from 103 sergeants compelled to share steerage with ordinary soldiers. 'The only redeeming feature of the whole thing,' Kemp cabled his officials, 'is that the O.C. of the ship is General McNaughton, a very level-headed officer, who may be able to remedy the blundering and incompetency which has been exhibited in connection with this sailing.'[23] In fact, as Harrington dutifully explained, the only confusion had come from an attempt to fill a few hundred last-minute vacancies with an extra draft from Kinmel.[24]

Thanks to the *Mauretania*, May sailings reached a total of 49,887 troops. Most of the Canadian staging camps were closed and their personnel joined the repatriation stream through Witley. By now most of the waiting Canadians were MSA men and other latecomers with a low priority for demobilization. Almost a thousand of the soldiers at Witley had been released from military prisons and detention barracks as a result of post-war amnesties and reprieves. Others had been dropped from earlier drafts because of disciplinary offences or venereal disease. To avoid scandal, the Militia Department had insisted that infected Canadians be cured in Britain rather than shocking their own communities.[25] Like Kinmel, Witley had become a dangerous mixture of conscripts, troublemakers, and homesick soldiers. The potential for trouble soared when British seamen and dockers welcomed June with a fresh round of strikes and disruptions.

The commander at Witley, Brigadier-General A.H. Bell, had no illusions about the problems of keeping order among his 20,000 disgruntled men. His staff of military policemen was overworked while the MSA men on his staff were unwilling to exert any authority. The answer, Bell insisted, would be a special unit of volunteers, well-paid and ready to maintain order. The appeal came too late.[26]

Gambling was the perennial pastime for bored, restless soldiers. At Witley a highly organized syndicate separated soldiers from their back pay. On Saturday 14 June military police stopped a car for a routine check and discovered that they had captured not only the week's take but a major gambling kingpin as well, a warrant officer from the Overseas Ministry staff. The indignant operators were promptly lodged in the nearest guardroom. Within an hour a large crowd had gathered. Prisoners, badly overcrowded in their cells, began shouting. The crowd replied. A few men smashed a board fence behind the guardroom and broke in. In a minute the prisoners had fled. Then a crowd of almost two thousand headed for the next guardroom. Witley's assistant provost marshal was caught by the crowd and given two minutes to order the release of all prisoners. With Bell's angry acquiescence, the order was given. Growing as it went, the mob surged across the camp, raiding messes and canteens. At the venereal hospital, soldiers battered a hole through the wire mesh fence and rolled in two barrels of beer for the patients. At last, rioters poured across the main London-to-Portsmouth road to raid the local Tin Town. Someone set fire to one of the tinder-dry structures. In moments flames caught hold and roared into the sky. The fire raced along the line of buildings and gutted the big garrison theatre. By dawn Witley's main Tin Town was a charred ruin.[27]

On Sunday morning, Turner arrived, toured the camp, and delivered a stern warning. That night there was more trouble. Again canteens were attacked and buildings in Lower Tin Town were set ablaze. This time rioters were met by strong, armed picquets. More than forty arrests were made. Kemp's officials had absorbed another lesson about riots: news blackouts would not work. News of the Witley riot reached London too late for the Sunday papers and there was time to dispatch a carefully briefed staff officer to each of the morning dailies. The resulting reports were as bland as Kemp could have wished. Unfortunately, there were exceptions. 'Troops Burn

Camp' proclaimed the *News Chronicle*, '20,000 Men Shelterless' announced the *Daily Mail*. Outflanked by such claims, backed up by photographs of the gutted Tin Towns, other newspapers could charge that they had been deceived by Kemp's emissaries.[28]

At Ripon trouble followed directly on the heels of the Witley riots. When men of the Twenty-third Reserve Battalion, a mainly French-Canadian unit, learned that their sailing had been cancelled, it was easy to believe that their ship had been switched to the Witley drafts. If rioting brought results, why not try? Moreover, they soon had a grievance. On 18 June officers ordered forty men who had spent the previous night on guard duty to don helmets and full packs and prepare for a long route march. The men refused. Others joined them. A few raided a nearby canteen and brought back some barrels of beer. When the camp commander, Brigadier-General D.M. Ormond, appeared, the trouble was over. The men listened respectfully and returned to duty. However, the brief resistance brought heavy penalties. Fifteen leaders convicted by courts martial received sentences totalling twenty-one years at hard labour.[29]

The most dynamic response of the Overseas Ministry to the series of disturbances during the spring of 1919 was to worry about British press coverage. It was also the cheapest alternative. Every significant suggestion from the successive courts of inquiry would have cost money, whether it meant providing richer bonuses for cooks and clerks required to work in the demobilization camps or recruiting more police and guards. However, it was not until June that the Canadian authorities received much sympathy for their complaints and it came from David Caird, head of the War Office's newly reconstituted publicity department. Acutely aware that one of the worst offenders in Canadian eyes was the *News Chronicle*, controlled by Lloyd George's chief whip, Captain Freddie Guest, Caird promised to raise the matter discreetly with Winston Churchill. It might well be argued that British-Canadian dissension could have 'a most serious effect on the Peace Conference at a very critical time.'[30]

However, not even Caird could hope to dampen response to the Epsom tragedy. Better known for its racing, Epsom had also become a Canadian convalescent centre. As elsewhere, relations between Canadians and their British hosts had deteriorated. Canadian visitors to the race track were hustled and jeered. On the evening of 17 June a Canadian soldier and his wife were surrounded and abused by a crowd. When two other Canadian soldiers came to their rescue, police arrested them and allegedly maltreated them on the way to the local station. When the story reached the Canadian depot, more than three hundred soldiers swarmed into the town, fought their way into the police station, and rescued their comrades. In the *mêlée*, eight Canadians and eight police were injured. One of them, Station Sergeant Thomas Green, died next day of his injuries.[31]

To respectable British opinion, there was no imaginable justification for the violent death of a policeman. Green's death came at a moment when the British press and official opinion badly wanted to rehabilitate police prestige tarnished by wartime dilution and postwar strikes. The death of an elderly veteran of the Surrey constabulary at the hands of a mob of rowdy, ill-disciplined Canadians was inspiration enough for the laziest editorial writer. The tone ranged from righteousness to the sneering inquiry from the *Sunday Herald*: 'And will the great victory of 400 over the formidable 17 ... be counted among the Canadian battle honours?'[32] Furious and humiliated, Sir Richard Turner stopped blaming the British press and turned to his own men. On 20 June a 'Special Order of the Day' was printed and distributed to each Canadian soldier in England. There would be no more condoning disorder. There would be no amnesty for military offenders. 'There can be no innocent spectators at a mutiny,' Turner warned, 'the man who, out of curiosity, hangs about at the outskirts of the crowd is, in the eyes of the law, almost as seriously involved as the actual ringleader.' No distinctions would be drawn: 'I am not going to remind you of our record in France. That point has been emphasized before – apparently without avail. I am not going to remind you of the distress which these outbreaks cause our families and friends at home. Of that you yourself must be fully aware. What I have to say to you now is that these disturbances must and shall cease and that whatever steps are necessary will be taken to ensure that they do cease.'[33]

Perhaps Turner's message worked. More probably it was the accelerated pace of sailings that guaranteed that there were no more Epsoms. By the end of August barely thirteen thousand Canadians remained in England, many of them officers, nursing sisters, and dependents entitled to first-class accommodation and unable to find it in the crowded troopships.[34] There was also an impressive and wholly unexpected outburst of pro-Canadianism. When King George v allowed his deep displeasure at the Epsom affair to be known to the Overseas Ministry, officials finally had an opportunity to report some of Canada's long-standing grievances about shipping, press coverage, and local relations. If no specific commitments emerged from a lengthy Whitehall meeting on 21 June, the wall of official indifference was breached.[35] When five Canadian soldiers, charged for their role in the Epsom riot, appeared at the Guildford assizes, the judge pointedly observed that their conduct had been no worse than that of many local troublemakers and sentenced them to only a year in prison without hard labour.[36] Lord Burnham of the *Daily Tele-*

graph allowed one of his staff, Sir Hall Caine, to publish a gushingly sympathetic account of the homesick Canadians. Sir Hamar Greenwood, an uprooted Canadian and Conservative politician, rushed into print with his own version of the problem. Canadian soldiers, he explained to his British readers, 'are like children. They learn to pout and do the opposite to what they are asked to do and soon they take great pride in their independence and arbitrariness. So soon as they get headed for Canada, they will be themselves again – the best soldiers in the British Empire.'[37] Greenwood's genius for mass psychology was soon to be tested, with even more disastrous results, on the people of Ireland.

By then, the Overseas Ministry would have passed into history. First, there was much to be accomplished. Afflicted by neuralgia and the complications of losing two of his sons-in-law within a few months, Kemp spent most of May, June, and July in Canada, leaving Harrington and Turner to wrestle with a variety of problems, from the repatriation programme to the inspection and transfer of military and aeronautical stores destined for Canada's postwar armed forces. No problem bulked larger or was more important to the reputation of the Overseas Ministry than the final settlement of the financial arrangements with the British. Few problems could be more complex.

The arrangement Sir George Perley had accepted in January 1917 had been simple enough: five shillings per man per day for each Canadian in France, an extra shilling to represent the cost of artillery ammunition, and payment for all but accommodation for Canadian troops in England. The ink was hardly dry before the War Office insisted that its estimates for artillery expenditure had been far too low and demanded a readjustment at least from 1 November. Perley refused. The rate might be re-opened but only from the date of the War Office notification on 2 March 1917. The argument had continued in a desultory fashion with the War Office pointedly reminding Perley by July that Canada was, in effect, defaulting on £4 million of real obligations by rejecting any retroactive settlement.[38]

By the time Kemp came on the scene, the issue was not only unresolved but increasingly complicated by a host of controversial transactions. The simple proposition, endorsed in 1914, that Canada would bravely meet her full costs had been transformed into high-level haggling about responsibility for half a million dollars in technical railway equipment supplied for Canada's railway construction units, $1,785,618 in spare parts for Colt and Canadian-made Lewis machine guns, forage for the British Remount Commission in Montreal, or the expenses of Serbian army contingents trained in Canada.[39] Not until 19 March 1918, after a three-man Canadian committee had examined and audited statements of artillery ammunition expended for Canada, was a higher capitation rate accepted. Even at that, the War Office refused to charge Canada for ammunition destroyed by enemy action or for artillery support provided by units like the Lahore Division artillery when Canada's gunners were still under-strength. By that stage, Canadian negotiators were more eager to limit their government's burdens than to echo the imperial spirit of 1914. On 15 August, the detailed examination of the artillery figures ended with acceptance of monthly rates ranging from one shilling to four shillings and fourpence with no concession on retroactivity.[40] The Canadian negotiators were just as adamant in rejecting a British bid to raise the daily maintenance rate from five shillings. If costs had risen, as the British insisted, they were counterbalanced by lower costs after the armistice. In the end, Overseas Ministry representatives reached a settlement that cost Canada $252,567,942 – a little more than the federal government had spent for all purposes in 1914.[41] The host of other claims for equipment, buildings, barrack damages, transportation, dead horses, and miscellaneous Serbians was finally settled, on Harrington's fervent recommendation on 27 May 1920, for half a million pounds sterling. 'Balance may not completely exhaust all matters both sides,' Harrington cabled, 'but is so nearly accurate does practical and substantial justice to both taxpayers England Canada.'[42]

Kemp's absence from most of the 1919 negotiations was a reflection of his failing health. When he returned in July he could see that other senior officials of his department were just as exhausted. In August Sir Richard Turner and his family left for Canada.[43] So did Thacker, Hogarth, and Colonel Ross. Turner's successor was Brigadier-General James MacBrien, a tough, no-nonsense officer who had impressed both generals and politicians. His qualities were needed. Homesickness or an impatience to re-establish interrupted lives had made most CEF members desperate to get back to Canada. Those who remained had a very different incentive amidst postwar unemployment and disruption. Some officers who had counted on postwar military careers suddenly realized that rivals in Ottawa had entrenched themselves even at the expense of those with overseas service. Colonel Ward, who had worked faithfully without promotion at the head of the overseas pay department, discovered that he would return only to a tiny retirement pension.[44] Amidst such spreading resentment and an accompanying urge to go slow, it took all of MacBrien's bustling insensitivity to close down departments, disband organizations, and prod ordnance staff to speed up the work of inspecting and packing the guns, ammunition, aircraft, and spare parts presented to Canada by a grateful and overburdened British government. By the end of 1919 less than five hundred Canadians remained in England and

France, not including, unfortunately, some 1,627 recorded deserters or the 22,318 CEF members who had taken their discharge in Britain. Even most of the prisoners court-martialled after the spring disturbances had been released and quietly returned to Canada.[45]

For all his efforts, MacBrien did not quite meet the deadline for the expiry of the Overseas Ministry – the end of the parliamentary session of 1920. However, the organization officially came to an end on 8 June. By then the surviving staff had been attached to the appropriate branches of the Militia Department. More than a year after other Canadians had returned to resume their broken lives, Harrington, Foster, and Ward rejoined postwar Canada. The flags and the welcoming parties had long since disappeared.[46]

There would have been no special celebration for those identified with the notorious Argyll House. To thousands of Canadian soldiers overseas, Argyll House had become a symbol of insensitive, arrogant bureaucracy, much like the comparable Australian establishment on Horseferry Road. 'I know scarcely an officer or a private who has ever had very much to do about Argyll House,' Major C.G. Power informed the House of Commons, 'but will say that it is one of the worst and most mismanaged institutions in the world.'[47] That reflected the inevitable bitterness of fighting men against those who work in safer and more comfortable places. It also echoed the resentment of young Canadians to whom officialdom and regulations were new and unwelcome experiences. They were, after all, wartime novelties for a great many Canadians. Complaints about Argyll House were profuse but also vague. They could be answered with that mixture of indignation and statistics familiar to all practised bureaucrats. Though Kemp's ministry was not staffed by shirkers in 'bombproof' jobs it was sprinkled with men whose political credentials were as important as their military achievements.

Yet the criticism of Argyll House was often the criticism of any head-quarters from which emanates a mixture of authority and confusion. A more significant and particular complaint was that the overseas minister was not answerable to Parliament or, indeed, to his cabinet colleagues. The difficulty was made greater by the creation of a wartime coalition government. In 1917 Kemp in Ottawa could at least represent a fellow Conservative, Sir George Perley, in a familiar partisan forum in the House of Commons. In 1919 Mewburn might be no less loyal an ally of his overseas minister but his problems were entirely apparent to his former Liberal friends. 'Why should there be two departments in one,' asked Jacques Bureau, 'and why should one man, if I may use the expression, wear the harness, draw the coat, be exposed here to all the criticism, and yet have no control over the other man?'[48] Bureau was not satisfied by the prime minister's explanation of the accounting system and by assurances that the auditor-general was agreeable to it. Less obvious but just as important was the overseas minister's isolation from cabinet colleagues. For Kemp, who had known the benefits of consultation and who suspected, perhaps with justification, that his colleagues had often abandoned him to his critics, cabinet solidarity was more than a constitutional theory. In an angry letter to Sir Thomas White (which he never sent) Kemp poured out his feelings:

Those of you who have been fortunate enough to carry on the Government by almost daily meetings of Privy Council can scarcely appreciate, I am sure, what it means to hold one of the most responsible positions in the Government without the advantage of daily contact with one's colleagues. Moreover, so far as I am concerned, I was thrust into this responsibility at a time when a new Government was formed, many of the members of which were either strangers to me or might have been considered in some cases political antagonists. (Evidence was not lacking at the outset that the latter, like the leopard, had not changed its spots, therefore I could not expect under such circumstances, very much sympathy in my work and this was manifested to me not only at the outset but at a later stage as well.)[49]

In the circumstances, such criticisms, for all their political and constitutional validity, do not outweigh the very real achievements of the Overseas Ministry. The circumstances, it goes without saying, should never have been allowed to develop. A minister too powerful to be removed and too unstable to fulfil his responsibilities, a system of appointments and promotions built on personal influence and patronage, and an organization built on principles of benign good fellowship were the antithesis of rational bureaucratic management.

The experiment was not repeated in the Second World War because the circumstances were not repeated. Mackenzie King's government included as many as three ministers of national defence but the armed forces overseas were commanded by service officers who reported to Ottawa. Why had the Borden government followed so innovative and constitutionally so questionable an initiative? What could a cabinet minister accomplish in London in the autumn of 1916 that a competent administrator, armed with the authority and confidence of the government could not have achieved? The answer at the time seemed clear. Only a cabinet minister could possibly have eliminated Sir Sam Hughes from responsibilities which he had demonstrably and egregiously mismanaged. Not even the strongest administrator, civil or military, could have accomplished the necessary reforms and revived the flagging confidence of Canadian soldiers in England while serving as Hughes's subordinate. The overseas ministry was conceived by Perley and Borden without the presumption that Hughes would be removed from his department though that alternative must surely have been explored by the two men during their discussions in August and September 1916.

Within the structure of Canadian government in the early decades of the century, only a cabinet minister could possibly have brought the necessary prestige to a major task of reform. Sir George Perley may have exaggerated the significance of his high commissionership but he was entirely right about the importance of cabinet rank. His own eclipse after the arrival of Sir Edward Kemp would be proof enough. Only a cabinet minister, backed by the rest of the government, could have removed unfit senior officers, disposed of surplus officers, or curbed the struggle for regional patronage which seems to have governed the promotion of Canadian generals. Only a member of the Canadian government could insist on direct access to British ministers, a power which Sir Richard Turner, for one, prized highly.

A third attribute which a minister could bring to the problems of Canada's overseas forces was the analytical capacity of an intelligent outsider. In 1916 it would have been difficult for the prime minister to have imposed a non-military authority in London of less than ministerial rank. It would have been much easier to select a senior officer like Currie or Turner but it is not obvious that their initial prestige would have survived the bruising and essentially political struggles necessary for the reform of the overseas military organization. It would also have been difficult for any senior Canadian officer to be divorced from the ties of friendship and faction which had become so significant in the Hughes-dominated CEF. Political influence, cabinet rank, and a detachment from preconceptions and factions helped to make the creation of an overseas minister a success.

Neither Perley nor Kemp eliminated political considerations from the management of the Canadian forces overseas. By 1916 and perhaps at any stage in the development of the Canadian Expeditionary Force, that would have been impossible and, in their view, not even wholly desirable. In a sense that was far less apparent in the more professional and experienced management of Canadian forces overseas in the Second World War, the CEF was a community in arms with all its strengths and limitations. What Perley, Kemp, and the officials of Argyll House proved was that politics could be incidental to reasonable efficiency and a sense of common purpose. Thanks to the ministry, long-festering sores healed or were surgically removed. A drastic comb-out of able-bodied officers and men, together with the dissolution of the 5th Canadian Division did not forestall the need for wartime conscription but it did guarantee that the Canadian Corps could face the casualties expected in 1919 with more confidence than any other fighting formation outside the American army. There is little doubt either that the Overseas Ministry, particularly under Kemp's management, achieved a respectable degree of financial control and accountability. The discovery of fraud and defalcation, ranging from the Officers' Kit Store to the forage and transport accounts of the Canadian Army Service Corps, was a painful consequence of overdue improvements in accounting.

Simply because the Overseas Ministry secured a firm grip on Canadian military administration and reduced it to a state of sometimes unlovable efficiency, it could also extend Canadian military autonomy. Kemp's insistence on formal liaison at British General Headquarters through Brigadier-General Embury demonstrated that Canada had become almost a sovereign, if junior, ally in the course of the war. It was both the formal counterpart of and the essential support for Sir Arthur Currie's own insistence that his formation was not an army corps like all the others in the British Expeditionary Force.

The basic achievements of the Overseas Ministry may easily be overlooked under its unpopularity with the troops and its involvement in noisy controversies, from Colonel Herbert Bruce's denunciation of medical services to the postwar demobilization riots. Like the rest of Sir Robert Borden's wartime government, the Overseas Ministry found itself on stormy and uncharted seas. Its businessmen-ministers and senior officials lacked either the breadth of experience or the gift of intuition which might have allowed them either to overwhelm their problems or to dissolve them by ingenuity. Canadians had not equipped themselves with that kind of leadership.

Nor did those most closely associated with the Overseas Ministry profit much from it. Sir Edward Kemp did not become lieutenant-governor of Ontario as he may have hoped. Instead, he spent much of 1920 in hospital and emerged without his gall bladder. He was called to the senate shortly before the Conservatives went down to humiliating defeat in the 1921 election. He died in August 1929, only months before his world of business and finance began to collapse in the Great Crash. His predecessor, Sir George Perley, ended his career as high commissioner in February 1922, shortly after the Liberals returned to power in Canada. He discovered that his English and French constituents in Argenteuil were perhaps more faithful to him than he had been to them. They elected Perley in 1925 and returned him faithfully until his death in 1938. In both the short-lived Meighen government of 1926 and the ill-fated Bennett régime of 1930-5, Perley held cabinet rank without the heavy burdens of office. Lieutenant-General Sir

Richard Turner returned to Quebec and the respectable obscurity of his pre-war business career, emerging only to help lead Canada's divided and quarrelsome veterans' organizations into the conservative respectability of a unified Canadian Legion in 1925. Gordon Harrington faced the daunting task of rebuilding his law practice in Sydney. 'I now make the statement,' he wrote to Kemp, 'and expect to make it again at some future time, that it did not advantage a man materially to serve our country in a high capacity overseas in the late war.'[50] Perhaps Harrington might have been content to have survived unscathed. For more than sixty thousand Canadians there would be no return; as many more would carry crippling mental and physical wounds to their graves.

Appendix

Overseas Forces from the Other Dominions

A logical question, for which there is no simple answer, is whether other self-governing dominions shared the Canadian experience in managing their contingents in France and whether they reached a similar solution.

Though the question is reasonable, it almost never seems to have been posed by those who devised the succession of expedients that became, in due course, the Ministry of Overseas Military Forces of Canada. Though information was easily available, Canadians preferred to consider their problems as their very own.

Some of the overseas contingents were so small that they were completely integrated in the British army. That was the case for the brave little battalion of infantry from Newfoundland. The South African infantry brigade, authorized in July 1915, was paid and administered by the British once it reached France although it remained under the nominal supervision of its original commander, Major-General Henry Lukin, as he rose to command the 9th British Division.[1]

Like Lukin, Sir Alexander Godley was a British officer who had established his dominion links before the war. Godley, commander of New Zealand's military forces from 1910, remained responsible for New Zealanders overseas throughout the war although, by the end of the war, he was also in command of the XXII British army corps. An austere, strict soldier, not particularly beloved by his New Zealand men, Godley was respected as an efficient, successful soldier whose prestige was seen as a protection for New Zealand interests.[2]

New Zealand's anglophile government might be expected to accept a British general as commander of its overseas forces. It was more surprising that Australia did the same. Senator George Pearce, the Commonwealth's minister of defence, was as nationalist as Sam Hughes and just as devoted to the virtues of universal military training. As a Labour politician, he had none of Hughes's propensity for British aristocrats.[3] However, in Sir William Birdwood, the Australians found a British general who was better attuned to their own casual attitude to military discipline and routine than most of their own senior officers. Birdwood's attitude may have won him the contempt of Sir Douglas Haig but it also contributed to the Australians' unquestioned fighting prowess and self-esteem.[4] Birdwood remained in over-all authority over the Australians even when in June 1918 he moved to the command of a reconstituted Fifth British Army. His chief of staff, Major-General Brudenell White, an Australian, argued that Birdwood was a necessary safeguard against the external political interference and internal rivalries which had so troubled the Canadian Expeditionary Force.[5]

Certainly the Australian Imperial Force was not free of many of the problems which afflicted the Canadians. Their original base in Egypt was plagued by inefficiency and inexperienced officers and the confusion was compounded when the survivors of Gallipoli joined 40,000 restless, undisciplined recruits at the end of 1915. Unlike Hughes, Senator Pearce was a shrewd administrator with skill in choosing subordinates. His choice for Egypt, a hastily created colonel, Robert M.McC. Anderson, transformed the Australian base by 'business principles.'[6] Although the Australian base in London was established by Brigadier-General V.C.M. Sellheim, Anderson followed him there in the summer of 1916, built a staff and organization and negotiated financial arrangements with the British government. Though Anderson was an intelligent, energetic man with a sense of humour, he lacked, in the view of the Australian official historian, 'the faculty of retaining the complete confidence of his colleagues ...'[7] He was replaced in 1917 by Major General James M'Cay, commander of the unfortunate Fifth Australian Division during the disastrous attack at Fromelles. Like Turner, General M'Cay purged his battlefield limitations by administrative service.

Unity of command meant that Senator Pearce could deal directly with General Birdwood who in turn remained the over-all authority for the Australian troops in Britain and France. That did not spare the Australians some of the problems familiar to Canadians. ANZACs regarded the 'bodgers in Horseferry Road' with all the contempt Canadians reserved for Argyll House. When the Australian Corps was formed in 1918, as C.E.W. Bean later confessed, officers and journalists conspired to secure the command for their favourite general. However, once Birdwood had decided on Sir John Monash, the competition was over.[8]

Rational command structures did not spare soldiers from the other dominions any of the miseries and mistakes of the war. The Newfoundlanders were annihilated on the first day of the battle of the Somme. The South African brigade was wiped out twice, once at Delville Wood during the Somme campaign and even more disastrously at Massières Wood on 24 March 1918 during the German offensives. Australian battalions, reduced to a shadow by lack of reinforcements, experienced mutinies during the final, exhausting weeks of the war. No other dominion went as far as Canada in establishing her military autonomy by the end of the war. Perversely, because he had forced his colleagues to extend political authority overseas to undermine his influence, Sir Sam Hughes might claim that autonomy as his final achievement.

Notes

CHAPTER 1

1 On the arrival, see A.F. Duguid, *Official History of the Canadian Forces in the Great War, 1914-1919*, General Series, I (Ottawa 1938) 118 and A.F. Duguid, *Appendices* (Ottawa 1938) 123, 134-5; Toronto *Globe* 16 October 1914; Toronto *News* 16 December 1914
2 *The Times*, 16 October 1914
3 C.P. Stacey, 'John A. Macdonald on Raising Troops in Canada for Imperial Service, 1885,' *Canadian Historical Review*, XXXVIII, 1, March 1957, 319-40; R.A. Preston, *Canada and 'Imperial Defense'* (Toronto 1967) 160-4
4 John English, *The Decline of Politics: The Conservatives and the Party System* (Toronto and Buffalo 1977) 89
5 *Ibid.* 88-90; Canada, House of Commons, *Debates*, 19 August 1914
6 On Borden, see R.C. Brown, *Robert Laird Borden: A Biography* (Toronto 1975) I; H.A. Wilson, *The Imperial Policy of Sir Robert Borden* (Gainesville, Fla. 1966) especially chap. 2
7 On the War Book and preparations, see Duguid, *Appendices* 1-3, 14. See C.P. Stacey, 'Canada's Last War and the Next,' *University of Toronto Quarterly*, 1938-9, 250
8 Duguid, *Appendices* 34-5
9 4 Edw. VII, c.23 s.70. See C.P. Stacey, *The Military Problems of Canada* (Toronto 1940) 76
10 Duguid, *Canadian Forces* 24-5
11 Canada, House of Commons, *Debates*, 21 August 1914, 56
12 Perley to Borden, 18 September 1914, PAC, Perley Papers, I
13 On the Quebec problem, see E. Armstrong, *The Crisis of Quebec* (New York 1937); Mason Wade, *The French Canadians*, 2d ed. (Toronto 1965) II, chaps. 11 and 12

14 On the war years in Canada, see B.M. Wilson, *Ontario and the First World War* (Toronto 1977); John H. Thompson, *The Harvests of War: The Prairie West, 1914-1918* (Toronto 1978); Michael Bliss, *A Canadian Millionaire* (Toronto 1978) chaps. 10-13; Daphne Read, ed., *The Great War and Canadian Society: An Oral History* (Toronto 1978)

15 Roger Graham, *Arthur Meighen*, II, *And Fortune Fled* (Toronto 1963) 209-13

16 Carl Berger, *The Sense of Power: Studies in the Ideas of Canadian Imperialism* (Toronto 1970) chap. 10 and Carl Berger, ed., *Imperialism and Nationalism, 1884-1914: A Conflict in Canadian Thought* (Toronto, 1969) 4-5

17 Noted by C.P. Stacey, *Canada and the Age of Conflict* (Toronto 1977) I, 176

18 Connaught to Harcourt, 1 August 1914, cited in C.P. Stacey, ed., *Historical Documents of Canada*, V, *The Arts of War and Peace* (Toronto 1972) 549

19 Ramsay Cook, *The Politics of John W. Dafoe and the Free Press* (Toronto 1963) 67

20 C.F. Winter, *Lieutenant-General The Hon. Sir Sam Hughes, K.C.B., M.P., Canada's War Minister, 1911-1916* (Toronto 1931) 32-6

21 Derby to Haig, 2 November 1917, cited in Robert Blake, *The Private Papers of Douglas Haig, 1914-1919* (London 1952) 266. See G.W.L. Nicholson, *C.E.F., 1914-1919: The Official History of the Canadian Army in the First World War* (Ottawa 1962) 381; Preston, *'Imperial Defense'* 488-92; Stacey, *Age of Conflict* 195-6

22 See, for example, R.C. Brown and Ramsay Cook, *Canada, 1896-1921: A Nation Transformed* (Toronto 1974) 213

23 Duguid, *Appendices* 122

24 Stacey, *Age of Conflict* 61

25 On the dispute, see Norman Penlington, *Canada and Imperialism, 1896-1899* (Toronto, 1965) chaps. 16 and 17

26 Stacey, *Age of Conflict* 62-71

27 Desmond Morton, *Ministers and Generals: Politics and the Canadian Militia* (Toronto 1970) 152-5; Desmond Morton, *The Canadian General: Sir Wiliam Otter* (Toronto 1974) 162-3, 166-7

28 On the dispute, see Minto to Laurier, 14 August 1899, PAC, Laurier Papers, C-768, 36477-82; PAC, Hutton Papers, 1100-77; PANS, F.W. Borden Papers, letterbook 11; PAC, Otter Papers; Hughes to Laurier, 23 October 1899, PAC, R.W. Scott Papers, IV, 1647-54

29 Morton, *Canadian General* 173-82 and chaps. 5 and 6. For a criticism see W.H. McHarg, *From Quebec to Pretoria with the Royal Canadian Regiment* (Toronto 1902); Russell G. Hubley, *'G' Company or Everyday Life of the R.C.R.* (Montreal 1901); O.C.C. Pelletier, *Mémoires, souvenirs de famille et récits* (Quebec 1940)

30 Canada, Department of Militia and Defence, *Supplementary Report, Organization, Equipment, Despatch and Service of the Canadian Contingents During the War in South Africa, 1899-1900* (Ottawa 1901)

31 Canada, House of Commons, *Debates*, 6 April 1900, 3334-5; 3 May 1900, 4560-4; Col W.H. Cotton to Otter, 23 December 1899, Otter Papers

32 Otter to Molly Otter, 5 April 1900, Otter Papers; W.D. Otter, 'Lecture on the Paardeberg Campaign,' Otter Papers, 6; Morton, *Canadian General* 206-8, 210

33 Toronto *Globe* 4 April 1900

34 *Supplementary Report* 12-13

35 Stacey, *Age of Conflict* 70

36 See Nicholson, *C.E.F.* 6-11; Preston, *'Imperial Defense'* 401 ff.; Carmen Miller, 'Sir Frederick William Borden and Military Reform, 1896-1911,' *Canadian Historical Review*, L, 3, September 1969. On Halifax, see Roger Sarty 'Halifax and the Defence of Canada 1906-1914,' paper delivered at the annual meeting of the Canadian Historical Association, 1981

37 Preston, *'Imperial Defense'* chap. 12

38 On the 'citizen army,' see Lord Dundonald, *My Army Life* (London 1926) 186-8; draft for Part II, Militia Report for 1902, Queen's University, Dundonald Papers; Morton, *Ministers* 178-9

39 Desmond Morton, 'The Cadet Movement in the Moment of Canadian Militarism, 1909-1914,' *Journal of Canadian Studies*, XIII, 2, Summer 1978. On Dundonald in Canada, see Morton, *Ministers* 174-92

40 On the Ross rifle, see Duguid, *Appendices* no. 111, 75-99; Morton, *Canadian General* 248-51, 290-2; Canada, House of Commons, *Debates*, 22 May 1908, 9028-66. Borden arranged for Hughes's promotion to colonel and created the post of railway staff officer to keep him on active duty

41 On the Oliver equipment, *Supplementary Report* 13; Duguid, *Appendices* no. 209, 146; Morton, *Canadian General* 157, 203

42 Morton, *Ministers* 193-5; Morton, *Canadian General* 292-4; Preston, *'Imperial Defense'* 335-6, 351

43 Miller, 'Military Reform' 274-5. On Lake, see Henry Borden, ed., *Letters to Limbo* (Toronto 1971) 251, for a list of reforms accomplished in his term

44 Nicholson, *C.E.F.* 14-15

45 On Gwatkin, see C.F. Hamilton's obituary, *Canadian Defence Quarterly*, I, 3, 1925, 226-30

46 Miller, 'Military Reform' 283, commenting on Donald Gordon, *The Dominion Partnership in Imperial Defence* (Baltimore, 1965) 276

47 On the plans, see Duguid, *Appendices* no. 11, 11; Nicholson, *C.E.F.* 14

48 On Hughes's appointment, see Sir Robert Borden, *Memoirs* (Toronto 1938) I, 33; Brown, *Borden* I, 202-4

49 On Hughes as minister, see Winter, *Hughes* 25-73; Morton, 'Cadet Movement' 64-7; Morton, *Canadian General* 310-13; *Canadian Annual Review*, 1913, 216-17, 222

50 On drinking, see *Canadian Annual Review*, 1912, 287; 1913, 217

51 'Memorandum re General MacKenzie,' Hughes to Borden, n.d., Borden Papers, OC 55, 741; Hughes to Borden, 12 February 1913, Borden Papers, OC 55, 742

52 Borden to Governor General, 1 May 1913, Borden Papers, OC 55, 78-83; Borden to Sir John French, Borden Papers, OC 55, 807. For British copies and comments, PRO, CO 537/498. A.B. Keith commented that Hughes was 'notoriously a very difficult person to deal with'

53 On conditions, see Brown and Cook, *Canada, 1896-1921* 198-200; Thompson, *Harvests of War* 13-24

54 *Canadian Liberal Monthly*, I, no. 1, September 1913; H.F. Gadsby in *Canadian Liberal Monthly*, I, no. 7, March 1914. Hughes's own defence is in Borden Papers, RLB 414, 99097-103; on overseas trip, Hughes to Borden, 18 March 1914, 99148-51

55 George Clare to Borden, 3 November 1913; Borden Papers, OCA 162, 784-95 and letters from E.L. Weichel MP and the Hon T.W. Crothers, Borden Papers, 78502, 78509

56 See Morton, 'Cadet Movement' 66; Toronto *Globe* 12 December 1913; for earlier comment, see Maurice Hutton, 'The Strathcona Trust,' *Proceedings of the 51st Convention of the Ontario Educational Association, 1912* 326-30

57 Desmond Morton, 'French Canada and the Canadian Militia, 1868-1914,' *Social History/Histoire Sociale*, no. III, June 1969, 49; Morton, 'French Canada and War: The Military Background to the Conscription Crisis, 1917,' in J.L. Granatstein and R.D. Cuff, eds., *War and Society in North America* (Toronto 1971) 94; Borden Papers, OC 190, 15614-19; *La Presse* 8 June 1914; Hughes to Borden, 1 June 1914, Borden Papers, OCA 155, 78146-7

58 For comments, see G.F.G. Stanley, *Canada's Soldiers: The Military History of an Unmilitary People*, 3d ed. (Toronto 1974) 308-9; Duguid, *Appendices* 12

59 Duguid, *Appendices* 13; Nicholson, *C.E.F.* 18

60 Stanley, *Canada's Soldiers* 309; on resources, see Nicholson, *C.E.F.* 11, 25; *Report on the Military Institutions of Canada by General Sir Ian Hamilton, G.C.B., D.S.O., Inspector General of the Overseas Forces* (Ottawa 1913)

61 PC 2068, 6 August 1914. See Duguid, *Appendices* 28-39, 69

62 PC 2067, 6 August 1914

63 PAC, RG 24, vol . 1220, file HQ 593-1-5

64 Canada, House of Commons, *Debates*, 26 January 1916, 292

65 On construction of Valcartier, see Hughes's speech, *ibid*. Duguid, *Canadian Forces* 34-8; Nicholson, *C.E.F.* 20-1

66 On training at Valcartier, see Nicholson, *C.E.F.* 21-5; Duguid, *Canadian Forces* 88-92; Winter, *Hughes* 144-5. Borden, *Memoirs* I, 462 reflects criticism: see Borden Papers, OC 165/11, 12468

67 On the composition of the CEF units, see Duguid, *Appendices* no. 85, 54-7. On other organizations, see Duguid, *Canadian Forces* 65-70

68 On senior officers, see Duguid, *Canadian Forces* 63-4. See R.C. Brown and Desmond Morton, 'The Embarrassing Apotheosis of a "Great Canadian": Sir Arthur Currie's Personal Crisis in 1917,' *Canadian Historical Review* LX, 1, March 1979, 50-1

69 On the consequences, see Morton, 'French Canada and War' 95-6; on the origins of the troops, see Duguid, *Canadian Forces* 49-53; Thompson, *Harvests of War* 24

70 Nicholson, *C.E.F.* 25-8; Duguid, *Canadian Forces* 77-87. On the MacAdam shovel, see Duguid, *Canadian Forces* 79-80; Hubard to H.W. Brown, 18 September 1914, PAC, RG 24, vol. 1202 HQ 130-19-2-3; OC 43d Bn to HQ. Shorncliffe camp 9, July 1915, RG 9 III, vol. 9, file 4-2-35

71 Nicholson, *C.E.F.* 29-30; Duguid, *Appendices* 106-9. R.C. Brown, *Robert Laird Borden: A Biography* (Toronto 1980) II, 13-14

72 Duguid, *Appendices*, no. 149, 123.

73 John English, *Borden: His Life and Times* (Toronto 1977) 103

CHAPTER 2

1 I.S. Bloch, *The Future of War in its Technical, Economic and Political Relations* (Boston 1902); R.A. Preston and S.F. Wise, *Men in Arms*, 2d rev. ed. (New York 1970) 259-60; Theodore Ropp, *War in the Modern World* (New York 1959) 218-22

2 On conditions, see Ropp, *War in the Modern World* chap. 8; Preston and Wise, *Men in Arms* chap. 16; John Ellis, *Eye Deep in Hell* (London 1976)

3 Roberts to Secretary of State for War, 28 June 1900, PRO, CO 42/879, 438. On performance, see 'Brig. Gen. Henry H. Settle's dispatch on the Prieska Rebellion, 24 April 1900,' PRO, WO 105/7 C in C 126, 48 and 49, 4, 6

4 Hughes's fullest account of his views and grievances is in Hughes to Secretary of State for War, 30 March 1903, CO 42/895, 497-515. See also Lord Minto to Sir Montague Ommanney, 1 July 1903, CO 42/895, 522-6

5 Hughes to Borden, 16 September 1914, Borden Papers, OC 190, 15651

6 Governor General to Secretary of State for the Colonies, 1 August 1914, in Duguid, *Appendices* no. 16, 14

7 Canada, House of Commons, *Debates*, 21 August 1914, 52-3 and passim

8 Some of the problems are summarized in Duguid, *Appendices* no. 8, 4-10; John Swettenham, *To Seize the Victory: The Canadian Corps in World War I*

(Toronto 1965) 124-42; Capt L.R. Cameron, 'The Administration of the C.E.F. in the United Kingdom, 1915-1916,' unpublished report in the Directorate of History, March 1959; D.M.A.R. Vince, 'The Development of the Legal Status of the Canadian Military Forces, 1914-1919,' *Canadian Journal of Economics and Political Science*, XX, 3, August 1954; D.M.A.R. Vince, 'The Acting Overseas Sub-Militia Council and the Resignation of Sir Sam Hughes,' *Canadian Historical Review*, XXXI, 1, March 1950; Preston, *'Imperial Defense'* chap. 15, 467-8, 477-81; Desmond Morton, '"Junior but Sovereign Allies": The Transformation of the Canadian Expeditionary Force, 1914-1918,' *The Journal of Imperial and Commonwealth History*, VIII, 1, October 1979

9 On the Canadian high commissioner, see Stacey, *Age of Conflict* 33-4; D.M.L. Farr, *The Colonial Office and Canada, 1867-1887* (Toronto 1955) chap. 8

10 On the roles played by Tupper and Strathcona, see Sir Charles Hibbert Tupper, *Supplement to the Life and Letters of the Rt. Hon. Sir Charles Tupper, Bart. G.C.M.G.* (Toronto 1926) chap. 6; E.M. Saunders, *The Life and Letters of the Rt. Hon. Sir Charles Tupper, Bart. G.C.M.G.* (London 1916) II, 1-189 passim; Beckles Willson, *The Life of Lord Strathcona and Mount Royal* (London 1915) 455-584 (or the bilious view of W.T.R. Preston, *The Life and Times of Lord Strathcona* [London 1914] or *My Generation of Politics and Politicians* [Toronto 1927] 352-3)

11 On Perley, see English, *Decline of Politics* 83. Brown, *Borden* I, 205-6

12 Borden to Lewis Harcourt, 6 June 1914, PAC, Perley Papers, I; PC 1421, 2 June 1914; Borden to W.L. Griffiths, June 1914, Borden Papers, OC 176, 13364

13 Perley to Borden, 15 August 1914, Perley Papers, I, file 16. See Wilson, *Imperial Policy of Borden* 28-9

14 Duguid, *Appendices* no. 49, 39

15 Perley to Borden, August 1914, Perley Papers, I; Lord Kitchener to Perley, 16 August 1914, Perley Papers, I

16 Hughes to Lord Roberts, n.d., Borden Papers, OC 176, 15652-3

17 Borden to Perley, 29 August 1914, Perley Papers, I

18 Duguid, *Canadian Forces*, 93; *Appendices*, no. 120. On Alderson in South Africa, see particularly Alderson to Hutton, 12 July 1901, BM, add. mss 50083, Hutton Papers

19 Kitchener to Perley, 5 September 1914, Perley Papers, I; Nicholson, *C.E.F.* 29

20 Duguid, *Canadian Forces* 93

21 Borden to Perley, 9 October 1914, Perley Papers, II, file 29

22 Hughes to Borden, 25 October 1914, Borden Papers OC 190, 15664-6

23 Militia General Orders no. 175, October 1914; Hughes to Borden, 25 October 1914, Borden Papers, OC 190, 15664. On previous pressure see, for example, 'Canadian members of the Militia Council' to Borden n.d. (February 1913),

Borden Papers, OCA 162, 78470-1; Maj-Gen D.A. Macdonald to Borden, 7 March 1913 and enclosures, Borden Papers, OCA 162, 78484-7 (Hughes's predecessor, Sir Frederick Borden, had been made a surgeon-general, a comparable rank, during his time as minister)

24 Borden to Perley, 20 October 1914, Perley Papers, II. See Borden *Memoirs*, I, 462-4; John W. Dafoe, *Clifford Sifton in Relation to his Times* (Toronto, 1931) 387-8; Brown, *Borden* II, 14-17

25 Perley to Borden, 23 October 1914, Perley Papers, II

26 Perley to Borden, 15 October 1914, 17 October 1914, Perley Papers, I, folder 4. See also Perley to Borden, 9 July 1914, 8 September 1914, 6 October 1914, Perley Papers, I, folder 4, on the election prospects; English, *Decline of Politics* 90, 101-2

27 On the Second Contingent, see Duguid, *Appendices* 127-9; Nicholson, *C.E.F.* 109-10; PC 2831, 7 November 1914

28 Morton, 'French Canada' 96-7; Col J.H. Chaballe, *Histoire du 22ᵉ Bataillon Canadien-Français* I, *1914-19* (Montreal 1952) 20-36; Duguid, *Appendices* no. 711, 344-5

29 Perley to Borden, 9 November 1914, Borden Papers, OC 176, 13382

30 Duguid, *Canadian Forces* 121-2

31 *Ibid.* chap. 4

32 *Ibid.* 128-9; *Appendices* no. 192, 137-8, PAC, RG 9, III B1, vol. 485, file R-16-1, vol. 1

33 On equipment problems, see Alderson to Carson, 28 March 1915, Duguid, *Appendices* no. 227, 159-60, nos. 210-24, 147-57

34 Alderson to Connaught, 4 December 1914, Borden Papers, OC 227, 22857

35 On Carson see H.J. Morgan, *Canadian Men and Women of the Time* (Toronto 1912), 205; Winter, *Hughes*, photo facing p. 39; Duguid, *Appendices* no. 188, 135-6

36 Perley to Borden, 25 June 1915, Borden Papers, OC 183 (1) 14788 ff.

37 First Canadian Contingent Order, 7 November 1914; Brown, *Borden*, II, p. 16

38 Carson to Borden, 25 January 1915, Borden Papers, OC 225, 22813-4

39 Nicholson, *C.E.F.* 35

40 Duguid, *Canadian Forces* 140-2

41 Borden, Diary (through the kindness of Professor R.C. Brown)

42 Carson to Borden, 7 January 1915, Borden Papers, OC 227, 22805-7

43 Perley to Borden, 25 January 1915, Perley Papers, III file 44, in reply to Borden to Perley, 12 January 1915, *ibid.*

44 *Ibid.*

45 See Stacey, *Age of Conflict* 180-2; Thompson, *Harvests of War* chap. 3; Bliss, *Canadian Millionaire* chaps. 10, 11; Gaddis Smith, *Britain's Clandestine Sub-*

marines, 1914-15 (New Haven, Conn. 1964). Borden to Perley, 27 November 1914, Perley Papers, III, file 38

46 Carson to Borden, 20 January 1915, Borden Papers, OC 225, 22824

47 Borden to Carson, 21 January 1915, *ibid.* 22830.

48 Nicholson, *C.E.F.* 38-9, 88

49 Gwatkin to Christie, 3 March 1915, Gwatkin Papers

50 Perley to Borden, 3 December 1914, Borden Papers, OC 178, 13588; Duguid, *Canadian Forces* 137; *Appendices* 4-10, 135-6, 361-5. On medical arrangements, see Sir Andrew Macphail, *Official History of the Canadian Forces in the Great War: The Medical Services* (Ottawa 1925) 25-35, 137-44

51 On Seely, see Lord Mottistone, *Adventure* (London 1930) chap. 11 and 217-19, claiming that Kitchener 'devised' the command for him. Perley to Borden, n.d., Perley Papers, III, file 56; Duguid, *Canadian Forces* 158-9

52 Militia Department to Alderson, 9 February 1915, PAC, RG 9, III A1, vol. 184, file 6-MC-153

53 Carson to Altham, 18 February 1915, *ibid.* vol. 44, file 8-5-10

54 Carson to Hughes, 27 February 1915, *ibid.* vol. 43, file 8-5-8

55 MacDougall to Carson, 19 February 1915, *ibid.* vol. 44, file 8-5-10

56 Carson to Hughes, 23 February 1915, *ibid.*

57 Carson to Hughes, 2 March 1915, *ibid.*

58 Adjutant General to MacDougall, 17 March 1915, *ibid.*

59 Hughes to MacDougall, 17 March 1915, *ibid.*

60 Hughes to Carson, 19 March 1915, *ibid.*

61 Duguid, *Canadian Forces* 128

62 MacDougall to Carson, 21, 26 March 1915; Carson to MacDougall, 25 March 1915, RG 9, III A1, vol. 44, file 8-5-10

63 Hughes to Carson, 26 May 1915, *ibid.*

64 On Steele, see S.B. Steele, *Forty Years in Canada* (Toronto 1915); Steele to Arthur Sifton, 10 January 1919, PAC, A.L. Sifton Papers, vol. 14

65 Hughes to Kitchener, 29 March 1915, copy in Perley Papers, III, file 66, with a notation from Kitchener, 'This seems extraordinary even for Hughes.' See also Hughes to Lougheed, 26 July 1915, in Nicholson, *C.E.F.* p. 112, for a less flattering view of Steele

66 Carson to Steele, 25 May 1915, RG 9, III A1, vol. 43, file 8-5-8; Carson to Hughes, 27 May 1915, *ibid.*

67 Carson to Steele, 27 May 1915, *ibid.*

68 RG 9, III A1, vol. 29, file 8-1-28 passim

69 Carson to Hughes, 18 February 1915, *ibid.* vol. 44, file 8-5-10

70 Gwatkin to Christie, 3 March 1915, Gwatkin Papers

71 Hughes to Borden, 28 May 1915, Borden Papers, OC 281, 31777

72 Turner to Alderson, 7 July 1915, RG 9, III A1, vol. 28, 8-1-10
73 Alderson to Carson, 7 July 1915, *ibid.* (A copy of Alderson's letter was sent through the High Commission to Borden. See Borden Papers, OC 281, 31780-8.) Alderson claimed that Hughes's statement that his information had come from a staff officer who had returned to Canada could only apply to one of Turner's officers who had gone out of his mind during the battle. See Borden Papers, OC 281, 31795. On the War Office *communiqué*, see Nicholson, *C.E.F.* 92
74 On the 2d Division, see Nicholson, *C.E.F.*, 109-13; Duguid, *Canadian Forces* chap. 16
75 Alderson to Hutton, 21 August 1915, Hutton Papers, add. mss 50088. Steele and Carson had agreed that Alderson was not the man for the job but Carson explained the British insistence: Carson to Steele, 24 June 1915, RG 9, III A1, vol. 43, file 8-5-8
76 On Landry, see Morton, 'French Canada' 97-8. For Quebec reaction, see Robert Rumilly, *Histoire de la Province de Québec*, XX, 99-100. See also Carson to Steele, 6 August 1915, RG 9, III A1, vol. 43, file 8-5-8. For Steele's reasons, see Steele to Carson, 2 August 1915, *ibid.*
77 Carson to Hughes, 16 June 1915, *ibid.*; Hughes to Carson, 18 June 1915, *ibid.* On Brooke, see Duguid, *Canadian Forces* 541-2; Nicholson, *C.E.F.* 112
78 On rearrangement of commands, see Nicholson, *C.E.F.* 112-13; Hughes to Lougheed, 26 July 1915, RG 9, III A1, vol. 78, file 10-8-52; Carson to Alderson, 13 September 1915, *ibid.* 8-5-8-A
79 Steele to Hughes, 10 April 1916, Borden Papers, OC 183(2), 14922-5
80 Carson memorandum to Steele, 27 August 1915, RG 9, III A1, vols. 74-5, file 10-8-22

CHAPTER 3

1 Nicholson, *C.E.F.* 114-16; H.M. Urquhart, *Arthur Currie: The Biography of a Great Canadian* (Toronto 1950) 1-28; A.M.J. Hyatt, 'The Military Career of Sir Arthur Currie' (Ph.D. diss., Duke University, 1965)
2 'Growth and Control of the Canadian Forces,' Borden Papers, vol. 298, 173820
3 *Supplementary Report*, 1900, 9-10; C.F. Winter, 'Some Recollections of Service with the Imperials,' *Canadian Defence Quarterly*, IV, 4, July 1927
4 Seely, *Adventure* 220-1; Duguid, *Canadian Forces* 455
5 Duguid, *Canadian Forces* 449-50; Winter, *Hughes* 163-5; PC 1593, 8 July 1915
6 On recruiting in Canada, see Wilson, *Ontario and the First World War* xxx-xxxvii, xlv-xlix; J.L. Granatstein and J.M. Hitsman, *Broken Promises: A His-*

tory of Conscription in Canada (Toronto 1977) chap. 2; Thompson, *Harvests of War* chap. 2; Morton, 'French Canadians' 96-103; Desmond Morton, 'The Short Unhappy Life of the 41st Battalion C.E.F.,' *Queen's Quarterly*, LXXXI, 1, 1974; W.R. Young, 'Conscription, Rural Depopulation and the Farmers of Ontario, 1917-1919,' *Canadian Historical Review*, LIII, 3, September 1972; R.J. Manion, *Life is an Adventure* (Toronto 1936) 172-3; R.M. Bray, 'The Canadian Patriotic Response to the Great War' (Ph.D. diss., York University, 1976) and '"Fighting as an Ally": The English-Canadian Patriotic Response to the Great War,' *Canadian Historical Review*, LXI, 2, June 1980

7 One vivid account of the experience in raising the 157th Bn, CEF is Leslie Frost, *Fighting Men* (Toronto 1967) 46-62. Harold Daly's unpublished memoirs provide a spirited view of Militia Headquarters and its personalities. See PAC, Harold Daly Papers, I 14-17

8 Duguid, *Canadian Forces* 547

9 Gwatkin to Christie, 13 March 1915, Gwatkin Papers

10 Duguid, *Appendices* no. 8, p. 7

11 Stacey, *Age of Conflict* 189-90; PC 2559; Duguid, *Appendices* no. 8, 7

12 Carson to Alderson, 13 September 1915, RG 9, III A1, vol. 43, file 8-5-8-A (See also Carson to Watson, 23 September 1915, *ibid.*)

13 Stacey, *Age of Conflict* 189-90; Borden, *Memoirs* I, 498-509; Preston, *'Imperial Defense'* 506-8

14 On Carrick, see Duguid, *Appendices* no. 111, 229; 'Thinks in millions,' *Canadian Men and Women* 1912, 203

15 Duguid, *Appendices* 162

16 Carson to Hughes, 9 July 1915, RG 9, III A1, vol. 125, file 6-C-12

17 Perley to Borden, 9 May 1915, Perley Papers, vol. 3, file 79

18 Carson to Ward, 6 September 1915, RG 9, III A1, vol. 125, file 6-C-12 and passim. See Borden to Perley, 24 November 1915, Perley Papers, vol. 4, file 117. On Carrick elsewhere, see Bliss, *Canadian Millionaire* 264

19 A.J.P. Taylor, *Beaverbrook* (London 1972). On the appointment, see pp. 81-90; Duguid, *Canadian Forces* 154-5; *Appendices* 161; PC 29, 6 January 1915; Hughes to Carson, 29 March 1916, RG 9, III A1, vol. 109, file 6-A-5

20 Beaverbrook to Borden, 11 September 1925, UNB Archives, Beaverbrook Papers, Borden Correspondence, no. 4. (His friend R.B. Bennett wondered whether Beaverbrook might not be fighting the wrong enemy at times. See Bennett to Borden, 7 December 1915, copy in Perley Papers, vol. 5, file 132)

21 Carson to Steele, 25 August 1915, RG 9, III A1, vol. 44, file 8-5-10-A; Carson to Lougheed, 30 August 1915, *ibid.*

22 Carson to MacDougall, 11 October 1915, *ibid.*; Carson to Hughes, 4 October 1915, 12 October 1915, *ibid.*

23 Carson to Aitken, 12 October 1915, *ibid.*, Hughes to Carson, 16 October 1915, and Hughes to Aitken, n.d., *ibid*; Turner to Carson, 1 December 1915, *ibid.*
24 Carson to Hughes, 1 December 1915, *ibid.*
25 'Administration of the Canadian Expeditionary Force' (ms report, Canadian Forces Historical Section, 1956), 16-17
26 Carson to Steele, November 1915, RG 9, III A1, vol. 44, file 8-5-10-A
27 Carson to Hughes, 15 November 1915, *ibid.* vol. 47, file 8-5-43
28 War Office to GOC in C, Aldershot, 12 December 1915, RG 9, III A1, vol. 44, file 8-5-10-B and passim
29 Carson to Steele, 16 December 1915, *ibid.* vol. 47, file 8-5-43
30 Carson to Steele, 9 January 1916, *ibid.* vol. 44, file 8-5-10-B; MacDougall to Carson, n.d., *ibid.*
31 Carson to MacDougall, 3 November 1915, RG 9, III A1, vol. 44, file 8-5-10-A
32 Carson to MacDougall, 19 November 1915, *ibid.*; also MacDougall to Carson exchange, 23 and 30 November 1915, *ibid.*
33 Carson to Hughes, 2 December 1915, *ibid.* vol. 29, file 8-1-26. On Carson's claim see Carson to Lt-Col E.W. Moor, 30 August 1915, *ibid.*
34 Hughes to Carson, 4 December 1915, *ibid.*
35 Carson to MacDougall, 22 December 1915, *ibid.* vol. 44, file 8-5-10-B; reply, 18 December 1915, *ibid.*
36 Carson to Hughes, 3 December 1915, *ibid.* vol. 34, file 8-1-87-A.
37 Carson to Hughes, 15 December 1915, *ibid.*; Carson to Hughes, 27 December 1915, *ibid.*
38 Alderson to Hughes (February 1916), *ibid.* vol. 44, file 8-5-8-D
39 Carson to Brade, 8 January 1915, *ibid.* vol. 43, file 8-5-8-B; Swettenham, *To Seize the Victory* 131. (The Fort Garry Horse won the place)
40 Carson to Hughes, 15 October 1915, RG 9, III A1, vol. 109, file 6-A-5
41 Carson to Hughes, 8 November 1915, *ibid.*
42 Steele to Carson, 1 December 1915, *ibid.* vol. 43, file 8-5-8-B
43 On the 3d Division, see Alderson to Carson, 24 November 1915, *ibid.*; Hughes to Carson, 2 November 1915, *ibid.*; Nicholson, *C.E.F.* 133-4
44 Carson to Alderson, 3 January 1916, RG 9, III A1, vol. 43, file 8-5-8-B; Alderson to Carson, 4 January 1916, *ibid.*
45 Gwatkin to Colonel James Mason, 3 July 1915, Gwatkin Papers
46 Carson to Alderson, 2 November 1915, RG 9, III A1, vol. 43, file 8-5-8-A; Carson to Hughes, 3 November 1915, *ibid.*
47 Granatstein and Hitsman, *Broken Promises* 34-9; Morton, 'French Canadians' 96-102
48 Hilliam to GOC, 8th CIB, 12 January 1916, RC 9, III A1, vol. 45, file 8-5-10-C. (The commanding officer and senior major had been dismissed after the bat-

talion dissolved in a panic. The incident forms a factual basis for Hugh MacLennan's novel, *Barometer Rising* [New York 1941; Toronto 1956]. See Perley Papers, vol. 4, file 102)

49 Currie to Carson, 21 January 1916, RG 9, III A1, vol. 45, file 8-5-10-C

50 Alderson to GOC Second Army, 8 February 1916, Borden Papers, OC 337, 39339; Carson to French, 29 February 1916, RG 9, III A1, vol. 45, file 8-5-10-C

51 Macdougall to Carson, 1 March 1916, RG 9, III A1, vol. 45, file 8-5-10-C

52 Nicholson, *C.E.F.* 504; *Report of the Ministry of the Overseas Military Forces of Canada, 1918* (London 1919) 345-6 (I gratefully acknowledge the advice of Dr W.A.B. Douglas, Director of History at National Defence Headquarters, on this point)

53 Hughes to Carson, 15 October 1915, RG 9, III A1, vol. 44, file 8-5-10-A

54 Carson to Hughes, 25 January 1916, RG 9, III A1, vol. 45, file 8-5-10-C

55 Steele to Carson, 28 January 1916, RG 9, III A1, vol. 45, file 8-5-10-C

56 Frost, *Fighting Men*, 84-92

57 Carson to Hughes, 8 November 1915, RG 9, III A1, vol. 109, file 6-A-5

58 Hughes to Carson, 19 November 1915, RG 9, III A1, vol. 30, file 8-1-55

59 Carson to Hughes, 20 November 1915, *ibid.* (with accompanying reports)

60 Ward to Carson, 27 November 1915, *ibid.*

61 Carson to Hughes, 15 December 1915, *ibid.*

62 Gwatkin to Christie, 15 January 1915, Gwatkin Papers

63 Gwatkin memorandum, 14 January 1916, Borden Papers, vol. 36, OC 183(2), 14862 ff.

64 Gwatkin to Christie, 14 January 1916, Gwatkin Papers; RG 24, vol. 502, file HQ 54-21-5-7, vol. 2. See Borden Papers, OC 183(2)

65 Borden to the governor general, 22 January 1916, *ibid.* 14865

66 Governor General to Colonial Office, 22 January 1916, RG 24, vol. 502, file HQ 54-21-5-7

67 PC 2138, 15 September 1915

68 Hughes to Aitken, 30 November 1915, Borden Papers, OC 279, 31365. See also Aitken to Borden, n.d. (November 1915), Perley Papers, vol. 5, file 132

69 Stacey, *Age of Conflict* 193; Borden, *Memoirs* II, 622-3; Preston, *'Imperial Defense'* 508-10

70 PC 273, 23 February 1916. For correspondence, see Borden Papers, OC 318(1); Preston, *'Imperial Defense'* 469 ff.

71 On the Ross rifle the best single reference is Duguid, *Appendices* no. 111, 75 ff

72 Nicholson, *C.E.F.* 155-7; Duguid, *Canadian Forces* 522-4

73 Alderson to Gwatkin, 6 February 1916, cited in Duguid, *Appendices* 94-5

74 Hughes to Alderson, 7 March 1916, cited in Duguid, *Appendices* 95-6 and comments, 96-7 (Several of the addresses plainly used Hughes's letter as a chance to win favour from the minister)

75 For example, on Hughes's abuse of the governor general, see Borden to Hughes, 18 March 1916, Borden Papers, OC 165(2), 12807 ff. On the Shell inquiry, see Borden to Hughes, 10 March 1916, *ibid.* OC 218(1), 35586

76 Borden to Perley, 14 March 1916, *ibid.* OC 190, 15790

77 Borden to Hughes, 14 March 1916, *ibid.* 15792. See Borden to Hughes, 14 March 1916, *ibid.* OC 318(1), 33587

78 Carson to MacDougall, 1 February 1916, RG 9, III A1, vol. 45, file 8-5-10-C

79 MacDougall to Carson, 3 February 1916, *ibid.*

80 Carson to MacDougall, 13 March 1916, *ibid.*; MacDougall to Carson, 15 March 1916, *ibid.*

81 Hughes to Borden, 24 March 1916, Borden Papers, OC 183(2), 14899-903.

82 *Ibid.* Col Harrington was presumably Brig-Gen Charles Harrington, Alderson's chief of staff. Such a disloyal comment seems incredible but Harrington's memoirs suggest no such affection for Alderson as he felt for his successor, Byng. Harrington played a later, more indirect role in Canadian history as the British officer at the heart of the Chanak crisis of 1923. See Gen Sir Charles Harrington, *Tim Harrington Looks Back* (London 1940). (On Alderson's plan for Carson, see Alderson to Carson, 18 February 1916, RG 9, III A1, vol. 109, file 6-A-55)

83 Memorandum, Hughes to Aitken, n.d., 'Beaverbrook File,' Canadian Forces Historical Section

84 Borden to Perley, 3 April 1916, Perley Papers, vol. 5, file 147. On the scandal, see Bliss, *Canadian Millionaire* 241-51 and passim; E.M. Macdonald, *Recollections, Personal and Political* (Toronto n.d.) 305-9; Borden Papers, OC 318(1) and 441(1)

CHAPTER 4

1 Sir Andrew Macphail, *History of the Canadian Forces in the Great War, 1914-1919: The Medical Services* (Ottawa 1925) 171

2 Alderson to Carson, 18 February 1916, RG 9, III A1, vol. 109, file 6-A-55

3 Aitken to Military Secretary, BEF, n.d., Perley Papers, vol. 3, file 132; Major R.M. Sims to Military Secretary, 7 December 1915, Borden Papers, OC 337, 39336

4 Alderson to Assistant Military Secretary, 13 December 1915, *ibid.* 39337

5 Aitken to Borden, n.d., Perley Papers, vol. 5, file 132

6 On Lowther, see Duguid, *Canadian Forces* 128; Hughes to Borden 25 October 1914, Borden Papers, OC 190

7 Borden to Perley, 30 October 1915, Perley Papers, vol. 4, file 107; Perley to Borden, 21 January 1916, *ibid.*

8 Borden to Perley, 24 November 1915, *ibid.* file 117

9 Borden to Perley, 2 December 1915 and 6 December 1915, *ibid.* file 119

10 Perley to Borden, 9 May 1915, *ibid.* vol. 3, file 79

11 Perley to Aitken, 19 November 1915, *ibid.* file 116

12 Perley to Borden, 6 December 1915, *ibid.* file 124A. See also Perley to Borden memorandum, 10 August 1915, *ibid.* file 94A; Borden, *Memoirs* II 498

13 Perley to Borden, 17 February 1916, Borden Papers, OC 183(2), 14876 ff. in reply to Borden to Perley, 22 January 1916, Perley Papers, vol. 5, file 129

14 Gwatkin memorandum, 11 March 1916, Borden Papers, OC 280, 31737

15 See undated memorandum, *ibid.*, OC 318(1), 35589-90

16 Gwatkin to Borden, 4 April 1916, *ibid.* 35588

17 Memorandum, 8 April 1916, *ibid.* 35562-4

18 Borden to Perley, 10 April 1916, *ibid.* OC 183(2), 14927-8

19 Nicholson, *C.E.F.* 206-7

20 Hughes to Lessard, 22 April 1916, Borden Papers, OC 183(2), 14944-6; Perley to Borden, n.d., *ibid.* 14942; Borden, *Memoirs*, II, 563

21 PAC, RG 9, III B1, vol. 2892, file 0-153-33, vol. 1

22 MacDougall to Aitken, 19 April 1916, RG 9, III A1, vol. 184, file 6-MC-153

23 Steele to Hughes, 10 April 1916, Borden Papers, OC 183(2), 14922-4

24 Oulster to Carson, undated memorandum, RG 9, III A1, vol. 30, file 8-1-55

25 See RG 9, III B1, vol. 2892, file 0-15-3-33, vol. 1

26 Perley to Borden, 3 April 1916, Borden Papers, OC 183(2), 14908-9

27 Perley to Borden, 25 April 1916, *ibid.* OC 318(1), 35638

28 James Muir to P.D. Ross, 1 May 1916, *ibid.* OC 165(2), 12720 and passim

29 Borden to Perley, 3 April 1916, and notes by J.W. Borden and H. Dunn, Perley Papers, vol. 5, file 145

30 Perley to Borden, 11 May 1916, Perley Papers, vol. 5, file 145

31 Carson to Steele, 18 April 1916, RG 9, III A1, vol. 45, file 8-5-10-C

32 Carson to Whigham, 18 April 1916, *ibid.*

33 Can 121/Overseas 1938, 12 April 1916, RG 9, III A1, vol. 45, file 8-5-10-D

34 Carson to MacDougall, 16 May 1916, *ibid.*

35 Steele to Carson, 18 June 1916, *ibid.*

36 Steele to Rogers, 13 May 1916, Borden Papers, OC 183(3), 14955-7

37 Nicholson, *C.E.F.* 137-45; 'St. Eloi Craters: Report on Operations,' PAC, Turner Papers, vol. I, no. 2, 247ff. Borden had a low opinion of Alderson. See *Memoirs* II, 606-7, 607n

38 Aitken to Hughes, 26 April 1916; Borden Papers, OC 183(2), 14966-7; Taylor, *Beaverbrook* 89-90

39 Blake, *Haig Diaries*, 21 April 1916
40 Aitken to Hughes, 26 April 1916, Borden Papers, OC 183(2), 14967. Borden and Hughes learned of the change in command some days after Aitken and Haig had settled the details. See Brown, *Borden* II, 63 and n9
41 Hyatt, 'Currie' 86-92 (Currie shared Alderson's assessment of Turner)
42 Blake, *Private Papers* 140. John Terraine, *Douglas Haig: The Educated Soldier* (London 1963) 217
43 Aitken to Hughes, 20 May 1916, Borden Papers, OC 183(3), 15045
44 Steele to Carson, 2 June 1916, RG 9, III A1, vol. 29, file 8-1-22; Alderson to Carson, 9 June 1916, *ibid.*
45 Carson to Watson, 20 June 1916, *ibid.*
46 Carson to Alderson, 11 July 1916, *ibid.*
47 Urquhart, *Currie* 137-8
48 War Office to Lord French, 5 July 1916, RG 9, III A1, vol. 45, file 8-5-10-E. See Steele to Carson, 23 June 1916, RG 9, III A1, vol. 45, file 8-5-10-D for his interpretation of MacDougall's status
49 Perley to Borden, 4 July 1916, Perley Papers, vol. 6, and Perley's recollections in Perley to Borden, 6 September 1916, Borden Papers, OC 318(1), 35722
50 On the Shell scandal, see Royal Commission on Shell Contracts, *Minutes of Evidence* (Ottawa 1916) and Borden Papers, OC 318(1) passim
51 On Camp Borden riots see Frost, *Fighting Men* 65; Hughes to Borden, 12 July 1916, Borden Papers, RLB 635, 103771-4; Wilson, *Ontario and the First World War* xlix-1
52 See Winter, *Hughes* 89; P.D. Ross, *Recollections of a Newspaper Person* (Toronto 1931)
53 Hughes was fortunate in the limitation of testimony according to Bliss, *Canadian Millionaire* 273-6, the best modern summary of the munitions problem and the 1916 controversy.
54 See Borden Papers, OC 190, 15806-9
55 Hughes to Borden, 15 July 1916, *ibid.*
56 PC 1720, 15 July 1916
57 Hughes to Borden, 24 July 1916, Borden Papers, OC 165a, 12738-40
58 Borden to Hughes, 3 August 1916, *ibid.* OC 190, 15817 passim. (The deplorable state of training in Canada was revealed by General Lessard's report. See PAC Lessard Papers, I)
59 Hughes to Borden, 15 August 1916, Borden Papers, OCA 189, 80895 (Australia and New Zealand by then had six divisions in France and strong mounted contingents in Egypt. See Appendix)
60 Borden to Hughes, 16 August 1916, Borden Papers, OC 190, 15820
61 Hughes to Borden, 16 August 1916, *ibid.* OCA 149, 77919

62 Borden to Hughes, 24 August 1916, OC 318(1), 35707. See Perley to Borden, 19 August 1916, *ibid.* OC 190, 15821
63 Steele to Carson, 21 July 1916, RG 9, III A1, vol. 45, file 8-5-10-E; Steele to Carson, 25 July 1916, *ibid.*
64 Ottawa *Citizen*, 5 August 1916; Borden Papers, OCA 189, 80885. Hughes' activities in England may be traced in RG 9, III A1, vol. 45, file 8-5-10-E and elsewhere.
65 Hughes to Borden, 10 September 1916, Borden Papers, OC 318(1), 35725. (On this episode see D.M.A.R. Vince, 'The Acting Overseas Sub-Militia Council and the Resignation of Sir Sam Hughes,' *Canadian Historical Review*, XXXI, 1, March 1950, 1-24)
66 Ottawa *Evening Journal*, 6 September 1916
67 Borden to Hughes, 7 September 1916, Borden Papers, OC 318(1), 35725
68 Hughes to Borden, 8 September 1916, *ibid.* 35780
69 Borden to Hughes, 8 September 1916, *ibid.* 35779
70 Hughes to Borden, 10 September 1916, *ibid.* 35785
71 Aitken to Borden, 11 September 1916 (2d cable), *ibid.* 35784 (Reference in the cable to Borden to Aitken, 16 August 1916, CFHQ 'Beaverbrook File')
72 Hughes to Borden, 8 September 1916, Borden Papers, OC 318(1), 35731-3
73 Hughes to Carson, 18 September 1916, CF 8-1-106; Carson to Hughes, 21 September 1916, *ibid.*
74 Minutes of the Sub-Militia Council, 8 September 1916, RG 9, III A1, vol. 107, folder 348
75 Hughes to Greene, 20 September 1916, RG 9, III A1, vol. 35, file 8-1-106
76 Perley to Borden, 28 November 1916, Borden Papers, OC 434, 45414
77 Minutes, 13, 18, 23 October 1916, RG 9, III A1, vol. 107, volder 348, passim. See Vince, 'Resignation' 15-16. For a more generous view see Nicholson, *C.E.F.* 208
78 Hughes to Carson, 8 October 1916, RG 9, III A1, vol. 35, file 8-1-106-A
79 Minutes, 13, 18 October 1916, RG 9, III A1, vol. 107, folder 348
80 *Ibid.* 27 October 1916

CHAPTER 5

1 Hughes to McCurdy, 21 September 1916, Borden Papers, OC 190, 15879; Hughes to Borden, n.d., *ibid.* 15832, indicated the minister's sense of optimism
2 Perley to Borden, 6 September 1916, *ibid.* OC 318(1), 35722-3
3 Newcombe memorandum, 18 September 1916, *ibid.* OC 434, 45406-9. See also D.M.A.R. Vince, 'The Development of the Legal Status of the Canadian

Military Forces, 1914-1919,' *Canadian Journal of Economics and Political Science*, XX, 3, August 1954

4 RG 9, III A1, vol. 35, file 8-1-106. See also Hughes to Boudreau, 23 October 1916, RG 24, vol. 430, file HQ 54-21-1-64

5 On Bruce see Herbert Bruce, *Varied Operations* (Toronto 1958) 86-90. Hughes to Borden, n.d., Borden Papers, OC 190, 15832-5 (on Bruce controversy, see below)

6 Perley to Borden, 11 October 1916, Perley Papers, vol. 6, file 183

7 Perley to Borden, 12 October 1916, Borden Papers, OC 318(2), 35807

8 White to Borden, 6 October 1916, *ibid.* 35805-6. See White to Borden, 30 August 1916, *ibid.* OC 318(1), 35718

9 Borden to Hughes, 18 October 1916, *ibid.* OC 318(2), 35808

10 Frost, *Fighting Men* 80; Vince, 'Hughes's Resignation' 17; Borden, *Memoirs* II, 568

11 Hughes to Borden, 23 October 1916, Borden Papers, OC 318(2), 35835-7 (seven pages)

12 Maj-Gen E.W. Wilson to Borden, 24 October 1916, *ibid.* OC 434, 45410; C.C. Ballantyne to Borden, 25 October 1916, *ibid.* OC 318(2), 35840

13 Lt-Col G.H. Bradbury to Borden, 25 October 1916, *ibid.* OC 165(3), 12840

14 Borden to Hughes, 26 October 1916, *ibid.* OC 318(2), 35841

15 Hughes to Borden, 26 October 1916, *ibid.* 35838

16 Borden to Hughes, 26 October 1916, *ibid.* 35845

17 Cited in correspondence published in Montreal *Gazette*, 17 November 1916, and in other newspapers, 15-17 November 1916

18 Borden to Perley, 6 November 1916, Borden Papers, OC 318(2), 35881

19 PAC, Foster diary, 26 October 1916; Borden, *Memoirs* II, 569

20 Hughes to Borden, 30 October 1916, Borden Papers, OC 318(2), 35853-4

21 Borden to Hughes, 31 October 1916, *ibid.* 35858-9

22 PC 2656, 31 October 1916, *ibid.* 35847

23 Hughes to Borden, 1 November 1916, *ibid.* 35860

24 Borden to Perley, 6 November 1916, *ibid.* 35881. On consultations, see Borden Papers, OC 318(2), 35896-7; Vince, 'Hughes's Resignation' 22

25 Borden to Hughes, 9 November 1916, *ibid.* 35884-5; Brown, *Borden* II, 57-8

26 Hughes to Borden, 11 November 1916, *ibid.* 35887-90; Borden, *Memoirs* II, 570; Vince, 'Hughes's Resignation' 22-3

27 Hughes to Borden, 15 November 1916, Borden Papers, OC 318(2), 35894. (Because of Hughes's pro-conscription speech to the Empire Club in Toronto on 9 November, some papers concluded that that was the basis for his dismissal. See Toronto *World*, 13 November 1916)

28 Hughes to Aitken, 6 December 1916, Beaverbrook Papers, F/1/24, letter 65 (Lord Birkenhead told Borden that Hughes had talked to him in August 1916 of 'overthrowing' the government. Borden, *Memoirs* II, 571)

29 Ottawa *Free Press*, 14 November 1916. On the resignation, see English, *Decline of Politics* 98-101; Nicholson, *C.E.F.* 209-10

30 P.D. Ross to Borden, 15 November 1916, Borden Papers, OC 127, 13738

31 See Toronto *Sentinel*, 23 November 1916; John Willison to Borden, 14 November 1916, Borden Papers, OC 177, 13731; H.C. Hocken to Borden, 15 November 1916, *ibid.* 13734

32 Borden to Kemp, 16 November 1916, *ibid.* OC 165(2), 12775

33 Perley to Borden, 1 November 1916, *ibid.* OC 318(2), 35873

34 Perley to Borden, 2 November 1916, Perley Papers, vol. 7, file 193

35 Borden to White, 2 November 1916, Borden Papers, OC 318(2), 35871. See also White to Borden, 6 November 1916, *ibid.* 35877

36 Perley to Borden, 27 January 1916, *ibid.* OC 176, 13638

37 Nicholson, *C.E.F.* 134. See correspondence, Watson to Carson, 10 May 1916, RG 9, III A1, vol. 44, file 8-5-8-E and Carson to Watson, 8 July 1916, *ibid.* 8-5-8-G passim

38 Proceedings of Sub-Militia Council, 8th Meeting, 27 October 1916, RG 9, III A1, vol. 107, folder 348

39 Col H.A. Bruce, *Report on the Canadian Army Medical Service* (London 1916). On the controversy, see Bruce, *Varied Operations* 89-94; H.A. Bruce, *Politics and the Canadian Army Medical Corps* (London 1919); Macphail, *The Medical Services* 156-69. On Bruce's appointment, see RG 9, III A1, vol. 107, folder 348

40 Hughes to Borden, 2 September 1916, Borden Papers, OC 331(1), 35863-6, on his views of faults in the Canadian administration. For other views, see A.M. Burke to Borden, 30 September 1916, *ibid.* 33880 and letters from Sir William Osler to Borden from 5 October 1916, *ibid.* 35884 ff. See also Perley to Borden, 24 October 1916, *ibid.* 33898

41 Perley to Borden, 1 November 1916, Perley Papers, vol. 7, file 194

42 Perley to Borden, 2 November 1916, *ibid.* file 195

43 Greene to members of the Acting Sub-Militia Council, 7 November 1916, RG 9, III A1, vol. 35, file 8-1-106

44 'Decisions,' RG 9, III A1, vol. 107, folder 348

45 Borden to Perley, 6 November 1916, Borden Papers, OC 318(2), 35878-81

46 Perley to Borden, 6 November 1916, *ibid.* 35879

47 Memorandum, 10 November 1916, RG 24, vol. 430, file HQ 54-21-1-64

48 Steele to Perley, 16 November 1916, RG 9, III A1, vols. 74-5, file 10-8-22; Steele to Perley, 19 November 1916, *ibid.*; Steele to Shaughnessy, 19 November 1916, *ibid.*

49 Ward to Perley, 7 November 1916, *ibid.*
50 Proceedings of Acting Sub-Militia Council, 16 November 1916, RG 9, III A1, vol. 107, folder 348
51 Perley to Borden, 22 November 1916, Borden Papers, OC 318(2), 35898
52 Perley to Borden, 22 November 1916, Perley Papers, vol. 7, file 205; Borden to Perley, 23 November 1916, Borden Papers, OC 318(2), 35899
53 Urquhart, *Currie* 189-91; Hyatt, 'Currie' 99-100 ff.
54 Perley to Turner, 24 November 1916, Perley Papers, vol. 7, file 206F; Perley to Borden, 28 November 1916, *ibid.* file 212; Turner to Perley, 30 November 1916, PAC, Turner Papers, 11-78, 7186
55 Perley to Borden, 22 November 1916, Perley Papers, vol. 7, file 205
56 Perley to Borden, 28 November 1916, *ibid.* file 212. On MacDougall's status, see Carson to Perley, 28 November 1916, RG 9, III A1, vol. 45, file 8-5-10-H
57 Perley to Steele, 24 November 1916, RG 9, III A1, vols. 74-5, file 10-8-22
58 Perley to Borden, 26 December 1916, Perley Papers, vol. 7, file 223
59 Perley to Borden, 5 December 1916, Borden Papers, OC 434, 45443; Perley to Borden, 16 December 1916, *ibid.* 45462
60 Perley to Borden, 2 February 1917, *ibid.* 45477; Borden to Perley, 18 January 1917, 20 January 1917, Perley Papers, vol. 8, file 233 on the deputy minister appointment
61 Borden to Perley, 2 December 1916, Borden Papers, OC 434, 45428 commenting on Rogers to Borden, 1 December 1916, *ibid.* On the structure, see 'Composition of the Headquarters of the Forces of the Overseas Dominions in the British Isles,' PRO, WO 33/814, March 1917
62 Borden to Perley, 29 November 1916, Perley Papers, vol. 7, file 210
63 Perley to War Office, 4 December 1916, Borden Papers, OC 434, 45436; Perley to Borden, 5 December 1916, *ibid.* 45443
64 Turner to Neill, Leckie, and Reid, 4 December 1916, Turner Papers, 11-81, 7503, 7414, 7415; Perley to Greene, RG 9, III A1, vol. 35, file 8-1-106-A
65 Perley to Borden, 27 November 1916, Perley Papers, vol. 7, file 198
66 Creelman Diary, 19 November 1916, PAC, Creelman Papers, 77
67 Perley to Borden, 4 December 1916, Borden Papers, OC 434, 45435. On Carson later, see RG 9, III A1, vol. 255, file 10-C-12, HQ 4556-2
68 Borden to Perley, 2 December 1916, Perley Papers, vol. 7, file 218. See also Perley to Borden, 8 December 1916, *ibid.*
69 Borden to Perley, 12 January 1917, Borden Papers, OC 279, 31656
70 See Granatstein and Hitsman, *Broken Promises* 37-47. The 246th Battalion was the last to be raised in the Maritimes (information supplied by Professor R.C. Brown)

71 Perley to Borden, 10 November 1916, Borden Papers, OC 332, 39103. (In fact, in March 1917 Perley learned that there were 125,465 Canadians in France and 125,478 in England)

72 On the 5th Division, see Borden to Perley, 26 January 1917, Perley Papers, vol. 8, file 235; Gow to Whigham, 15 March 1917, Turner Papers, 10-66, 6793. See also Chief of the Imperial General Staff to Kemp, 25 May 1917, *ibid.* On pressure for inclusion, see Borden Papers, OC 332 passim

73 Carson to MacDougall, 11 September 1916, RG 9, III A1, vol. 45, file 8-5-10-F; Carson to Hughes, 15 September 1916, *ibid.* (MacDougall was shifted to a new headquarters in Brighton to get him away from Shorncliffe and to place him in the centre of the new cluster of Canadian camps)

74 On the reorganization, see Nicholson, *C.E.F.* 223-8, 'Memorandum on Absorption of Quebec and B.C. Battalions,' Borden papers, OC 335, 39224 ff.; Perley to Turner, 26 December 1916, *ibid.* 39226; 'Memorandum on Breaking up Battalions in England,' *ibid.* 39240-50

75 See Borden Papers, OC 418 for the pressure involved in disposing of one battalion, the 199th Irish Canadians, despite the patronage of the minister of justice, Charles Doherty. See also, on the 206th (Beavers) Battalion, Lt-Col W.H. Price MLA to Borden, 10 April 1917, *ibid.* OC 335, 39256-61

76 S.F. Wise, *Canadian Airmen and the First World War: The Official History of the Royal Canadian Air Force* (Toronto 1980) I, chap. 19

77 Lt-Col W.E. Thompson to F.B. McCurdy, 17 February 1917, Borden Papers, OC 415, 43545-9

78 Perley to Borden, 27 January 1917, Perley Papers, vol. 8, file 229

79 Perley to Borden, 26 January 1917, *ibid.* file 235

80 See, for example, Borden to Rogers, 26 May 1917, Borden Papers, OC 434, 45510. On Greene's later career, see Hughes to Beaverbrook, 17 August 1917, Beaverbrook Papers, F/1/25, no. 2

81 The Babtie report is cited in full in Bruce, *Politics and the CAMC* 155-86. See also Macphail, *Medical Services* 157-67

82 Perley to Borden, 6 January 1917, Perley Papers, vol. 8, file 227; on Babtie, see Bruce, *Politics and the CAMC* 249-56; Macphail, *Medical Services* 176-9

83 Macphail, *Medical Services* 196

84 See House of Commons, *Debates*, 6 February 1917, 538-40 and 15 April 1919, for Brig Gen Smart's charges. (Bruce's own comments on 'matrimonial agencies' proved ironic: he met and married a VAD nurse during his later service in France. See *Varied Operations* 101-2)

85 Borden to Perley, 6 November 1916, Borden Papers, OC 318(2), 35879

86 Perley to Borden, 16 December 1916, 6 January 1917, Perley Papers, vol. 8, file 227; Borden to Perley, 31 December 1916, *ibid.*

87 Borden to Perley, 7 January 1917, *ibid.*
88 Perley memorandum, 9 February 1917, RG 9, III A1, vol. 76, file 10-8-30

CHAPTER 6

1 A.J.P. Taylor, *English History, 1914-1945* (Oxford 1965) 73
2 Borden, *Memoirs* I, 506; Borden diaries, 16 June 1915, 24 August 1915;
  Preston, *'Imperial Defense'* 506
3 On the progress of the war and the British effort, see Taylor, *English History*
  chap. 2
4 On the Canadians on the Somme, see Nicholson, *C.E.F.* chap. 6; on Canada's
  war effort, see R.C. Brown and G.R. Cook, *Canada, 1896-1921: A Nation
  Transformed* (Toronto 1974) chap. 12
5 Philip Wigley, *Canada and the Transition to Commonwealth: British-Canadian
  Relations, 1917-1926* (Cambridge 1977) 24. See also Borden, *Memoirs* II, 621;
  Preston, *'Imperial Defense'* 507-9
6 Borden to Perley, 4 January 1916, Perley Papers, vol. 5, file 127A. On
  Borden's anger, see Stacey, *Age of Conflict* 191-2; R.C. Brown, 'Sir Robert
  Borden, the Great War and Anglo-Canadian Relations' in J.S. Moir, ed.,
  Character and Circumstance; Essays in Honour of Donald Grant Creighton
  (Toronto 1970) 211-12; Brown, *Borden* II, 34-5
7 On Asquith's removal, see Beaverbrook, *Politicians and the War* 206-27;
  Taylor, *English History* 66-70; Christopher Addison, *Politics from Within*
  (London 1924)
8 Taylor, *English History* 73-9. Wigley, *British-Canadian Relations* 26-8
9 David Lloyd George, *War Memoirs* (London 1938) I, 148
10 S.W. Roskill, *Hankey: Man of Secrets* (London 1970) I, 148. Wigley, *British-
   Canadian Relations* 31-2
11 Brown, *Borden* II, 70, 73-5; Borden diaries, 25 January 1917; Borden,
   Memoirs II, chap. 30
12 On the Imperial War Cabinet, see C.P. Stacey, *Historical Documents of Canada*, V, *The Arts of War and Peace* (Toronto 1972) 363-9; Preston,
   'Imperial Defense' 514-21; Brown, *Borden* II, 75-82
13 Stacey, *Age of Conflict* 207-10. Borden's speech is found in PAC, Loring
   Christie Papers, II, file 3. See Brown, 'Borden and Anglo-Canadian Relations'
   217-24 on Resolution IX. R.C. Brown and Robert Bothwell, 'The "Canadian"
   Resolution' in Cross and Bothwell, *Policy by Other Means* 165-76
14 Brown and Cook, *Canada, 1896-1921* 282, citing G.L. Cook, 'Sir Robert
   Borden, Lloyd George and British Military Policy, 1917-1918,' *Historical
   Journal*, XIV, 2, Spring 1971, 375

15 Stacey, *Age of Conflict* 210-12. Wigley, *British-Canadian Relations* 33-7
16 Canada, House of Commons, *Debates*, 30 January 1917, 253-69
17 *Ibid.* 228
18 See, for example, Borden to Perley, 19 April 1917, Borden Papers, OC 415, 43677
19 Kemp to Borden, 1 February 1917, *ibid.* OC 417, 43383-6. See also Kemp to Borden, 24 February 1917, *ibid.* 43396-7
20 McRae to Perley, 12 March 1917, RG 9, III A1, vol. 80, file 10-9-20; Perley to Borden, 26 March 1917, Borden Papers, OC 414, 43498
21 Kemp to Borden, 24 March 1917, *ibid.* 43495
22 Perley to Borden, 2 April 1917, *ibid.* 45414
23 The problems of the Steacy era are presented in somewhat partisan form by Col Almond to Turner, 28 February 1917, RG 9, III A1, vol. 4648, DCS, GA 1/9417
24 Burke to Perley, 2 February 1917, RG 9, III A1, vol. 104, folder 339. On relations with the British, see, for example, Maj-Gen J.M. Simms to Perley, 20 April 1917, PAC, Kemp Papers, vol. 110, file 10
25 Workman to Perley, 29 December 1916, RG 9, III A1, vol. 104, folder 339
26 Borden to Perley, 28 January 1917, *ibid.* in reply to Perley to Doherty, 23 January 1917, *ibid.* See also Bishop Morrison to Borden, 4 September 1916, *ibid.*; Burke to Perley, 3 February 1917, Perley Papers, vol. 8, file 244
27 On subsequent problems with the two chaplains, see Major O'Gorman to Kemp, 25 July 1917, Kemp Papers, vol. 118, file 10; Borden, *Letters to Limbo* 147
28 See Deputy Minister to War Office, 17 February 1917, Turner Papers, vol. 11, file 79, 7264; Turner to Perley, 27 January 1916, *ibid.* 7263; Preston, *'Imperial Defense'* 474. General staff officers were responsible for operational planning as opposed to the personnel and supply matters dealt with 'A' and 'Q' staff officers
29 Perley to Long, 21 February 1917, Perley Papers, vol. 8, file 243
30 Nicholson, *C.E.F.* 359-60
31 Governor General to colonial secretary, 26 April 1915, Borden Papers, RLB 997(1), 117488; PC 767, 8 September 1915
32 Perley to Borden, 16 February 1915, *ibid.* 117471
33 Memorandum, January 1916, *ibid.* 117551-7; 'War Office Estimate of the Maintenance Expenses of Canadian Forces in the Field,' Borden papers, OC 415, 43614. Hospital care was billed at three shillings a day, reciprocally. See Macphail, *Medical Services* 138
34 RG 24, vol. 923, file HQ 54-21-23-13, vol. 2. (Both Carson and Perley had objected to any clause recognizing that the issue could ever be re-opened. See

Carson to Perley, 8 January 1916, Borden Papers RLB 997[1], 117601; Perley to Borden, 5 January 1916, *ibid.* 117613)

35 Sir Charles Harris to Perley, 2 March 1917, *ibid.* OC 415, 43606
36 Perley to Harris, 7 March 1917, *ibid.* 43609; Harris to Perley, 10 March 1917, *ibid.* 43610 ff.
37 Taylor, *Beaverbrook* 121-7
38 On the office, see *Report of the O.M.F.C.*, 1918, 453-460; Taylor *Beaverbrook* 88-9
39 Perley to War Office, 25 January 1917, Turner Papers, 8-51, 5885
40 Memorandum, n.d., *ibid.* 5874-94. See PC 1251, 15 May 1917, in RG 9, III A1, vol. 71, file 10-8-1
41 Gow to War Office, 13 March 1917, RG 9, III A1, vol. 72, file 10-8-7; G. Elliott to Gow, 4 April 1917, *ibid.*
42 Gow to War Office, 24 April 1917, *ibid.*
43 Currie to Turner, 29 July 1917, Turner Papers, 8-5, 5872; Montague to Turner, n.d., *ibid.* 5868
44 Turner to Currie, 9 August 1917, *ibid.* 5870
45 Brig-Gen Farmar to Turner, 9 January 1917, *ibid.* 11-81, 7331; W.S.P. Hughes to Perley, 20 March 1917, Borden Papers, OC 415, 43552-4
46 Turner to Carson, 15 January 1916, Turner Papers, 11-81, 7330 (explaining why he had earlier hesitated to recommend Hughes for promotion)
47 On Vimy, see Nicholson, *C.E.F.* chap. 8
48 *Ibid.* 283
49 W.B. Kerr, *Arms and the Maple Leaf* (Seaforth, Ont. 1943) 27-8, 44-5. See also W.B. Kerr, *Shrieks and Crashes, Being Memories of Canada's Corps, 1917* (Toronto 1929) 40
50 Seely, *Adventure* 234-5
51 On the change of command, see Urquhart, *Currie* 159-61; Hyatt, 'Currie' 115-20; Nicholson, *C.E.F.* 283-4; R.C. Brown and Desmond Morton, 'The Embarrassing Apotheosis of a Great Canadian: Sir Arthur Currie's Personal Crisis in 1917' 43-4
52 Sims to Perley, n.d., Perley Papers, vol. 9, file 258; Perley to Borden, 9 June 1917, *ibid.* On Perley's judgment of the two men, see Perley to Borden 22 November 1916, *ibid.* vol. 7, file 225. For a military assessment, see Hyatt, 'Currie' 76-7, 86-8
53 Urquhart, *Currie* 163
54 Perley had certainly made no written commitment, whatever Turner's obvious impression. See Perley to Borden, 9 June 1917, Perley Papers, vol. 7, file 258
55 See 'Notes on conversation with Maj-Gen G.B. Hughes, Toronto, 11 January 1934,' RG 24, vol. 1812, file GAQ, 4-6

56 Urquhart, *Currie* 165
57 *Ibid.* 64. On Macdonnell see Seely, *Adventure* 218-19. On Hughes see A.M.J. Hyatt, 'Sir Arthur Currie and Conscription: A Soldier's View,' *Canadian Historical Review*, L, 3, September 1969
58 Hughes's claims were certainly urged. See Borden to Perley, 13 June 1917, Perley Papers, vol. 9, file 258. Later Borden denied any involvement whatsoever. See correspondence beginning Macdonnell to Borden, 14 December 1933, Borden Papers, additions, folder 82, 150458 ff. See Perley to Borden, 15 June 1917, RG 9, III A1, vol. 107, folder 348
59 On the clothing scandal, see Brown and Morton, 'Currie's Personal Crisis' 48-57. The relevant file is RG 24, vol. 5871, HQ 7-52-5, vol. 1
60 Morton and Brown, 'Currie's Personal Crisis' 57-8. See Currie to Forsythe, 25 June 1917, PAC, Forsythe Papers; J.H. Pangman to Dudley Oliver, 17 June 1936, PAC, Urquhart Papers, vol. 2. See Daly to Currie, 31 August 1917, PAC, Daly Papers, vol. 1. For an argument for the Hughes' conspiracy, see Hyatt, 'Currie' 120; Swettenham, *To Seize the Victory* 72-3
61 Perley to Borden, 21 July 1917, Perley Papers, vol. 9, file 264
62 Borden to Perley, 27 July 1917, *ibid.*
63 Brown and Morton, 'Currie's Personal Crisis' 60-3
64 Perley to Borden, 28 June 1917, RG 9, III A1, vol. 107, folder 348. See Steele to Rogers, 15 June 1917, *ibid.*
65 Memorandum, 14 June 1917, *ibid.* vol. 72, file 10-8-7
66 Sims to Perley, 18 June 1917, *ibid.* vol. 107, folder 348
67 Gow to Perley, 29 June 1917, *ibid.* vol. 72, file 10-8-7
68 Currie to Perley, 4 August 1917, *ibid.*
69 Perley to Currie, 16 August 1917, *ibid.*; Perley memorandum, 3 September 1917, Turner Papers, 8-51, 5722A-23
70 Militia to OMFC, 23 May 1917, RG 9, III A1, vol. 77, file 10-8-43
71 Canada, House of Commons, *Debates*, 30 January 1917, 268. Perley resented the detailed questions posed by Hughes, presuming that they were intended for nuisance purposes. See Perley to Borden, 9 August 1917, RG 9, III A1, vol. 77, file 10-8-43, on a question demanding the number of cases of drunkenness in the CEF since the landing of the First Contingent.
72 Thacker to Perley, 16 August 1917, *ibid.* Later, Turner would claim even lower figures for August 1917. See Turner memorandum, 17 July 1918, Turner Papers, 5376
73 Canada, House of Commons, *Debates*, 7 August 1917, 4195-208
74 *Ibid.* 4195-6
75 *Ibid.* 13 August 1917, 4418
76 *Ibid.* 4420

77 *Ibid.* 4419
78 Only R.B. Bennett launched a strong personal counter-attack on Hughes. See Canada, House of Commons, *Debates*, 7 August 1917, 4428-30. Third reading was on 18 August 1917
79 Borden, *Memoirs* II, 681
80 Perley to Kemp, 14 May 1917, Perley Papers, vol. 9, file 255
81 Kemp to Perley, 8 May 1917, *ibid.*; also 19 and 26 May 1917

CHAPTER 7

1 Maurice Hankey, *The Supreme Command, 1915-1918* (London 1961) II, 662-3
2 See Desmond Morton, 'The Supreme Penalty: Canadian Deaths by Firing Squad in the First World War,' *Queen's Quarterly*, LXXXI, 3, Autumn 1973. On officers, see, for example, RG 9 III, vol. 294, 10-2-4
3 Macphail, *Medical Services*
4 Cited by A.M. Willms, 'Conscription, 1917: A Brief for the Defence,' *Canadian Historical Review*, XXXVII, 4, December 1956, 348
5 Canada, House of Commons, *Debates*, 20 September 1917, 6086-91; Nicholson, *C.E.F.* 219-20
6 Morton, 'French Canada' 102. On French Canadian recruiting, see Mason Wade, *The French Canadians, 1760-1945* (Toronto 1955) 648-58, 667-86, 708-35. For another view, see D. Morton, 'The Limits of Loyalty: French Canadian Officers and the First World War' in Edgar Denton II, ed., *The Limits of Loyalty* (Waterloo 1980)
7 On the CDF see Canada, House of Commons, *Debates*, 3 May 1917, 1038-9; also Borden Papers, OC 317(2), 35563. R.C. Brown argues that the voluntary recruiting effort outside Quebec was, in fact, impressively successful. See 'The Impact of Wartime Manpower Policy in Western Canada,' unpublished paper, Western Studies Conference, 1981
8 Granatstein and Hitsman, *Broken Promises* 63
9 On conscription politics the best summary is English, *Decline of Politics* 123-203. See also Elizabeth Armstrong, *The Crisis of Quebec* (New York 1937); Ramsay Cook, 'Dafoe, Laurier and the Formation of Union Government,' *Canadian Historical Review*, XLII, 3 September 1961; Willms, 'Conscription' 338-51
10 On the overseas election, see Desmond Morton, 'Polling the Soldier Vote: The Overseas Campaign in the Canadian General Election of 1917,' *Journal of Canadian Studies*, X, 4, November 1975, 39-58; Granatstein and Hitsman, *Broken Promises* 71, 79-81; English, *Decline of Politics* 193-5, 198-9, 204-5
11 See, for example, E.L.M. Burns, *Manpower and the Canadian Army* (Toronto 1956) 5-6; Granatstein and Hitsman, *Broken Promises* 210-17; J.L. Granat-

stein, *Canada's War: The Politics of the Mackenzie King Government, 1939-45* (Toronto 1975) 345-6

12 See Willms, 'Conscription' 338-42

13 On Australia see, for example, Bill Gammage, *The Broken Years* (London and Sydney 1976)

14 Perley to Borden, 15 October 1914, Perley Papers, vol. I, file 4

15 Dr F.L. Schaffner to Borden, 13 March 1915, Borden Papers, OC 180(1), 13960. See also Neil Watson to Borden, 25 February 1915, *ibid.* 13957

16 *Canadian Annual Review*, 1915, 269

17 See 5 Geo. V., c. 11. See also Canada, House of Commons, *Debates*, 22 February 1915; 1 April 1915; Borden memorandum, 27 March 1915, Borden Papers, OC 130(1), 13969

18 Canada, House of Commons, *Debates*, 8 April 1915, 2218

19 *Ibid.* 2208 (Laurier's argument may even have been constitutionally sound until 1931 but it was illustrative of the change in public attitude between 1915 and 1917 that the argument was not even mentioned in the debate on the Military Voters' Act)

20 Daly to Rogers, 12 May 1915, Borden Papers, OC 180(1), 14051; Perley to Borden, 13 May 1915, *ibid.* 14042. On Daly, see English, *Decline of Politics* 99, and for another of Daly's missions see Brown and Morton, 'The Embarrassing Apotheosis of Sir Arthur Currie' 54

21 On the British Columbia voting, see Martin Robin, *The Rush for Spoils: The Company Province* (Toronto 1972) 160; *Canadian Annual Review*, 1916, 789-91. See Bowser to H.S. Clement MP, 12 June 1916, Borden Papers, OC 180(2)

22 *Canadian Annual Review*, 1917, 772-3, 804-6. (The figures may be compared with 20,630 Alberta and 15,668 Saskatchewan votes polled overseas for the 1917 federal election.) Miss McAdams came by her politics understandably, being the niece of the Hon W.J. Hanna, an Ontario Conservative.

23 Henry Pope to Rufus Pope, 15 October 1916, Perley Papers, file 199

24 Lt-Col George B. McLeod to Laurier, 23 January 1917, PAC, Laurier Papers, 194615

25 Perley to Borden, 27 July 1917, Borden Papers, OC 180(2), 14239 and see memorandum by Meighen, n.d., *ibid.* OC 233, 125358

26 O'Connor memorandum, 'Summary of Changes in the Military Voters' Act between 1915 and 1917,' n.d., PAC, O'Connor Papers. See also O'Connor to Meighen, 10 May 1918, *ibid.*

27 Borden, *Memoirs* II, 707

28 Canada, House of Commons, *Debates*, 20 August 1917, 4690; 24 August 1917, 4892

29 *Ibid.* 20 August 1917, 4721. For Meighen's view, see Roger Graham, *Arthur Meighen,* vol. I, *The Door of Opportunity* (Toronto 1960) 256-7
30 Canada, House of Commons, *Debates,* 31 August 1917, 5196
31 See 'Memorandum on election preparations,' n.d., O'Connor Papers; 'Memorandum for the Minister of Customs,' 6 August 1917, Borden Papers, OC 370(1), 41069. See also Borden to Perley, 24 October 1917, file 285
32 Perley to Borden, 29 November 1916, Borden Papers, OC 180(1)
33 Perley to Borden, 22 June 1917, Perley Papers, vol. 9, file 257
34 Perley to Borden, 24 September 1917, Borden Papers, OC 370(1), 41073
35 Perley to Borden, 14 September 1917, *ibid.* 41070-1
36 Borden to Perley, 2 September 1917, Perley Papers, vol. 9, file 272
37 Borden to Perley, 18 June 1917, Perley Papers, vol. 9, file 258; A.M.J. Hyatt, 'Sir Arthur Currie and Conscription: A Soldier's View,' *Canadian Historical Review,* L, 3 September 1969, 285
38 Perley to Borden, 13 September 1917, Perley Papers, vol. 9, file 273 and Manly Sims to Perley, 8 September 1917, *ibid.*
39 McCurdy to Borden, 9 October 1917, Borden Papers, OC 370(1), 41086-8
40 Perley to Borden, 24 June 1917, *ibid.* 41116-7
41 Perley to Borden, 14 September 1917, Perley Papers, vol. 9, file 274 and see file 268
42 Perley to Borden, 9 October 1917, *ibid.* file 279 and see file 278
43 Borden to Perley, 13 October 1917, *ibid.* file 281; W. Stewart Wallace, *The Memoirs of the Rt. Hon. Sir George Foster PC GCMG* (Toronto 1933), 188
44 Perley to Borden, 13 October 1917, *ibid.*
45 Borden to Perley, 3 November 1917, *ibid.* vol. 10, file 288; Borden to Perley, 15 October 1917, Borden Papers, OC 176, 13646
46 Perley to Borden, 18 November 1917, *ibid.* OC 370(1), 41122-3
47 On the overseas election organization, see Perley to Borden, 19 December 1917, *ibid.* 41143
48 McCurdy to E.N. Rhodes, n.d., PANS, Rhodes Papers; McCurdy to Hayes, 30 October 1917, Borden Papers, OC 370(1), 41106-7
49 See Taylor, *Beaverbrook* 137; McInnes to Blount, 23 November 1917, Borden Papers, OC 370(1), 41139; Borden to Beaverbrook, 17 January 1918, Beaverbrook Papers, Borden correspondence, no. 3; Perley to Borden, 10 December 1917, Perley Papers, vol. 10, file 307, on the overseas Unionist organization
50 On Macphail, see Borden to Perley, 2 September 1917, Perley Papers, vol. 9, file 282; Perley to Borden, 11 September 1917, *ibid.,* Macphail to Perley, 2 October 1917, *ibid.* See also Borden to Macphail, 30 October 1917, PAC, Macphail Papers, vol. 11
51 Perley to Borden, 5 November 1917, Perley Papers, vol. 10, file 290

52 Lt G. Earle Logan to Perley, 7 October 1917, Borden Papers, OC 370(1), 41082-5. On Logan and other New Brunswick election agents, see J.D. Hazen to Perley, 9 August 1917, Perley Papers, vol. 10, file 300
53 Borden to Perley, 29 October 1917, *ibid.* file 286
54 Reid to Borden, 12 November 1917, Borden Papers, OC 370(1), 41120
55 See Laurier to Dandurand, 25 September 1917, Laurier Papers, 197201; Laurier to Hyman, 17 September 1917, *ibid.* 197027 and 11 October 1917, *ibid.* 197396; Hyman to Laurier, 13 October 1917, *ibid.* 197397; Laurier to D.D. Mackenzie, 12 November 1917, *ibid.* 198124; Laurier to Borden, 3 November 1917, *ibid.* 197928; Borden to Laurier, 7 November 1917, *ibid.* 198146
56 See Preston to Laurier, 30 May 1917, *ibid.* 195380. On Preston, see W.T.R. Preston, *My Generation of Politics and Politicians* (Toronto 1927) and P.D. Ross, *Recollections* 126-33
57 Alexander Smith to Laurier, 1 October 1917, Laurier Papers, 197257. See G.P. Graham to P.C. Larkin, 24 September 1917, *ibid.* 197467
58 Laurier to Alex Clément, 25 September 1917, *ibid.* 197800; 22 October 1917, *ibid.* 197997-9; Clément to Laurier, 5 December 1917, *ibid.* 198859
59 Turner to Preston, 10 November 1917, Turner Papers, file 89, 8201. See also PC 3011, 20 October 1917; Routine Orders no. 2872, Overseas Military Forces of Canada, 13 November 1917, OS 10-14-24
60 Langlois to Laurier, 23 November 1917, Laurier Papers, 198427; 7 December 1917, *ibid.* 198893. Langlois lacked funds and instructions and he received a list of contacts only 10 days before the polls closed. See RG 9, III A1, vol. 99, file 10-14-24
61 Preston to Turner, 21 November 1917, Turner Papers, vol. 10 and Laurier papers, 198596. See also Preston to Earl of Derby, 21 November 1917, RG 9, III A1, vol. 99, file 10-14-24
62 Preston to Turner, 3 December 1917, Turner Papers, vol. 10
63 *Ibid.* 8130
64 Turner to Preston, 3 December 1917, *ibid.*
65 On Thompson, see Thompson to Laurier, 25 December 1917, Laurier Papers, 199144. For the Unionist perspective, see McInnes to Blount, 23 November 1917, Borden Papers, OC 370(1), 41130:

'We are told over and over again that the soldier does not care and does not know what the issue is; that he won't read literature, but we are doing the best we can to impress them with the seriousness of the case.

'All the officers are sympathetic but properly they want to be within the regulations. They would like to help us if they could, but they don't want to take an active part in any propaganda.'

66 Derby to Haig, 9 November 1917, cited by Blake, *Private Papers of Douglas Haig* 266; Nicholson, *C.E.F.* 338

67 See *Instructions for the Guidance of Electors under the Military Voters Act, 1917* 1-3. (On voting for a party rather than a candidate, the instructions indicated: 'It will be safer but it is not obligatory ...')

68 The process was revealed when Meighen was publicly implicated by his Manitoba lieutenant, Senator W.H. Sharpe. See Graham, *Meighen* I, 255-9

69 McInnes to Blount, 30 November 1917, Borden Papers, OC 370(1), 41142

70 For their message, see Turner Papers, 8118; *Canadian Annual Review*, 1917, 634. For examples of other material, see PAC, RG 9, III, B1, vol. 1484, file E-2-7, vol. 3

71 Lt-Col Hayes to McCurdy, 18 December 1917, Borden Papers, OC 370(1), 41180A-B

72 See Canada, House of Commons, *Debates*, 22 May 1918; *Canadian Annual Review*, 1917, 535. See also Preston circular, Laurier Papers, 198925, indicating that Laurier actually favoured conscription

73 O'Connor memorandum, n.d., Borden Papers, OC 370(1), 41361; Col Frank Reid to Purney, 30 November 1917, PAC, Charles Murphy Papers, 16046 ff.

74 *Ibid.* 16053

75 Seely, *Adventure* 283-4. For some references to the overseas vote, see Kim Beattie, *The 48th Highlanders of Canada, 1891-1928* (Toronto 1932) 282; C.S. Rosenholt, *Six Thousand Canadian Men* (Winnipeg 1932) 133; H.C. Singer, *History of the 31st Infantry Battalion, C.E.F.* (n.p. 1938) 284; G.R. Stevens, *A City Goes to War* (Edmonton n.d.) 108; H.C. Urquhart, *History of the 16th Battalion, C.E.F.* (Toronto 1932) 242

76 On Currie and the election, see Hyatt, 'Currie and Conscription' 285-93; Hyatt, 'Military Career' 158-62; Urquhart, *Currie* 185-91; Currie to Col J.G. Creelman, 30 November 1917, PAC, Creelman Papers

77 Currie to Perley, 10 December 1917, Currie Papers, vol. 1; Nicholson, *C.E.F.* 346

78 Currie to Daly, 10 December 1917, PAC, Daly Papers, vol. 1

79 Oliver to Currie, 4 December 1917, Currie Papers, vol. 1. For Currie's belated message, see *Canadian Annual Review*, 1917, 636

80 *Canadian Annual Review*, 1917, 635-6

81 Langlois to Laurier, 17 December 1917, Laurier Papers, 198848-51; Preston, *Politics and Politicians* 370

82 On the events, see RG 9, III B1, vol. 2792, file E-323-33; Preston to Laurier, 21 December 1917, Laurier Papers, 199082 (Preston's main source of scrutineers and encouragement appears to have been the 150th Battalion, the French-speaking battalion in the 5th Division)

83 Perley to Borden, 10 December 1917, Borden Papers, OC 370(1), 41143-4
84 Laurier to Aylesworth, 6 December 1917, Laurier Papers, 198838; Preston to Laurier, 19 December 1917, *ibid.* 198985-6; Laurier to Preston, 3 January 1918, *ibid.* 198988
85 See *Instruction for the Guidance* ... and see photographs, PAC, 'Wartime Elections'
86 Laurier to Preston, 18 January 1918, Laurier Papers, 199249. See also O'Connor memorandum, Borden Papers, OC 370(1), 41363-6; Edward Dewart to Laurier, 25 January 1918, Laurier Papers, 199267
87 Langlois to Laurier, 15 January 1918, *ibid.* 199377. See also Edward Dewart to Laurier, n.d., *ibid.* 199425-40, W.T.R. Preston, *The Prime Minister's Offence: Electoral Debauchery Overseas* (Peterborough 1919) 9-11; Preston, *Politics and Politicians* 368-9
88 Langlois to Laurier, 30 January 1918, Laurier Papers, 199636
89 See N.W. Rowell to Borden, 2 February 1918, Borden Papers, OC 370(1), 41182. See also Lt-Col H.C. Pratt to Purney, 21 February 1918, RG 9, III A1, vol. 99, file 10-14-24; Pratt to Kemp, 21 February 1918, *ibid.*; PAC, Sir George Foster diaries, 1 February 1918
90 For an estimate of the ballots rejected for this reason, since no official record was kept, see Langlois to Laurier, 10 March 1918, Laurier Papers, 199085; Preston to Laurier, 26 February 1918, *ibid.* 199845; Report by W.R. Hearn, n.d., Charles Murphy Papers, 1335 ff. The government's own estimate, offered by Martin Burrell during the debate, was 17,000 out of 104,000 votes cast in England and 19,000 out of 52,000 cast in Canada with no estimate for France. See Canada, House of Commons, *Debates*, 22 May 1918, 2438
91 Borden to Perley, 18 December 1917, Borden Papers, OC 370(1), 41158.
92 See Sir Charles Matthews to Perley, 2 March 1918, *ibid.* 41234A; Perley to Borden, 4 April 1918, and enclosures, *ibid.* 41234 ff. For Preston's version, see Preston to Laurier, 15 March 1918, Laurier Papers, 200083-4 and enclosures, 200085-6
93 For the debate, see Canada, House of Commons, *Debates*, 22 May 1918, 2200-47; Preston, *Politics and Politicians* 386; Morton, 'Soldier Vote' 52-6
94 W.L.M. King to Laurier, 14 January 1918, Laurier Papers, 199367
95 Ward, *Party Politician* 61

CHAPTER 8

1 On Kemp, see Morgan, *Canadian Men and Women of the Time* (Toronto 1912); B.M. Greene, *Canada Who's Who* (Toronto 1921)
2 On the mood, see Lord Beaverbrook, *Men and Power, 1917-1918* (London 1956); Taylor, *English History* 102 ff.

3 Kemp to Borden, 4 January 1918, Borden Papers, OC 485D(1), 51129
4 *Ibid.* and Kemp to Borden, 9 December 1917, Kemp Papers, vol. 129, B-3
5 See, for example, Currie to Perley, 15 December 1917, Borden Papers, OC 176, 13658
6 Perley to Borden, 12 December 1917, Perley Papers, vol. 10, file 308; Borden to Perley, 18 January 1918, *ibid.* file 317 See McInnes to Perley, 29 January 1918, vol. 11, 20.
7 Kemp to Borden, 3 January 1918, Borden Papers, OC 419, 43932. Kemp's report ignored the main burden of the meeting: Lloyd George's statement of British war aims. Kemp played no further diplomatic role. See Wigley, *British-Canadian Relations* 56
8 Kemp to Borden, 4 January 1918, Borden Papers, OC 485D(1), 51129
9 Hunter to Mewburn, 5 November 1917, Turner Papers, 7-39, 5334; Mewburn to Kemp, 4 January 1918, *ibid.* 5331
10 *Ibid.* 7-34, 5120
11 Turner to Kemp, 2 February 1918, *ibid.* 7-39, 5328
12 Kemp to Mewburn, 7 February 1918, Kemp Papers, vol. 161, S-6
13 Kemp to Borden, 7 January 1918, Borden Papers, OC 332, 39145-6
14 Kemp to Borden, 25 January 1918, Kemp Papers, vol. 182, file 62; Nicholson, *C.E.F.* 231-2
15 Beaverbrook, *Soldiers and Politicians*
16 Urquhart, *Currie* 198
17 Borden to Perley, 7 November 1917, Borden Papers, OC 332, 39139A; see Borden to Kemp, 17 January 1918, *ibid.* 39154
18 Perley to Borden, 5 January 1918, *ibid.* 39146
19 Urquhart, *Currie* 198
20 Kemp to Borden, 25 January 1918, Kemp Papers, vol. 169, file 12
21 Borden to Kemp, 31 January 1918, Borden Papers, OC 98, 73868. In his figures Borden included a pioneer battalion which had been incorporated into the establishment of an infantry division.
22 Currie to Kemp, 11 January 1918, Kemp Papers, vol. 182, file 62. See also Currie to Harold Daly, 23 January 1918, Daly Papers, vol I
23 Urquhart, *Currie* 198
24 *Ibid.* 199-200
25 *Ibid.* 201-2
26 Memorandum, 6 January 1918, Turner Papers, 8-54
27 Currie to Turner, 7 February 1918, *ibid.* 6046-51; Currie to Kemp, 7 February 1918, *ibid.* and in Borden Papers, OC 494, 52798-52802
28 Kemp to Derby, 20 February 1918, Kemp Papers, vol. 182, file 621; Derby to Kemp, 21 February 1918, *ibid.*; Kemp to Borden, 8 February 1918, *ibid.* See Hyatt, 'Military Career' 172-80

29 Borden to Kemp, 6 February 1918, Borden Papers, OCA 98, 73871
30 Currie to Kemp, 21 February 1918, Kemp Papers, vol. 161 reply to Lt-Col Murdie memorandum, 18 February 1918, *ibid.* On criticism, see Frost, *Fighting Men* 97-8
31 Mewburn to Kemp, 21 February 1918, Kemp Papers, vol. 182, file 61; Kemp to Mewburn, 21 February 1918, *ibid.*; Kemp to Borden, 24 February 1918, *ibid.*
32 Kemp to Borden, 26 February 1918, Borden Papers, OCA 98, 73946
33 See Hyatt, 'Currie and Politics' 148; Preston, *'Imperial Defense'* 202; Currie to Loomis, 27 January 1918, Currie Papers, vol. 1; Currie to Daly, 23 June 1918, Daly Papers, vol. 3. See Hughes in Canada, House of Commons, *Debates*, 18 April 1918, 879; *Report of O.M.F.C. 1918* 3331-4
34 On the background, see Desmond Morton, *Ministers and Generals: Politics and the Canadian Militia, 1868-1904* (Toronto 1970)
35 Memorandum, 14 June 1917, RG 9, III A1, vol. 72, file 10-8-7; Perley to Kemp, 30 June 1917, *ibid.*
36 See, for example, Currie to Perley, 14 August 1917, *ibid.*; Perley to Currie, 16 August 1917, *ibid.*
37 Deputy Minister, OMFC to Secretary, War Office, 27 November 1917, *ibid.*
38 Kemp to Borden, 2 April 1918, Borden Papers, OCA 98, 73957
39 Kemp to Borden, 24 February 1918, Kemp Papers, vol. 129, B-3. See also Gow to Kemp, 11 March 1918, RG 9, III A1, vol. 107, folder 348, file 822
40 On the Australian problems, see C.E.W. Bean, *Official History of Australia in the War of 1914-18*, III, *The A.E.F. in France, 1916* (Sydney 1929) 145-71. See also Appendix
41 Urquhart, *Currie* 214-15; Hyatt, 'Military Career'
42 Turner memorandum, n.d., Turner Papers, 8-52, 5917-8
43 Borden to Kemp, 28 March 1918, Borden Papers, OCA 98, 73892
44 PC, 885, 11 April 1918, see Kemp to Borden, 2 April 1918, OCA 98, 73958; Kemp to Borden, 8 April 1918, *ibid.* 73968. Boudreau to Kemp, 12 April 1918, RG 9, III A1, vol. 107, folder 348, file 822
45 Kemp to Mewburn, 1 May 1918, *ibid.*
46 Minutes of Overseas Military Council, 14 May 1918, Kemp Papers, vol. 177; Kemp to Turner, 10 May 1918, Turner Papers, 10-74, 7086 ff.
47 'Report covering the Constitution and Activities of the Overseas Military Council,' RG 9, III A1, vol. 78, file 10-8-49
48 Kemp to Borden, 24 February 1918, Kemp Papers, vol. 182, file 61. Nicholson, *C.E.F.* 499-500; *Report of the O.M.F.C.*, 1918 xii
49 Wise, *Canadian Airmen* 593, and see Appendix C for an ingenious attempt to derive final statistics, concluding that the figure of 22,812 Canadians in the

British flying services, recorded in the Memorial Chamber of the Parliament Buildings, is an exaggeration.

50 Thacker to Turner, 17 September 1917, Turner Papers, 8-52

51 Hyatt, 'Military Career' 165-6

52 See Currie to Turner, 11 March 1918, Turner Papers, 8-51, 5759; Currie to Turner, 19 March 1918, *ibid.* 5751

53 Gow to Kemp, 11 March 1918, RG 9, III A1, vol. 107, folder 348, file 822

54 Minutes of a conference, 19 March 1918, RG 9, III A1, vol. 72, file 10-8-7

55 Urquhart, *Currie* 216

56 *Ibid.* 207

57 Nicholson, *C.E.F.* 309-10, 378-80

58 On the British retreat, see William Moore, *The Great Retreat* (London 1976)

59 On Currie and Gough, see Blake, *Private Papers* 272; Nicholson, *C.E.F.* 312 and 312n

60 Currie to Lawrence, 27 March 1919, in Nicholson, *C.E.F.* 381

61 Currie to Kemp, 27 March 1918, cited in Urquhart, *Currie* 208

62 Kemp to Derby, 29 March 1919, in Kemp Papers, C-25

63 Blake, *Private Papers* 303. (The allegation was made by General Horne of the First Army, Currie's immediate superior, not by Haig)

64 On the Canadians during the German offensive see Nicholson, *C.E.F.* chap. 12

65 Harrington to War Office, 29 March 1918, Borden Papers, OC 485D (2), 51360

66 Minutes of a conference, 2 April 1918, RG 9, III A1, vol. 72, file 10-8-7

67 War Office to Overseas Ministry, 4 April 1918, *ibid.*

68 War Office to Sir Douglas Haig, 16 April 1918, Turner Papers, 8-52, 5907

69 Gow to Turner, 25 April 1918, *ibid.* 5927; Gow to Turner, 29 April 1918, *ibid.* 5923

70 Memorandum, 12 April 1918, RG 9, III A1, vol. 72, file 10-8-7

71 *Ibid.* n.d.; Urquhart, *Currie* 215-16; see Currie to General Headquarters, 24 April 1918, Urquhart Papers, vol. 3

72 Memorandum, n.d., Turner Papers, 8-52, 5906-8 and in Borden Papers, OC 485D(2), 51363-75

73 Lawrence to Overseas Ministry, 23 June 1918, RG 9, III A1, vol. 72, file 10-8-7

74 Overseas Ministry to General Headquarters, 28 June 1918, *ibid.*

75 Beaverbrook to Kemp, 26 March 1918, Kemp Papers, vol. 161, C-11; Kemp to Currie, 23 April 1918, *ibid.* Currie despised Sims as an intriguer. See Hyatt, 'Military Career' 165-6

76 Kemp to Currie, 23 April 1918, *ibid.*

77 Perley to Lord Milner, 15 June 1918, RG 9, III A1, vol. 72, file 10-8-7

78 Embury memorandum, n.d., *ibid.*

79 Currie to Kemp, 13 July 1918, *ibid.*; Currie to Kemp, 14 July, 1918, *ibid.*

80 Embury memorandum, 22 September 1918, *ibid.*
81 Harrington to Paymaster General, 22 July 1918, *ibid.*
82 Turner to Gow, 14 September 1918, *ibid.*
83 PC, 2209, 22 September 1918
84 Kemp speeches, n.d., Kemp Papers, vol. 181, file 51. See also *Report of O.M.F.C. 1918* 1-8

CHAPTER 9

1 Kemp to Borden, 24 February 1918, Borden Papers, OC 485D, 51153
2 On the conscripts see Nicholson, *C.E.F.* 35-353. On special problems of French Canadians, see Currie to Turner, 14 March 1918, Currie Papers, vol. 8; Borden Papers, OC 209 passim
3 English, *Decline of Politics* chap. 11
4 Ottawa *Citizen*, 31 January 1918, 2 February 1918
5 Col W.R. Ward memorandum, n.d., RG 9, III A1, vol. 77, file 10-8-43; Kemp to Borden, 14 March 1918, *ibid.*
6 *Saturday Night*, 2 March 1918
7 Toronto *Daily Star*, 27 March 1918
8 Kemp to Borden, 8 January 1918, Kemp Papers, vol. 175, file 31a. On Kemp and Rowell, see J.R. Robinson to Kemp, 3 January 1918, *ibid.* vol. 161, R-15; Robinson to Kemp, 6 March 1918, *ibid.*
9 Kemp to Mewburn, 26 March 1918, *ibid.* vol. 175, file 31a. See Manitoba *Free Press*, 20 February 1918
10 Maj W.R. Creighton to Maj E. Bristol, 20 February 1918, RG 9, III A1, vol. 77, file 10-8-43
11 Kemp to Borden, 14 March 1918, *ibid.* On numbers, see Turner memorandum, 17 July 1918, Turner Papers, 5376, 5392-3
12 Kemp to Borden, 20 March 1918, RG 9, III A1, vol. 77, file 10-8-43; Canada, House of Commons, *Debates*, 21 March 1918, 56; Borden, *Memoirs* II, 780
13 Canada, House of Commons, *Debates*, 6 May 1918, 1488
14 *Ibid.* 10 April 1918 (Jacques Bureau); 18 April 1918, 881 (Thomas Vien)
15 On the furlough issue, see Canada, House of Commons, *Debates*, 18 April 1918, 883; Perley to Borden, 7 September 1917, Borden Papers, OC 397, 43744 ff.
16 J.R.L. Stairs to Borden, 10 April 1918, Borden Papers, OC 397, 43754; Borden to W.F. Nickle, MP, 4 September 1918, *ibid.* 43786; Borden *Memoirs* II, 822
17 Borden, *Memoirs* II, 809
18 *Report of the O.M.F.C., 1918* xii, 9-14
19 Borden, *Memoirs* II, 809-15

20 *Ibid.* 814-15. On the Imperial War Cabinet 1918, see Wigley, *British-Canadian Relations* 60-5

21 On Smart, see below. On problems of shifting officers, see Currie to Turner, 25 May 1918, Turner Papers, 8-47

22 On Currie's reputation, see Urquhart, *Currie* 218-25; Kerr, *Shrieks and Crashes* 40; Kerr, *Arms and the Maple Leaf* 27-8, 44-5

23 Currie to Rowell, 27 November 1918, PAC, Rowell Papers, vol. 3, folder 15, 1648. See also Currie to Daly, 26 October 1918, Daly Papers, in the same spirit

24 See Borden Papers, OC 485A, 50897-50942; Kemp to Borden, 8 August 1918, *ibid.* OC 485D(2), 51455

25 Gow to Kemp, 30 August 1918, *ibid.* 51478

26 Kemp to Gow, 17 September 1918, *ibid.* 51480

27 Gow to Kemp, 18 September 1918, *ibid.* 51481

28 Kemp to Gow, 24 September 1918, *ibid.* 51482

29 Kemp to Borden, 28 September 1918, *ibid.* 51480-9

30 Gow to Kemp, 26 October 1918, Turner Papers, 7-39, 5351-3

31 Turner to Kemp, 4 November 1918, *ibid.* Currie sympathised with Gow. See Hyatt, 'Military Career' 163-4

32 Nicholson, *C.E.F.* 386-483

33 On demobilization railway problems and arrangements, see J.A. Swettenham, 'The End of the War' (Directorate of History report), *The Return of the Troops: A Plain Account of the Demobilization of the Canadian Expeditionary Force* (Ottawa 1920) 14-16, 76-7

34 Canada, House of Commons, *Debates*, 10 March 1919, 323 ff.; 15 April 1919, 1524-5

35 'Report of the Overseas Demobilization Committee,' 22 July 1918, Borden Papers, OC 485A, 50921

36 Kemp memorandum, 20 July 1918, Kemp Papers, vol. 137, D-2. See also Kemp to Mewburn, 24 July 1918, *ibid.* D-2a

37 Director of Records to Kemp, 26 March 1919, *ibid.*; *Canadian Demobilization Instructions* (London 1918) I; *Report of the O.M.F.C., 1918* 520-1

38 Currie to E.H. Macklin, 4 October 1918, Currie Papers; Currie to Kemp, 6 November 1918, Kemp Papers, vol. 137, D-2; Nicholson, *C.E.F.* 528

39 White to Borden, 5 December 1918, Kemp Papers, vol. 137, D-2 and enclosures, D-3

40 Currie to Kemp, 18 December 1918, *ibid.* D-2 (A dissenting opinion came in a petition from 89 men of the Forty-fourth Battalion and addressed to Perley in London. See Kemp Papers, vol. 135, C-63)

41 Currie to Kemp, 23 November 1918, *ibid.* vol. 137, D-2

42 *Demobilization Instructions* 26-8; *Return of the Troops* chap. 1; Nicholson, *C.E.F.* 528-9

43 *Report of the O.M.F.C., 1918* 473-506 passim

44 On the British experience, see Paul B. Johnson, *Land Fit for Heroes* (Chicago and London 1968) chaps. 13 and 14; Arthur Marwick, *The Deluge: British Society and the First World War* (London 1965) 266-71; Martin S. Gilbert, *Winston S. Churchill*, IV, *1916-1922* (London 1975) 181; S.R. Graubard, 'Military Demobilization in Great Britain Following the First World War,' *Journal of Modern History*, XIX, 1947. On British troubles, see Dave Lamb, *Mutiny, 1917-1920* (Oxford n.d.) 21-7; Thomas Gibson memorandum, 30 July 1919, Borden Papers, OC 515, 62615 ff.

45 A.F. Duguid, 'Disturbances in Canadian Camps and Areas, 1918-1919' (Directorate of History report), RG 24, vol. 1841, GAQ 10-39F, no. 7 (hereafter 'Disturbances'); Desmond Morton, 'Kicking and Complaining: Demobilization Riots in the Canadian Expeditionary Force, 1918-1919,' *Canadian Historical Review*, LXI, 3, September 1980. See Maj F.R. Jones to HQ Kinmel Park, 21 November 1918, Borden Papers, OC 515, 55746; Kemp to Borden, 6 January 1919, Kemp Papers, vol. 137, D-2

46 Brig-Gen J.S. Stewart to HQ IV Corps, 14 December 1918, RG 9, III B1, vol. 2232, file D-6-29 and passim

47 On the leaders, see Capt. H.H. Ellis to Capt. R.S. Law, 20 August 1919, *ibid.* vol. 93, file 10-12-50, vol. 1; H.H. Stevens to Kemp, 14 June 1919, Kemp Papers, vol. 163; Kemp Papers, vol. 155 for subsequent disposal

48 White to Borden, 30 December 1918, *ibid.* vol. 135, D-2; PC, 3210, 31 December 1918; Kemp to Borden, 31 December 1918, Kemp Papers, C-63

49 *Report of the Royal Commission on the Northland*, 25 January 1919, Kemp Papers, vol. 155, C-6. See also Kemp to White, 24 February 1919, Borden Papers, OC 515, 55813-4

50 On shipping problems, see Col E. Duffin to Quartermaster-General, 6 March 1919, Kemp Papers, vol. 135, C-63; memorandum, 7 March 1919, *ibid.*; *Return of the Troops* 56-9

51 Kemp to Borden, 8 March 1919, Borden Papers, OC 515, 55847

52 Turner to Kemp, 11 February 1919, Kemp Papers, vol. 137, D-2. See Borden to Kemp, 3 March 1919, Borden Papers, OC 515, 55835

53 Churchill to Kemp, 2 February 1919, Borden Papers OC 515, 55822; Col R.M. Dennistoun to Quartermaster-General, 17 February 1919, RG 9, III A1, vol. 95, file 10-12-85x

54 'Disturbances,' no. 2; Report of court of inquiry, Borden Papers, OC 515, 55822-49; memorandum to Kemp, n.d., *ibid.* 55849

55 Memorandum, *ibid.* 55852
56 Adjutant General to Secretary, OMFC, 27 December 1918, RG 9, III A1, vol. 95; Thacker memorandum, 25 February 1919, Borden Papers, OC 515, 55854
57 Sir Graeme Thompson to Kemp, 15 February 1919, Kemp Papers, vol. 137, D-2. See also E.J. Foley to Hogarth, 20 January 1919, *ibid.* D-3
58 *Return of the Troops* 48-55; *Report of the O.M.F.C., 1918* 521-5
59 Kemp to Mewburn, 6 February 1919, Kemp Papers, vol. 137, D-2
60 On Colquhoun, see Carson to HQ, Canadian Corps, 21 November 1916, RG 9, III A1, vol. 127, file 6-C-181; Byng to Perley, n.d., *ibid.* vol. 259. 10-C-252
61 See Morton, 'Kicking and Complaining' 342-3 and n 36
62 Maj. G.V. Collier to OC Canadian Troops, Kinmel Park, 10 January 1919, RG 9, III, vol. 1709, D-3-13, vol. 6; Robin Winks, *The Blacks in Canada: A History* (Montreal 1971) 319 is, unfortunately, a largely erroneous account. On guard-room scuffle, see RG 9, III B1, vol. 1708, file D-3-13, vol. 2
63 On conditions, see *Report of the O.M.F.C., 1918* 322; 'Proceedings of the Court of Inquiry on Disturbances at Kinmel Park,' RG 9, III B1, vol. 2770, file D-199-33, vol. 5 (hereafter 'Kinmel Inquiry'), Toronto *Daily Star* 12 March 1919, 3 April 1919
64 Testimony, Maj F.C. Biggar, Lieut C.R. Gilpin, 'Kinmel Inquiry;' Biggar to Secretary, OMFC, 3 March 1919, exhibit 'N', *ibid.*
65 See Kemp Papers, vol. 169, file 13; Report of the *O.M.F.C., 1918* 518
66 On the *Haverford*, Col Duffin to Ministry of Shipping, 3 March 1919, Kemp Papers, vol. 137, D-3; Testimony of Maj H.W. Cooper, Capt J. Corbit, C.S.M. Williams, 'Kinmel Inquiry'
67 Testimony of Brig-Gen Hogarth, Col Colquhoun, Lt-Col Thackeray, Lt-Col McCormick and exhibits, 'Kinmel Inquiry'
68 Testimony of Col Colquhoun, Maj St George, Maj R.S. Worsley, Maj H.V. Allen, and others, 'Kimmel Inquiry;' Biggar to Colquhoun, 5 March 1919, RG 9, III B1, vol. 1708, D-3-13, vol. 1 (hereafter 'Riot Reports')
69 Testimony of Col Colquhoun, Maj St George, R.S.M. Wilson, R.H. Davis, Maj Worsnop and others, 'Kinmel Inquiry,' 'Riot Reports,' passim; Morton, 'Kicking and Complaining;' Liverpool *Echo*, 20 March 1919, 27 March 1919
70 Testimony of Capt R.J. Davidson, 'Kinmel Inquiry;' Turner to GHQ, Forces in Great Britain, 7 March 1919, Turner Papers, 5689
71 See especially *The Times, Daily Chronicle, Morning Post, Daily Telegraph,* Liverpool *Echo*, 7-8 March 1919; *Evening News*, 8 March 1919 reports Colquhoun's effort to suppress reports
72 *The Times*, 8 March 1919, *Morning Post*, 8 March 1919; Morton, 'Kicking and Complaining' 66

73 R.E. Henley to Brereton Greenhous, n.d. (Directorate of History)
74 Borden Diary, 8-9 March 1919; Kemp to Borden, 12 March 1919, Borden Papers, OC 515, 55882
75 See Colquhoun to Secretary, OMFC, 12 March 1919, RG 9, III B1, vol. 1708, file D-3-13, vol. 3, passim
76 Findings, 'Kinmel Inquiry.' (MacBrien's initial findings and testimony were revised to eliminate any suggestion of responsibility on the part of officials of the Overseas Ministry. See Kemp Papers, vol. 147, D-11; RG 9, III A1, vol. 45, file 10-12-85)
77 For figures see 'General Demobilization of the C.E.F., 1918-1919' (Directorate of History report) 27

CHAPTER 10

1 *Report of the O.M.F.C., 1918* 524-5
2 Kemp to Borden, 8 March 1919, Borden Papers, OC 515, 55857
3 See *The Times*, *Morning Chronicle*, 10 March 1919
4 Borden to Kemp, 10 March 1919, Borden Papers, OC 515, 55873; see also Borden Diary, 10 March 1919
5 Kemp to Borden, 12 March 1919, Borden Papers, OC 515, 55882
6 On the trials, see Morton, 'Kicking and Complaining;' Kemp Papers, vol. 155; RG 9, III A1, vol. 1708, D-3-13, vols. 1-4
7 Capt George Black to Borden, 29 June 1919, Kemp Papers, vol. 155, P-11
8 Maj Weyman to Deputy Minister, OMFC, 10 September 1919, *ibid.* On origins, see Morton, 'Kicking and Complaining' n 79
9 On Smart's charges, see *Canadian Annual Review*, 1919, 54-5; Memorandum, 14 March 1919, RG 9, III A1, vol. 77, file 10-8-43; *Saturday Night*, 29 March 1919
10 'Review of Press Comment,' RG 9, III A1, vol. 77, file 10-8-43
11 See Turner to Harrington, 7 April 1919, Turner Papers, 5651
12 Turner to Kemp, 3 April 1919, *ibid.* 7-39, 5359
13 Maj-Gen G.L. Foster to Deputy Minister, OMFC, 6 April 1919, OS 30-0-0 (c), 9. See Foster to Kemp, 1 May 1919, Kemp Papers, file 6a
14 Fotheringham to Foster, 8 July 1919, PAC, Fotheringham Papers
15 Macphail to White, 5 March 1919, PAC, Macphail Papers, vol. 11, Foster to Macphail, 21 April 1919, *ibid.*
16 Canada, House of Commons, *Debates*, 15 April 1919, 1524, 1484-527 passim
17 *Return of the Troops*, appendix B, 154; Kemp to Mewburn, 24 April 1919, Kemp Papers, vol. 137, D-2; Kemp to Sir Joseph Maclay, 14 April 1919, *ibid.*

18 See 'Disturbances,' no. 11; Col J.G. Rattray to Turner, 13 May 1919, Turner Papers, 5624; 'Canadian Troops and British Press,' Borden Papers, 62595
19 Rattray to OC's, Units, n.d. Turner Papers, 5627
20 'Disturbances,' no. 12; APM to Headquarters, Witley, 20 June 1919, RG 9, III B1, vol. 2085, file R-1-23, vol. 2. On comparative pay scales, see Kemp Papers, vol. 181, file 54. A Canadian private earned $1.10 a day, approximately twice the British rate.
21 'Canadian Troops and British Press' 62602
22 'Statement by Overseas Ministry,' 13 May 1919, Borden Papers, 62597; News-Chronicle, 13 May 1919, Sketch, 14 May 1919, Daily Mail, 21 May 1919
23 Kemp to Harrington, 3 May 1919, Kemp Papers, vol. 135, C-63
24 Harrington to Kemp, 9 May 1919, ibid.
25 Fotheringham to Foster, 8 July 1919, Fotheringham Papers, file 24
26 Report of the Court of Inquiry on Disturbances at Witley Camp, RG 9, III B1, vol. 2084, file R-1-23, vol. 4, exhibit P
27 Ibid.; 'Disturbances,' no. 6
28 'Canadian Troops and British Press' 62603-4; see also RG 24, vol. 1841, GAQ 10-39F
29 'Disturbances,' no. 9; Ripon Observer, 19 June 1919. For sentences see Kemp Papers, vol. 155
30 'Canadian Troops and British Press' 62604-7
31 'Disturbances,' no. 13. See Turner Papers, 5613
32 Sunday Herald, 22 June 1919; 'Canadian Troops and British Press,' 62609-10
33 'Special Order of the Day,' Turner Papers, 5595-6 or RG 24, vol. 1841, GAQ 10-39F
34 'Memorandum on shipping,' 1 August 1919, Kemp Papers, vol. 137, D-2; Kemp to Borden, 31 July 1919, ibid.
35 Memorandum of conference, 21 June 1919, Turner Papers, 5600-04
36 Morning Post, 24 July 1919; Dennistoun's notes, Kemp Papers, vol. 155
37 Greenwood memorandum, 27 June 1919, Turner Papers, 5597; Daily Telegraph, 8 July 1919
38 See Nicholson, C.E.F. 359-60; Perley to Borden, 21 March 1917, Borden Papers, OC 415, 43604-5
39 'Memorandum respecting Accounts with the Imperial Government,' 25 October 1917, Kemp Papers, vol. 176, file 40
40 D. McK. McClelland to Kemp, 13 December 1918, ibid.; 'Report on Maintenance of Canadian Troops in France,' 3 July 1919, Kemp Papers, vol. 166, file 1d
41 Nicholson, C.E.F. 361; RG 24, vol. 923, file HQ 54-21-23-13 vol. 2

42 Maj L.P. Sherwood for Harrington to Kemp, 27 May 1920, Kemp Papers, vol. 177, file 40

43 Turner to Kemp, 22 April 1919, Turner Papers, 11-78, 7190; Kemp to Borden, 31 July 1919, Kemp Papers, vol. 137, D-2

44 Harrington to Kemp, 13 December 1920, Kemp Papers, vol. 173, file 20

45 *Canadian Annual Review*, 1919, 48; Canada, House of Commons, *Debates*, 2 October 1919, 778-9

46 Harrington to Kemp, 22 November 1920, Kemp Papers, vol. 173, file 28; PC, 1705, 26 July 1920; Borden to Kemp, 30 June 1920, Kemp Papers, vol. 176, file 40; Gibson to Kemp, 15 February 1920, *ibid.*, vol. 176, file 42

47 Canada, House of Commons, *Debates*, 15 April 1919, 1524

48 *Ibid.* 10 April 1919, 598

49 Kemp to White, n.d. draft, Kemp Papers, vol. 135, C-63

50 Harrington to Kemp, 13 December 1920, *ibid.* vol. 173, file 28. (See also Kemp to MacBrien, 31 October 1919, PAC, MacBrien Papers, vol. 1, file 1.) Harrington succeeded in law and in politics, winning election to the Nova Scotia legislature in 1925 and appointment to the Rhodes government. He became premier of the province in 1930 only to meet the harshest impact of the depression. He lost power in 1933, resigned as leader of the opposition in 1937, and died in 1943.

APPENDIX

1 On the South Africans, see John Buchan, *The History of the South African Forces in France* (London 1920) 15; R.E. Johnston, *Ulindi to Delville Wood: The Life Story of Maj. Gen. Sir Henry Timson Lukin* (London 1931); John Ewing, *The History of the 9th (Scottish) Division* (London 1921)

2 Sir Alexander Godley, *Life of an Irish Soldier* (London 1939); *Dictionary of National Biography, 1950-1960* (London 1971) 44-5

3 Peter Heydon, *Quiet Decision: A Study of George Foster Pearce* (Carlton, Victoria 1965) has disappointingly little to say about Pearce in the war years.

4 On Birdwood and the Australians, see Preston, *'Imperial Defense'* 482-3

5 C.E.W. Bean, *Official History of Australia in the War of 1914-1918*, III, *The A.I.F. in France, 1916* (Sydney 1929) 150-1

6 *Ibid.* 145-6

7 *Ibid.* 171. On Anderson, see also Preston, *'Imperial Defense'* 484-5

8 C.E.W. Bean, *Two Men I Knew: William Bridges and Brudenell White: Founders of the A.I.F.* (Sydney 1957) 166, 169-73

Index